Molly Keane

Molly Keane

Essays in Contemporary Criticism

Eibhear Walshe & Gwenda Young

EDITORS

FOUR COURTS PRESS

Set in 10.5 on 12.5 point Ehrhardt for
FOUR COURTS PRESS LTD
7 Malpas Street, Dublin 8, Ireland
e-mail: info@four-courts-press.ie
http://www.four-courts-press.ie
and in North America by
FOUR COURTS PRESS
c/o ISBS, 920 N.E. 58th Avenue, Suite 300, Portland, OR 97213.

ISBN (10 digit) 1-85182-956-3
ISBN (13 digit) 978-1-85182-956-9

A catalogue record for this title
is available from the British Library.

Printed in England
by MPG Books, Bodmin, Cornwall

Contents

Foreword

VERA KREILKAMP

Molly Keane's fourteen novels span more than six decades of the twentieth century, the last three appearing in the 1980s under her own name, twenty years after she had ceased publishing under the gender-neutral pseudonym, M.J. Farrell. Although these remarkable late works rapidly generated international praise for the septuagenarian author, film versions of two of them, and Virago reprints of the eleven earlier (M.J. Farrell) novels, substantial critical recognition has emerged more slowly. This first volume devoted exclusively to Keane appears a quarter of a century after the appearance of *Good Behaviour* in 1981; in it participants investigate her contributions to a variety of genres and suggest sources for the steadily increasing interest in her work.[1] Although several of the collection's analytic essays focus on the late novels, more than half turn to Keane's earlier ones; thus the M.J. Farrell novels, dismissed by some readers as apprentice works for the later tours de force, are now firmly integrated into the critical corpus of Keane's accomplishments. The range of contributions to this volume demonstrates that classifying Molly Keane's fiction is no easy matter: readers describe her work, for example, as illustrating the genre of Big House fiction, the post-Big House novel, and the Gothic; as subversive feminist writing; and as central to the development of the contemporary lesbian novel. Mary Breen insists that Keane's work belongs not to the tradition of realistic fiction, but to the Irish comic tradition of Swift and Edgeworth. Ironically, both the novelist's complex straddling of multiple genres and her popularity among general as well as academic readers may well account for the slow critical acknowledgment of her fullest achievement.

Keane sets all of her novels in Anglo-Irish gentry homes in the period spanning the Edwardian interlude before World War I, the Easter Rebellion, the War of Independence and the Civil War – through the long twentieth-century aftermath of accelerating gentry decline. Composed with an insider's intimate apprehension of Anglo-Irish life, the fiction circles around settings marketed today as grand country hotels or tourist sites commemorating a failed imperial ruling class. From Maria Edgeworth's *Castle Rackrent* in 1800 through Somerville and Ross and Elizabeth Bowen's novels in the late nine-

---

1 For example, *Literature Online* lists more than six doctoral dissertations about Keane since 1993.

teenth and early twentieth centuries, the Big House genre, preoccupied with
the social and political decline of an improvident Ascendancy before a rising
native middle class, inescapably shapes our responses to Keane's fiction. But
as essayists in this collection make clear, Keane offers subversive complica-
tions of earlier conventions. In all but two of her novels, for example, she
elides any significant consideration of the political trauma facing the Big House
and leading to its collapse. Instead she depends on domestic plots to chart
the delusions and claustrophobic maladjustments of twentieth-century Anglo-
Irish life.

The Irish critical response to the Big House genre has long been ambivalent. Given that recent commentators can still describe twentieth-century
practitioners of it as producing works in an Anglophone end-of-empire tradition,[2] Keane's exclusion from the *Field Day Anthology of Irish Writing* in
1991 seems predictable. Both her gender and engagement with twentieth-century Anglo-Irish society failed to engage a criticism still liberating itself from
decades of a nationalist hegemony. As Carolyn Lesnick observes in her contribution to this volume, assumed historical narratives have too often been
used 'to marginalise and exclude' Ascendancy novels from the canon of Irish
fiction. Keane's achievement attests to the inadequacy of Seamus Deane's dismissal of modern Big House fiction as written in the shadow of a Yeatsian
nostalgia.[3] Her increasingly savage evocations of gentry society register as
light-years from Yeats's deification of the Ascendancy landed estate in his
middle poetry. We might, however, as Sinéad Mooney suggests here, turn to
the poet's darkest reading of Anglo-Ireland in the late *Purgatory*, rather than
to his nostalgia for a high culture he imagined residing in the eighteenth-century Ascendancy house. Keane's savage exposures of Big House society in
Good Behaviour, *Time after Time*, or *Loving and Giving* are closer in spirit to
the subversive gaze on the gentry estate of *Castle Rackrent* than to invoca-
tions of Anglo-Irish culture as a stay against modern disorder.[4]

Readers exploring decaying Anglo-Irish houses (and bodies) in the late
fiction describe Keane as exploiting and transforming the conventions of Big
House literature.[5] Silvia Diez Fabre and Derek Hand compare Keane's most

---

2 Joe Cleary, for example, reads the twentieth-century Big House novel as a conservative form,
with 'a rueful emphasis on the grace of a lost civilization tending to soften memories, sometimes to the point of willed amnesia, of the violent monopoly of power that sustained the
Ascendancy world': Joe Cleary, 'Postcolonial Ireland', in Kevin Kenny (ed.), *Ireland and the
British Empire* (2004), 271.   3 'The Big House surrounded by the unruly tenantry, culture
besieged by barbarity, a refined aristocracy beset by a vulgar middle-class – all of these are
recurrent images in twentieth-century Irish fiction which draws heavily on Yeats's poetry for
them': Seamus Deane, 'The literary myths of the Revival', *Celtic revivals* (London, 1985), 32.
4 A discussion of Keane's intertextual relationship to Edgeworth appears, for example, in Ann
Weekes, *Irish women writers: an uncharted tradition* (1990), 156–8.   5 See Vera Kreilkamp, 'The
persistence of illusion in Molly Keane's fiction', *The Anglo-Irish novel and the Big House* (1998),

explicitly political novel, *Two Days in Aragon*, to fiction by Somerville and Ross or Elizabeth Bowen. Indeed Éibhear Walshe argues that *Good Behaviour*, the publication that brought Keane acclaim in her seventies, is a novel of termination, a dark 'swan song for the Ascendancy novel', offering a lacerating vision of Anglo-Irish social and moral collapse before a kinder, more nurturing, and feminising bourgeois morality. In another view of the fiction as chronicling cultural decline, Ellen L. O'Brien explores Keane's recurring preoccupation with the bodily materiality of her protagonists. Drawing on Kristeva and Bakhtin, O'Brien focuses on Keane's attention to, for example, vomit, diarrhoea, ageing bodies, and corpses – an emphasis rupturing the symbolic order identified with Anglo-Irish class position. Shifting its attention from the moldering house to the body of its inhabitants as the central metonym for cultural decline, the essay provides a politically attuned reading of Keane's fascination with abject bodily functions – an attribute more typically viewed as contributing to the dark comedy of her fiction.[6] In O'Brien's reading, the coloniser's historical apprehension of the native Catholic Irish – savage and grotesque in their fetid hovels – is turned on its head. From *Castle Rackrent* to Keane's *Time after Time* the domestic disarray of the Ascendancy house in Big House fiction eerily replicates that of the notoriously slipshod rural cabin which pre-Famine English tourists and Ascendancy landowners transformed into a trope of Ireland's baffling 'otherness'. Thus Keane's abject Anglo-Irish bodies shatters those layers of ritualised good behavior purportedly separating elite gentry landlords from their tenants.

Just as Keane's novels seemingly destabilise any nostalgia invoked by the category of end-of-empire anglophone fiction into which some would place her, her handling of gender subverts easy feminist pieties. The recuperative 2002 *The Field Day Anthology* volumes IV and V on Irish women's writing includes an autobiographical piece by Keane and an excerpt from *Good Behaviour*, both depicting the unhappy lives of Anglo-Irish children. The editor of the 'Contemporary Fiction' section of volume V notes that the Big House genre, dominated by socially advantaged Anglo-Irish women, represented a rare female literary form making its way into the Irish canon.[7] From Edgeworth to Keane, women novelists, seemingly writing in dialogue with one another, exploited the ironic potential for an inward-looking social criticism by anatomising domestic gentry life. But as Kelly McGovern's essay on women's relationship to abjection in the later fiction makes clear, although Keane is remarkably attuned to female suffering, she holds little truck with a feminism focusing on victimhood. Her recurring attention to patriarchal

174–94. 6 See Rachel Jane Lynch, 'The crumbling fortress: Molly Keane's comedies of Anglo-Irish manners', in Theresa O'Connor (ed.), *The comic tradition in Irish women writers* (1996), 73–98. 7 Ruth Carr, 'Contemporary Fiction', *Field Day anthology of Irish writing, volume V*, ed. Angela Bourke et al. (2002), 1132.

decline, accompanied by portrayals of children's defenselessness before their coldly egocentric mothers, offer strikingly un-nostalgic images of the Anglo-Irish family romance, that emotional cauldron of guilt, sadism, and child sacrifice explored by Margot Backus in *The Gothic Family Romance*.[8] Building on and developing suggestions of several earlier critics, Mooney's study of the Gothic elements in Keane's work explores the women characters as vampirish and sadistic perpetuators of the abuses of colonialism, never solely as victims of it. Many of the novels depict doomed heterosexual and homosexual liaisons enacted amid an eroticised fixation on horses and fox hunting. Cumulatively, Keane's often numbing textual zeal for blood sports appears to signal compensations for Anglo-Ireland's failures, not just of political power, but also of sexual, maternal, and paternal love. (Rachael Sealy Lynch's essay on the equestrian themes reminds us, however, that in its obsession with the bloodlines of livestock and hounds, fox hunting also reflects the defensive snobbery of a society obsessed with its rapidly fading status.)

Keane's depictions of transgressive passion – most centrally in the 1934 *Devoted Ladies*, a novel with multiple homosexual protagonists, but also in *Good Behaviour* and *Time after Time* published almost a half century later – have generated increasing interest in the field of lesbian and gay studies. Gender critics have begun to explore the recurring appearances of lesbian figures in Irish fiction, for example, Harriet Freke in Edgeworth's *Belinda*, Cecilia Cullen in George Moore's *Drama in Muslin*, Marda in Bowen's *The Last September*, and a range of characters in Kate O'Brien's and Keane's novels.[9] Typically, socially transgressive pairings – both lesbian and gay – become evidence of Anglo-Irish decline. As the children of the Big House form relationships failing to perpetuate the family line, they undermine their society's dependence on an orderly genealogical transmission of property and cultural values. But moving beyond political readings, Moira Casey turns to Keane's *Devoted Ladies* in 1934 as a significant precursor of the twentieth-century lesbian novel, a form generally viewed as emerging with the publication of Radclyffe Hall's *The Well of Loneliness* six years earlier. Although Breen argues that Keane does not marginalise same-sex desire, both she and Casey note the author's insistent and problematic presentation of homosexuality as a doomed deviancy. In Keane's Ireland, as Casey observes, 'sexual alternatives are literally killed off'.

Despite Keane's savage exposure of those delusions sustaining Anglo-Irish society, her evocations of the surface of Ascendancy life often invite other, even contrasting, responses. In her introduction to the Virago reprint of

---

8 Margot Backus, *The gothic family romance: heterosexuality, child sacrifice, and the Anglo-Irish colonial order* (1999).   9 See, for example, Ellen Crowell's 'Ghosting the Llangollen Ladies: female intimacies, ascendancy exiles, and the Anglo-Irish novel', *Éire-Ireland* 39:3&4 (Fall/Winter 2004) 202–27.

Conversation Piece, Polly Devlin described Keane chronicling, not a dark Gothic maelstrom of sadistic mothers, helpless children, and loveless couplings, but 'the beauty and atavistic qualities of Irish great houses, marooned dreams of tranquility and decaying splendour standing in their depleted demesnes'.[10] Devlin registers Keane's sensuous receptiveness to the landscape and architecture of the Irish country estate, a strand of near-ecstatic pleasure with the gardens, drawing rooms, and remnants of classical design that endures throughout the fiction. Often coexisting somewhat uneasily with the dark Gothic subversions of the work, this aesthetic delight in texture, color, and line nevertheless assumes a role, even in the parodic late fiction. In this volume Molly Keane's daughters provide context for their mother's ambivalence toward Big House culture, expressing itself in what I once, rather unkindly, expressed as the *Architectural Digest* side of Molly Keane, her unfailing responsiveness to physical beauty (and its decay) in the novels. Recollections by Sally Phipps and Virginia Brownlow suggest the conflicts facing a twentieth-century Anglo-Irish woman choosing a writing life, tensions undoubtedly contributing to the powerful ambivalences evident in Keane's responses to her society. Phipps describes the choices confronting her mother: one directing her to an active social life, domestic concerns, and the sensuous pleasures of food, houses, and gardens that were to become so embedded in her fiction; the other to the socially frowned upon and lonely labour of the writer's private imperatives to strip a domestic world of its sustaining illusions. Such biographical material implies at least one source of Keane's receptiveness to the beauty of domestic Big House life and her simultaneous recognition of its seductive dangers.

A number of essayists in this collection reject reading Keane's fiction exclusively through a historical focus of big Ascendancy decline; exploring several of the M.J. Farrell novels and the late *Time after Time*, they suggest that the novelist frequently undermines her own darkest narratives, in essence creating a new post-Big House form. For example, Sarah McLemore's reading of *Mad Puppetstown* describes how its plot, by omitting the expected scene of conflagration, challenges our assumptions of Big House defeat in the Troubles. Keane instead depicts the survival of the house in the early 1920s and even its modernisation for a new age. In a similar vein, Carolyn Lesnick observes that *Full House* fails to provide readers with the 'tropes or signifiers of decline in the Big Houses' political, economic, or cultural status'. These new readings undoubtedly have been encouraged by significant cultural changes in Ireland since the 1980s: a growing receptiveness to ideals of hybridity that contest exclusions of Protestant Ireland from Irish identity; an atten-

---

10 Polly Devlin, 'Molly Keane: an interview with Polly Devlin', in Molly Keane (M.J. Farrell), *Conversation Piece* (1991), n.p.

tion to the legitimacy and political implications of women's domestic voices in literature; and above all, a revision of an essentialising nationalist dominance of Irish cultural criticism, emerging in no small part from feminism and historical revisionism. In these readings, in other words, the Anglo-Irish are not all that bad. Ellen Wolff prefaces her analysis of *Time after Time* by arguing for an anti-essentialist interpretation of Anglo-Irish literature, exploring Keane's 'striking dynamic and self-divided fiction'. If, she suggests, that novel 'evokes Keane's rejection of Anglo-Ireland, it suggests, too, her continued and complicated bond'.

Other contributors to this volume respond to Keane's sympathy for flawed Big House characters who manage to construct futures for themselves. The novelist breaks with the paradigmatic historical narrative of Ascendancy social and political losses to dramatise that an impoverished gentry carries on and – as with the Swifts in *Time after Time* – even thrives in a post-Independence Ireland. On occasion, as in the optimistic ending of *Two Days in Aragon*, the destroyed Big House will simply arise from its ashes, but more frequently (and convincingly) Keane dramatises the new relationships her protagonists must establish with those living outside the demesne walls. Although Andries Wessels acknowledges that many of Keane's works operate within the tradition of Anglo-Irish decline, he notes a competing narrative of history in both early and late works, *Mad Puppetstown, Treasure Hunt,* and *Time after Time.* In these novels, he finds that Keane creates characters who negotiate with history, moving out of its 'debilitating shadow' of glamour to find 'a legitimate place in contemporary Ireland'. Rachael Sealy Lynch also disputes the necessary linkage of Keane's novels set in the Big House with a historical focus on Ascendancy degeneration or decline. Such responses offer new interpretative directions for Keane's readers, suggesting, in Lesnick's words, how 'Keane lays the groundwork for ... [the] continuation of the Big House novel as a vital and vibrant generic form into and beyond the late twentieth century'.

A Molly Keane chronology

1904   Molly Skrine born in Co. Kildare. Her mother was Moira O'Neill, author of *The Songs of the Glens of Antrim*. She was the youngest child and was brought up in Wexford. She was educated at home and at a boarding school in Bray, Co. Wicklow, a large part of her childhood being spent at Woodruff, Co. Tipperary, the residence of the Perry family.

1910   Birth of Robert Keane whom Molly meets and marries in the 1930s.

1921   Writes her first novel, *Knight of Cheerful Countenance*

1926   Mills & Boon publishes her first novel, *The Knight of Cheerful Countenance*, written under the pseudonym M.J. Farrell, a name she used until 1981.

1928   *Young Entry* published by Elkin Mathews & Marrot

1929   *Taking Chances* published by Elkin Mathews & Marrot

1931   *Mad Puppetstown* published by W. Collins & Sons

1932   *Conversation Piece* published by W. Collins & Sons

1934   *Devoted Ladies* published by W. Collins & Sons

1935   *Full House* published by W. Collins & Sons

1937   *The Rising Tide* published by W. Collins & Sons

1938   Collaborates with John Perry on a play, *Spring Meeting*, which is produced in London and directed by John Gielgud

1940   Birth of Sally, first daughter of Molly and Robert Keane in Dublin. She is raised in Belleville, Cappoquin, Co. Waterford

1941   *Two Days in Aragon* published by W. Collins & Sons

1942   Keane writes a play, *Ducks and Drakes*, which is produced in London under the direction of John Gielgud

1945   Birth of Virginia, second daughter of Molly and Robert

1946   Death of Robert Keane following an operation in London

1949   Debut on the London stage of *Treasure Hunt*, written with John Perry. The play is later published in 1952 by W. Collins & Sons

1951   *Loving Without Tears* published by W. Collins & Sons

1952   *Treasure Hunt* published by W. Collins & Sons

1952   Molly and her daughters move from Belleville to Ardmore, Co. Waterford

1952–61   Keane works on a number of play ideas and translations from French to English

1961   *Dazzling Prospect*, written with John Perry, debuts on the London stage but receives poor critical responses.

1961–81   Disappointed by the response to *Dazzling Prospect*, Keane retreats to Ardmore where she concentrates on raising her daughters. She also begins work on the novel that would become *Good Behaviour*.

1981   Keane's 'comeback' novel, *Good Behaviour*, written under her real name, Molly Keane, is published by Andre Deutsch.

1981   Keane is nominated for the Booker prize for *Good Behaviour*.

1983   *Time after Time* is published by Andre Deutsch.

1983   *Good Behaviour*, adapted by Hugh Leonard and filmed in Dunkathel House, Cork, and Coolemore House, is made into a television mini-series by the BBC.

1985   *Time after Time* is produced as a film, directed by Bill Hays and starring John Gielgud and Googie Withers.

1988   *Loving and Giving* (published in the USA as *Queen Lear*) published by Andre Deutsch.

1989   Molly Keane is awarded an honorary doctorate in Literature by the National University of Ireland and attends the ceremony at University College Cork.

1993   Publication by HarperCollins of *Molly Keane's Ireland*, an anthology written in collaboration with her daughter, Sally Phipps.

1996   Molly Keane dies in Ardmore, Co. Waterford

2004   University College, Cork hosts the Molly Keane Centenary Conference, which is attended by Molly Keane's daughters, Sally and Virginia, and by many of her friends and relatives from Ireland and abroad.

Editors' preface

EIBHEAR WALSHE & GWENDA YOUNG

Molly Keane was born Molly Skrine in Co. Kildare in 1904, part of what she herself described as 'a rather serious hunting, fishing church going family'. Her mother, Moira O'Neill, was a well-known writer, called the 'Poetess of the Glens', and Keane herself wrote *The Knight of Cheerful Countenance* in 1921 when she was just seventeen; it was later published by Mills and Boon in 1926. She used the name of M.J. Farrell as a pen name, reputedly the name of a pub she spotted one day while out hunting. For Keane, the male name became a screen for her literary work, a necessary self-protection within the distinctly unliterary anti-intellectual hunting world of the Anglo-Irish in the 1920s. Comic novels like *Young Entry* (1928), *Mad Puppetstown* (1931), *Devoted Ladies* (1934) and *Full House* (1935) established her reputation, as did her most dramatic novel of the Irish war of Independence, *Two Days in Aragon* (1941). At the same time, Molly Keane was also a successful dramatist in London's West End, working with John Perry and John Gielgud between 1938 and 1961 to produce a series of commercial hits. Then, after the death of her husband and with the later failure of a play, *Dazzling Prospect*, in 1961, Molly Keane moved back to Ardmore, Co. Waterford, with her two daughters and gave up writing as M.J. Farrell. Finally, in 1981, she published, under her own name, the novel that is considered her masterpiece, *Good Behaviour*, and found new inspiration as a novelist in her old age with later novels such as *Time after Time* (1983) and *Loving and Giving* (1988). Molly Keane died in 1996.

In November 2004, the Department of English at University College Cork held an international conference on Molly Keane with scholars from Ireland, the UK, North America and South Africa participating, marking a renewed scholarly interest in Keane's writings. Many of the essays in this collection are drawn from this conference and in addition, we decided to reprint two influential essays on Keane by Ellen L. O'Brien and Mary Breen and we also commissioned an original essay by Moira E. Casey on Keane's lesbian representation. In assembling this collection, we structured the essays thematically to contextualise the novels of one of the most distinctive and subversive voices within twentieth-century Irish writing, a novelist charting the end of her class and the immanent collapse of a literary genre. These essays are informed by current feminist and post-colonial critical theories and situate Keane's place in contemporary Irish studies. This is the first collection of scholarly essays on Molly Keane's fictions, dealing with all of her important novels and, throughout, the contributors address questions concerning the representation of gender and sexuality, the Gothic, and the demise of the Big House tradition in her writing. Overall, we feel that this volume of essays enables the contemporary reader to engage with the darkly ironic, comic and original imaginative world of M.J. Farrell/ Molly Keane with a fuller sense of insight and enjoyment.

In putting together this volume we have been greatly helped by a number of people and we wish to express our gratitude for all the support and help. Thanks to Michael Adams, Martin Fanning, Anthony Tierney and Aoife Walsh of Four Courts Press for publishing the volume. We acknowledge the assistance of the Arts Faculty Publication Fund, UCC, and the NUI Publication Fund in producing the book. Molly Keane's family was a great support and encouragement to us and we want to mention Sally and George Phipps, Virginia, Kevin and Julia Brownlow, and Molly Keane's friend, Thomas McCarthy. We were also indebted to the English Department, UCC, the Arts Faculty, Professor G.T. Wrixon and the Munster Literature Centre, Cork. In addition, we were helped by UCC friends Anne Fitzgerald, Elaine Hurley, Cal Duggan, Pat Coughlan, Jennifer Crowley, Clíona Ó Gallchoir, Mary Breen, Carol Quinn, John Fitzgerald, Tina O'Toole, Carmel Quinlan, David Cox, Eamon Ó Carragáin, Nuala Griffin, Marie McSweeney, Kevin Barrett, Daniel Kennedy and Aoife Healy.

We would like to thank the contributors for all their patience and helpfulness, Sarah Farrelly for the wonderful design of the cover, Vera Kreilkamp for agreeing to write the excellent foreword and, in particular Brian Cliff and Julie Anne Stevens for being such careful and thorough readers. The editors would like to thank John and Celine Walshe, Keith and Phil Young, and their respective families.

Memories of Molly Keane

SALLY PHIPPS & VIRGINIA BROWNLOW

SALLY PHIPPS

I think my first awareness of my mother as a writer was in the 1940s when I was three or four, at Belleville near Cappoquin. She wrote and slept in a pale green room floating above the valley at the top of the house. I would arrive there with Lizzie, our maid. We brought tea, and a hot water bottle. We would put the tray on the table, and slip the hot water bottle into her sheepskin foot-muff. Molly was accompanied by Soo, her little black barge dog. We didn't speak, and got out as soon as possible. She often blew us a kiss. When she came from writing, you were aware of a tenseness if she suffered from blocks, and a sweetness and sense of freedom if it had gone well.

This was war time. Most families had people away in the fighting, but for those of us left behind in the Blackwater Valley, eerily shielded from war, social life continued. People visited each other's houses for Poker games, lunches and hunts, or just to see the lilies in bloom. They travelled by bicycle, or pony trap (sometimes with hunters or retired racehorses between the shafts). Standards were kept up. Molly said of local chatelaines, 'We vied with each other in the forcing of bulbs.' Hospitality had a competitive aspect. Molly – a perfectionist and social animal – was drawn into this world. It conflicted with her writing. In a notebook of that time, she says: 'If only people and life did not matter quite so much to me, I would write better and give my writing the passion I give my living. Not always, but often, I live passionately, inspired about food, and doing flowers, and being amusing, and all the fire that ought to eat me up over my writing goes into those things.' It is moving to me that in this statement she nods towards the fact that she is unfair to her writing. She did not often admit she had a gift. It was a burden she carried that kept her alienated (she who feared to be left out) upstairs in her bedroom, struggling to earn a crust in the most grinding manner possible. Her writing called to her with the spoilsport tone of a strict governess. She complained about the suffering, and she was mostly silent about any happiness or satisfaction involved. She hid her love of writing from others, and herself, until the process began to unravel in old age, when it became obvious that she was grief stricken. Unquestionably, you are in a hard place when the stuff of your life is also the clay of your creation as totally as hers was, the cutting off point, and the refocussing is anguish. 'In writing, you have to achieve this awful separation from living, and still write about life,' she said.

Marguerite Yourcenar puts it another way: 'Books are not life, only its ashes.' In retrospect, she added, 'Books are also a way of learning to feel more acutely. Writing is a way of going to the depths of being.' Molly tried to ignore this painful truth in the surface of her mind, but she seldom evaded it in her work, and that is why her writing, like her living, was passionate, and has the power to transcend its conversational mode and small social world, and reach out to all its readers.

Gardening grounded her when she was stretched too thinly between her two worlds. It was very important to her. She loved plants and digging. It assuaged the depressive moods of her artist's temperament. Its imagery pervades her work, and is part of a wider, intense response to the natural world of the Irish landscape which manifests itself in the novels, and is, I think, one of the main sources of energy which feeds her writing, both in overt and hidden ways. There are gardeners in every book. Aunt Diana is the only happy person in *The Rising Tide*. Her rich and bossy mothers, jealous for their power, often have their few creative, self-forgetful moments when they are tending their beds of irises of lilies. In *Time after Time*, Jasper Swift's 'elegant, lengthy figure, is bent like a reed in a cool breeze ...' His negativity is only revoked when he is in his garden, attempting to make order in the wilderness, which is bound to engulf him.

Anyone who has read one of her books will be aware of her love of houses and rooms, and objects in rooms. The rooms in her novels were often taken from life. They have mostly gone now, so it is good that she, almost their last recorder, had so much relish and affection for them, combined with a sharp, poetic eye for detail. She herself created many rooms. Her favourite was the drawing room at Belleville, which she and Bobby, my father, arranged together. Drawing-room life has vanished. I expect most people have never heard of it unless they are readers of Jane Austen. I, myself, would only barely remember it if I had not spent a lot of time in this room in early childhood. Like her dress, it had a 1930s flavour. It was sort of glamourous, with plump cushions and a cocktail shaker in the corner. It was decorated in peaceful shades of pale grey, dark blue, and rust colours. It had tall windows, crossed with thin glazing bars, facing to the south. Many visitors came to this room, relatives, neighbours, with their silk stockings and narrow-waisted coats, mud-besmattered after hunting, writers, actors, monks from Mount Melleray, ladies dressed in the beautiful speckled tweed of those days, and prone to Chanel No. 5 perfume. A Garda superintendent called regularly, and kept Molly and Bobby up to date on the progress of the war. He was said to be in touch with secret intelligence.

I remember Molly biting the stems of flowers, and fixing them in huge bouquets, which fanned out against the gable walls. She sewed a lot, deftly and speedily, embroidering daisies in white silk button-hole stitch on blue linen, and mending sheets and clothes. She sat with me and the little dog, in an armchair, reading out loud. When friends came to play cards, she spread a table with a cloth tasselled at the corners. She never took to Bridge, but she loved Poker, because of its elements of secrets and danger. The drawing-room was a place of real hospitality, warmth, and informality: I remember Elizabeth Bowen lying on the floor in the front of the fire, smoking elegantly, not guiltily like people do today.

Molly was, of course, well able for conversational abrasiveness and wickedness. Nobody has ever recorded the cruel jungle that the drawing-room could become more painfully and hilariously than she. She was sometimes torn by opposing forces – her stiletto-like sharpness, and her infinite kindness. She was a person very beguiled by the beauty of the world, besieged also by dark forces, fascinated and sharp-eyed concerning human nature, and above all, amused. Laughter, for her, was the great healer. Asked if she put her friends into books, she replied: 'I think there is a touch of the Judas in every writer, but it had better go hand in hand with invention.' Friendship was one of the most important things in her life. Sometimes she struggled to keep her friends in the face of her over-quick wit, but she nearly always succeeded. She was completely generous when people were in trouble, and in good times she was exciting, sympathetic company, full of mischief and insight. She offered champagne cocktails to celebrate a joy, and as an anaesthetic for grief. Even when she couldn't afford it, she proffered this elixir if the need was great.

Although she said she never put people undisguised into her novels, her aunts May and Lou were the exception. She described them as the bane of her childhood, and they, too, might have had a difficult time with her. Aspects of them appear in almost all her novels. At a lecture in Paris in 1984, she acknowledged her debt to her aunts in a way that is illuminating about her whole ironic approach to human nature: 'I have written, and I expect I shall go on writing, about people like them. I find their manner of getting through life, their avoidance of turmoil and disappointment, their grip to the last on the fantasies that support them interesting, even dramatic.' I see shards of herself in her template characters; in the girls (full of innocence and guile), in the grand and bossy mothers, in the lonely governesses, in the brilliant gardeners and cooks, in the rakish, charming people who understand. Eliza in *Full House* is the nearest she came to a self-portrait. Eliza is both simple and sophisticated in the way she was herself, and she has several connections with the Molly of that era. She is an artist, an outsider and an insider. She is a seer, aware of people's inner being, and the need to deal obliquely with it in accordance with the demands of 'Good Behaviour'. She is a giver, prepared to use her trivial drawing room skills in a greater cause.

After my father died, our lives changed. She was in awful pain at his sudden loss, and so was I. He had died in London, so whenever she went to

London, I thought she was going to die too. We clung to Virginia (a baby of
1) as a sign of hope. Eventually we moved to a smaller house, and lived in
much closer contact. Most of Molly's energy and time was focussed on us.
Before, our relationship had been diluted by my father, and by the microcosmic village, which Big House life consisted of at the time. Now we became
more exclusively dependent on her. Good can come out of sadness. We moved
to Ardmore, where she lived for forty-four years (longer than anywhere else).
My father had gone to Ardmore every summer since childhood. Like a lot of
people from inland, he was at his happiest there. I always think so many
Anglo-Irish people chose to be buried in Ardmore because it was a place
where they had felt free, away from the shadow of the Big House. Molly put
down her deepest roots at Ardmore, and was sustained by the sea, and by the
people. She said, 'The sea awakens my imagination'. Eventually in old age
she moved her work into a new realm there, with *Good Behaviour*.

This novel brought her fame in the modern sense of the word, and the
media exposure involved in selling books today, which is quite at odds with
the lonely, risky business of writing them. In a way she made a success of her
relationship with the press. I think it was because she was so interested in real
hospitality but also in social life (with its combination of joy in people and net-
working). She seemed to regard the arrival of journalists in her life as an extension of that. She acquired many new friends, some of them quite unlikely, but
the tightrope of writing, in any form, is an intuitive link. We went to Paris
together. For me it was carefree, looking at paintings, walking the lovely streets,
drinking champagne at receptions for her. She was helping to promote the
French publication of *Time after Time*. 'I am too old for this sort of thing,' she
said nervously, awaiting an interviewer. When he arrived, he seemed to be from
a different planet to her. He was intellectual, cool, dressed in leather, possibly
a Maoist, and more than half a century younger than her. She gathered up her
possessions – bag, umbrella, red scarf – uncertainly, and accompanied him to
a nearby café, like a lamb to the slaughter, casting an envious look at me, dash-
ing off to see Van Gogh's *La Meridienne*. I returned to find her lying down,
although already dressed to go out in the evening and much refreshed. 'Well,'
she said, 'in spite of the fact that he looked so peculiar and had not shaved, he
was extraordinarily nice and very intelligent. What can he have made of me?'
I remember being touched by love and admiration for the spirit in which she
encountered the world. Of course, he, too, became a friend, and kept in touch,
sending her books and literary journals.

She spent some of her happiest times in her kitchen at Ardmore. She said
if she had not been a writer, she would have been a housewife, adding that
she would have preferred to have been one anyway, only it didn't pay! She
delighted in domesticity, and was brilliant at it. For a long period, she stopped
writing, and I think she replaced it by cooking. She cooked with the preci-

sion and care she spent on words, balancing sweet and sour, and creating subtle unique flavours. Her food really was extraordinary. It was light, and had a recognisable style, like her prose. She loved risky dishes, involving a sleight of hand. We would observe her, half praying and half swearing, as she turned out her custard at the last moment, set it in a lake of sauce, covered it in soft cream, and broke up a sheet of caramel with a hammer to scatter over the top. We called it 'Broken Glass Pudding'. Despite a fondness for troublesome, dramatic dishes, she also valued simplicity. Virginia and I were touched when Thomas McCarthy, in her funeral address, mentioned that she had advised him years ago to add a pinch of sugar to carrots and he had done so ever since. She preferred wild, seasonal ingredients. When she became too infirm to gather them herself, other people brought them to her door. In her last years, she awaited the carrigeen, picked by her friend Tony Gallagher, with the anticipation some people might bestow on the premier cru of the Medoc. Another friend, Dennis Fitzgerald, brought her the herbs he grew, and she would hold them in a bouquet as she sat by the fire, long after he went home. Having to stop cooking caused her suffering. She passed many of the tricks of her trade on to Nora and Brigitta, who helped her after she got ill. She made marmalade with Brigitta almost to the end. After she died, this note dropped out of *Le Grande Meaulnes*, one of the last books she had been reading: 'Well-being returns when I see sunlight glittering through a new batch of marmalade on the kitchen table.'

The comparison drawn between her and Elizabeth Bowen is inevitable, but a bit of a cul-de-sac, I feel. They practise a different art, although they hold subjects in common. They both see the house as having a presence or personality that is stronger than the people who live in it. This intense sense of place pervaded Anglo-Irish life, and often led to a crushing of individual sensibility. Conversely, it nurtured the imagination, and formed many writers. To me, Elizabeth's is a literature of ideas and essences, almost poetry sometimes. Her style is subtle, and has a fruitful opaqueness. Above all, her view is shaped by history. Molly tremendously admired Elizabeth's writings, and felt it was superior to what she did. Her world was impinged on by its fuller, immediate past, and the losses of its future, but beyond that, she did not see things historically or politically. She blamed this on her lack of education. It was as much a question of temperament. She was not drawn to the overall view, but to the luminosity of detail (in the Proustian way). She filters her writing sensuously and emotionally, and then structures and calms it with the measure and craftsmanship of her language.

Her long life almost spanned the century. She has to be the last of the Anglo-Irish writers, because she bore witness to the dying away of her world. It is partly this, running parallel with her own fading, and its unreconciled sense of life's splendour, which gives to her late books their fierce autumnal colours.

VIRGINIA BROWNLOW

When I started thinking about what I should say this evening, I came to the conclusion that although I love my mother's work, I have nothing new or erudite to say about it. Maybe, however, I can try to illuminate from the point of view of her child, some of the ways in which aspects of her life are reflected in her books. As a child I tended to equate my mother writing with being unwell, as she would spend the morning in her bedroom and emerge looking green.

So much of the person she was, and so many of both the tangible and intangible things she gave me, reoccur in her books. The infinite pains she took in order that my experience of horses and riding should be positive is a typical example. The ponies she found for me gave me a rich sense of achievement and joy. I had the pleasure without the terrors she often describes in her books and which she had to endure on huge, out-of-control hunters in her own childhood.

Sally and I grew up with a strong sense of the importance of special places. Her passionate appreciation of wild landscape always moves me in her books. On many walks and picnics she conveyed and shared with us a lyrical delight and excitement in fey foxglove-filled glens and heathery mountainous places. I remember when I was four, the intense green of the mosses we collected from the ditch of a rocky mountain path above Ballymacarbury. She was nearly as interested as I was in my plan to make moss houses for the fairies. She fostered our creativity in many ways.

In the same way in which she initiated my love of wild landscape, she lit the spark of my pleasure in the sea and the mystique of boats. She read me *Twenty Years a Growing* more than once. She writes about trips to the sea as a liberation. She sympathised with my intoxication when jumping in the waves, until I turned blue from the cold. Prawning was a serious pursuit. We felt like proud primitive fishermen, when we gave her buckets of prawns to boil for us to eat with brown bread for tea. I loved the status and importance given to my endeavours to bring home fish, blackberries, mushrooms and primroses.

On long car journeys, in the forties and fifties, we had no car stereos, and she made up serial stories. One was about a character called Miss Pink, who had a most ambiguous and anarchic way of eventually doing a good deed. Her 'Crotty the Robber' stories could last from Dungarvan to Dublin.

She writes so well about the details of practical things. In her life she gave her full attention to practicalities – how to embroider a flower; do a perfect yarn in a linen sheet; restore a dessicated eighteenth-century table; how to create a beautiful, imaginative and comfortable house. She was interested in every area of domestic life, from dogs' worms to flower arranging.

The garden, plants and flowers in her books are enormously evocative. It's only since I've inherited her garden and done some horticultural courses, that I've discovered the extent of her horticultural knowledge and intelligence. These days in her overgrown, jungly garden, I find that she always put the right plant in the right place, although many have now grown grotesquely out of proportion.

She wrote about clothes and magical dressmakers, who could transform hand-me-downs. She was very interested in clothes, although she never had new clothes in my childhood. She dressed with great style from what she called 'Mercy Parcels', which often came from Fred Astaire's sister, Adele, in America. She had them altered by clever dressmakers and her own unerring eye.

I suppose for many of us our mother's food is central to our sense of home. It's certainly so in my case. Her books and life were both full of food. She spoke of the disgusting food in her childhood. We, on the other hand, grew up with delicious and sophisticated food. She gave us a culture of food. There was a sense of ritual around celebration food, comfort food and everyday food. I remember a feast of lobsters and mayonnaise that she made with a wooden spoon, stirring in drop after drop of olive oil. It was a summer's evening in the garden. The lobsters had cost 7s. 6d. a pound. This was before her books had begun to generate an income – and she had a huge overdraft at the bank – but all of us knew it was worth every single, expensive mouthful. She was a perfectionist in most areas of her life. It's evident in her writing and it was always part of her cooking. Even when she was in her eighties, the quality of the meal she created was of far more importance to her than her inevitable exhaustion. It could entail certain ruthlessness. If a vital ingredient was missing, we had to drop everything and go and get it. She wrote vividly about delicious meals and created so many in her kitchen. The focus on dogs' dinners in *Time after Time* was echoed in her attention to her beloved Zephy, Tessa and Hero's meals, although I don't think their dinners often ended up on our plates!

Food was of course at the centre of the social life, which she loved. When she was old, she would alarm us by driving long miles on frosty roads to see her friends. She had a boundless interest in people from dukes to dustmen and a piercingly sharp tongue and eye, as well as great empathy and delight in both her old and new friends.

Her perfectionism over food and social life reminds me of trips to the Blackwater estuary to collect mussels and the less romantic aspects of scraping off their barnacles and scrubbing away the mud before they became a superb *moules mariniere* for a dinner party. We accepted our role of mussel cleaners, as we were always included in the dinner party. There was no sense of generation gap. We genuinely felt that we were the friends of her adult friends. Our lives were full of interesting people and so many stories about people and so much wit. Social life floated on alcohol. It was a potent part of our lives. I remember glasses of champagne to get us into the dentist in Cork; no wages were ever paid without a shared whiskey. After hunting I would soak in a deep, hot bath, so different from the tepid bathwater of her youth that frequently occurs in her books. She would come in with a hot milk, whiskey and cloves for me to sip, while I recounted my day's adventures. On car journeys there was always a slim silver flask of whiskey in the picnic basket, along with the thermos of soup and neat packets of sandwiches wrapped in greaseproof paper. Once, on a snowy day, she rubbed whiskey into my freezing feet.

A few weeks ago, Eibhear and Gwenda asked me what she'd have thought of this event. I know she'd have been surprised and flattered by the appreciation of her work, but equally important to her would have been the fun she undoubtedly would have had – the stories, jokes and confidences. She'd have felt very nervous beforehand and she'd have had a really good time when she got here. She would have been thoroughly delighted by it and would probably have ended up inviting several new friends to lunch, tea, dinner, and to stay the night.

Keane and the Anglo-Irish

Resolving history: negotiating the past in Molly Keane's Big House novels

ANDRIES WESSELS

In a William Trevor short story, 'Beyond the Pale', a traumatised English visitor to Ireland concludes that:

> History is unfinished in this island; long since it has come to a stop in Surrey ... A language was lost, a faith forbidden. Famine followed revolt, plantation followed that. But it was people who were struck into the soil of other people's lands, not forests of new trees; and it was greed and treachery that spread as a disease among them all. No wonder unease clings to these shreds of history and shots ring out in answer to the mockery of drums. (78)

This notion of unresolved history is not only pervasive in Irish literature but, as Tom McAlindon has pointed out (293), articulates an idea that runs through Trevor's own *Fools of Fortune* (1983) and indeed through some of his other novels like *The Silence in the Garden* (1988), and more recently, *The Story of Lucy Gault* (2002). All of these deal with the decline of the Anglo-Irish Protestant Ascendancy, the very people who were 'struck into the soil of other people's lands' through successive waves of English colonisation from the invasion of Henry II's Norman barons in 1172, through later 'plantations' and the dispropriation of native landlords, to the settling of Cromwell's conquering army on seized land after 1690 (Magnusson 13–15). The Ascendancy effectively dominated Ireland until the twentieth century, when they would in their turn be dispossessed and marginalised in terms of the main thrust of Irish history, prompting Elizabeth Bowen to comment:

> In the life of what we call the new Ireland – but is Ireland ever new? – the lives of my own people [the Ascendancy] become a little thing; from 1914 they began to be merged, already into a chapter of different history. (*Bowen's Court* 437)

Irish novelists like Bowen, Trevor and Molly Keane all use the format of the Big House novel to demonstrate how the Ascendancy, the class that maintained their dominant position through the oppression of others, themselves became the victims of the relentless and paralysing hold of their own history of oppression. In *The Last September*, Bowen comments on the stranglehold the

unresolved past has on the Ascendancy: 'The unbelievable future became as
fixed as the past ...' (52). The immutable past gains a debilitating power that
holds members of the Ascendancy in helpless thrall. In her essay on 'The Big
House' (1940), Bowen characterises the power the past exercises as 'a spell':

> ... life in the Big House, in its circle of trees is saturated with char-
> acter: this is, I suppose, the element of the spell. The indefinite ghosts
> of the past, of the dead who lived here and pursued this same rou-
> tine of life in these walls add something, a sort of order, a reason for
> living, to every minute and hour. This is the order, the form of life,
> the tradition to which Big House people still sacrifice much. (28–9)

In William Trevor's *The Silence in the Garden*, the debilitating force of
the past is demonstrated. The high-handed arrogance of the privileged
Ascendancy is dramatised by and distilled into the case of Cornelius Dowley,
a local boy who is hunted like a quarry by the Rolleston children of the
Carriglas island demesne one summer. To the Ascendancy children it is an
intermittent game, great fun, to the boy a terrifying nightmare, which precipitates his eventual political activism. As a direct consequence of his suffering, he sets off a bomb at Carriglas years later, which tragically kills the
butler, rather than the young Rollestons, his erstwhile persecutors. Mrs
Rolleston, the grandmother of the careless and uncaring children, realises the
moral implications of this deed, namely that 'history has moral consequences
that must be faced' (Schirmer 157), and thereafter presides over the self-
imposed extinction of the family. The family shoulders the responsibility for
its past actions and accepts the need for the expiation of historical transgres-
sions. The two Rolleston sons lead utterly meaningless and isolated lives on
the declining estate, while the daughter renounces her love for a cousin and
marries instead the family solicitor on condition that they have no children
nor try to restore the estate. Tom, the illegitimate, Roman-Catholic son of
the murdered butler, inherits Carriglas, signifying the advent of the new dispensation and the extinction of the old.

In Trevor's earlier novel, *Fools of Fortune*, the possibility of making an
individual choice against the compelling thrust of history is investigated. The
novel has been called a 'kind of parable', dealing with the making of modern
Ireland (Hildebidle 114). As Vera Kreilkamp has pointed out, the genre of
the Big House novel usually reveals a 'connection between the private domestic world of the landlord's decline and the world of history - the political
transformations of Ireland in the nineteenth and twentieth centuries' (454).
Accordingly, the fate and experience of the Quintons of Kilneagh - as of the
Rollestons of Carriglas – are representative of the fate and experience of their
class and society. Willie Quinton, who would wish to escape the fate of his

class and lead a fulfilled personal life at Kilneagh, the family home, is forced by the thrust of history to avenge his father's and sisters' death by murdering the officer responsible for the burning of Kilneagh, thus sacrificing any hope he may have had of salvaging a happy and fulfilling life for himself and his loved ones. The inescapable stranglehold that history has on the helpless and insubstantial individual in its grip - and by extension on the class the individual represents - is confirmed by the title of the novel: 'After each brief moment there was as little chance for any of us as there was for Kilneagh after the soldier's wrath. Truncated lives, creatures of the shadows. Fools of fortune, as his father would have said; ghosts we became' (186). Trevor appears to confirm that – in spite of possible individual innocence – the only heartbreaking redemption from the heavy hand of communal past responsibility and culpability for this class is extinction.

Like William Trevor, Molly Keane also depicts the theme of the unhealthy hold of the past on her Ascendancy characters in her Big House novels. Unlike Trevor's Big House novels, Keane's novels mainly function in the mode of comedy (even though the comedy can be quite dark at times) and her depictions involve a quirky, humorous and individualised analysis of the dilemmas facing the members of her class, allowing for the possibility of more constructive resolutions to their troubled condition. In some of her novels like *Good Behaviour* (1981) and *Loving and Giving* (1988), she does reveal the same pessimistic grasp as Trevor with regard to her people's fate. Describing the Anglo-Irish novels of Elizabeth Bowen, Hermione Lee says that these works are shaped by 'a preoccupation with loss, betrayal and dislocation' and characterises Bowen's vision of contemporary (Ascendancy) life as 'dislocated, dispossessed and denatured' (4). So, too, in these novels by Keane, a marginalised class finds itself in thrall to a powerful past and reveals itself unable to cope with the hand that history has dealt it, resorting to deception and illusion in order to keep the unpleasant reality of the present at bay. In *Good Behaviour*, Aroon St Charles is the only survivor in the Ascendancy family, and she can only exist in a fantastic fortress of self-delusion. However much pity the unloved and unlovely Aroon may evoke, this dark comedy remains deeply pessimistic and even sinister, as it depicts a society where there is no escape from the debilitating hold of the past on the Ascendancy. In *Loving and Giving*, Keane goes even further to show the destructive patterns of self-delusion as the heroine, Nicandra, dies in the headlong pursuit of her self-delusive fantasy that she is loved by her husband. Her obsessive and unfulfilled need to be loved points to the tragic condition of a class that finds its legitimacy and its place in history rejected, struggling in vain for an affirmation of its very right to exist in the new Ireland. As in Trevor's novels, the Ascendancy is shown to pay a heavy price – extinction – for the burden of its past.

However, in other novels, like *Mad Puppetstown* (1931), *Fortune Hunt* (1952) and *Time after Time* (1983), Keane suggests the possibility of resolving the historical problems of her class, so that the individual can move out of the debilitating shadow of an unfinished history (even if it is only into the uncertain daylight of a not particularly congenial present), to negotiate for himself or herself a legitimate place in contemporary Ireland.

Mad Puppetstown (1931) is set during the Troubles of the early 1920s and the decade thereafter. It starts with a typical depiction of the idyllic existence of the Chevington family on their Irish demesne, Puppetstown, hunting, fishing, dancing and drinking, and then gradually shows the reality of political insurrection impinging on this paradisiacal existence, so that the children's freedom of movement becomes restricted, words have to be counted in front of the servants, security measures have to be taken. This sense of foreboding is fulfilled when a party from the house is attacked by political activists. The widowed Brenda and the three children of the demesne flee in consternation to England. As a result of the flight, Easter Chevington and her cousin, Basil, grow up in England, but find that they are never at home there:

> 'England,' Basil said ... 'she's too *crowded*. We want a littler, wilder sort of place ... We don't have the settled, stable drop of blood that goes down with the English. Easter, the thing is we don't see quite the same *jokes* ... My dear, don't think me an ass, but you do laugh in the wrong places for them. You'll never be a success here.' (232)

A bold escape to their motherland turns out to be futile, for what they are longing for is not Ireland as such, but their irreclaimable past in another Ireland, now lost. The house and estate are in a state of decay and the remembered familiar world has become alien and unknowable: 'There they stood, the pair of them, having tried confidently to sail their ships into the harbour of Yesterday, only to find that harbour silted up against anchorage' (252). As always in the Big House novel, the house symbolises or represents the family or society associated with it, and the decay of Puppetstown signifies the irreversible decline, perhaps demise of the Ascendancy as they had known it, the extinction of their class as required by an unmerciful history. In the history of her own family, *Bowen's Court*, Elizabeth Bowen suggests that the Ascendancy had always been alien in Ireland, but had lived with an illusion of belonging:

> If Ireland did not accept them, they did not know it – and it is that unawareness of final rejection, unawareness of being looked out at from some secretive, opposed life, that the Anglo-Irish naïve dignity and, even, tragedy seems to stand. Themselves, they felt Irish, and acted as Irishmen. (160)

Similarly, in her memoirs, *Seventy Years Young*, the Countess of Fingall, when commenting on the burning of Big Houses in the 1920s, states:

> People, whose families had lived in the country for three of four hundred years, realised suddenly that they were still strangers and that the mystery of it was not to be revealed to them - the secret lying as deep as the hidden valleys in the Irish hills, the barrier they had tried to break down standing as strong and immovable as those hills, brooding over an age-long wrong. (414)[1]

Bowen and Lady Fingall's historical accounts confirm the element of self-delusion in Ascendancy culture, so uncompromisingly depicted by Keane in *Good Behaviour* and *Loving and Giving*. In terms of *Mad Puppetstown*, the heartbreaking implications are that not only is 'Yesterday' not accessible to Basil and Easter anymore, but the 'Yesterday' they yearn for is in itself characterised by delusion. Keane depicts the crisis of identity and belonging of the young Chevingtons as extremely anguished. On encountering the reality of post-independence Puppetstown, Easter states initially: 'Tomorrow ... I'll go back. All this is more than I can bear' (261). They stay, however. They have to adapt to new circumstances, but will presumably be happier doing that in Ireland, than they would be in exile in England: 'They had come to find a refuge and had found instead Adventure' (265). By implication, Keane endows her Ascendancy characters with the potential to find a psychological and cultural home in the new Ireland, even though this can be achieved only with considerable effort on the part of those characters who wish to do so. Like Trevor, Keane depicts the Ascendancy as irretrievably displaced in the new Ireland. However, Keane's depiction differs from Trevor's in that she shows individual characters to have the potential and the option to move away from or out of the confinement of their Ascendancy identity in order to achieve personal autonomy and fulfilment.

In *Treasure Hunt* (1952), the decline of the Ascendancy is dealt with in terms of three generations of the family of Sir Roderick Ryall: a vital older generation from a vigorous aristocratic past that can only exist by complete negation of the present; a decadent, devitalised, middle generation, who are incapable of coping with the arduous present, and a modern generation who are faced by the 'fixed', unpalatable present as an inheritance from their elders. The older, vital generation is represented by Aunt Anna Rose, a delightful, vivacious old lady, with an 'indefinable air of arrival and departure – a look of absolute virility and concentration, enchanting in one so old' (90), who

---

1 Cf. also Margot Backus's discussion of Fingall's statement in her book *The Gothic family romance: heterosexuality, child sacrifice and the Anglo-Irish colonial order* (214).

spends a great deal of her time in a sedan-chair which has to do service in
turn as a nest, or a train, an ocean liner or aeroplane, taking Aunt Anna Rose
on frequent imaginary trips to destinations as exotic and far-flung as Honolulu,
Constantinople, St Petersburg or Budapest, a woman through whose apparent lunacy a keen intelligence and broad sanity shimmer, suggesting that Aunt
Anna Rose's fantasy world is only a self-protective bubble she maintains in
order to survive the uncongenial present. In terms of the conjunction of the
historical and the personal, Aunt Anna Rose's delusions are explained on a
personal level as the result of a traumatic experience she had on the Orient
Express during her honeymoon, which she cannot face psychologically, and
which impels her to blot out reality. (It turns out that she killed her elderly
husband by pushing him off the train.) However, in terms of the appease-
ment of history, her delusions suggest that Aunt Anna Rose, embodying all
those positive qualities that enabled the Ascendancy initially to establish a
vigorous aristocratic class in Ireland, has no place in the new Ireland where
her social group has become 'dislocated, dispossessed, denatured'.

The inadaptable, middle generation is represented by the late Sir
Roderick's siblings, Hercules and Consuelo, spoilt, selfish and decadent, completely incapable of even grasping the predicament of their race and class in
a changed Ireland, though attired in an insouciant charm and indefinable
glamour which makes them irresistibly attractive, even in their displacement
and selfishness. These two engaging sexagenarians never grow up or accept
any responsibility. Their pleasure in recalling their glamorous days at the
gaming tables of the Riviera – 'Do you remember the night we were cleaners – absolutely out, at Monte, and you left everything on red and it came
up fourteen times ...' (160) – is as acute as their pleasure in finding eggs for
the breakfast table:

> They went their opposite ways, prowling and poking along the racks
> of hay and straw-filled corners and hollowed earthly places as they
> had done since they were five years old. They knew they were bet-
> ter at finding eggs than any two people in the world and of all things
> they loved the game. A hot egg in the palm of the hand sent shivers
> of pleasure through them. (204)

It is thus left to the younger generation, Phillip and his cousin, Veronica,
to divest themselves of the paralysing historical encumbrances in order to deal
with reality in purely practical and personal terms:

> [The] outlook [of Phillip and Veronica] ... was not unlike that of two
> plumber's mates looking back without much interest or rancour to an
> illegitimate ducal grandfather. The present struggle to live and con-

tinue to live blinded them to their family's yesterdays and days before yesterday. They were depressingly factual and sensible in their accept-ance of the present. (154)

While Keane acknowledges that this divestment of past glamour is the only way to survive in the new Ireland, she nevertheless mourns the tran-sience of the beauty and harmony of a lost past, embodied by Hercules and Consuelo. The scholarly and aesthetically perceptive English guest, Eustace, thinks to himself that Phillip and Veronica 'seemed ... like the Victorian age succeeding the age of elegance' (155). The loss of allure is reflected in both the appearance and the spirit of the younger generation:

> Although in features [Phillip] was a blunt edition of his elders, he did not have that air of cosseted glamour which they wore with their clothes, without their clothes and under their skins. There was a com-moner colour about him ... there was no grace, inherited, studied, or forgotten. There was no leisure or dalliance with amusing thoughts by the way ... There was something useless yet valuable which had been cut out of his life. (26–7)

Though gracious and glamorous, the cigars and champagne generation (of Hercules and Consuelo) does not have an intimation of the resources nec-essary to help resolve the personal crisis of the solvency of the estate. Their own personal crisis represents in microcosmic form the historical crisis of their place in Ireland. It is left to Aunt Anna Rose, representing a more vital past, to resolve the family's predicament. The comic climax of the novel is a hilarious game of 'hunt the thimble' with the entire household participating in a search for Aunt Anna Rose's long lost rubies – believed by some to be mythical – which she is supposed to have worn on that fateful day on her honeymoon on the Orient Express. With the discovery of the jewels, Phillip and Veronica's financial security and their place in a new dispensation in Ireland are assured, and they move out of the shadow of the past into the daylight of present reality. At the same time, the magic of a glorious past – both Aunt Anna Rose's personal past of Viennese waltzes and imperial grandeur, and the wider historical past of the Anglo-Irish as a dazzling aris-tocracy – are lost.

Although *Time after Time* (1983) was published thirty years after *Treasure Hunt*, it has more in common with that novel – both as regards comic style and theme – than with its chronological predecessor, the much darker *Good Behaviour* (1981). *Time after Time* focuses on the Swift family of Durraghglass (possibly an ironic reference to the lost intellectual vitality of the Ascendancy represented by Jonathan Swift), another aristocratic Ascendancy family, displaced in modern Catholic Ireland, consisting of a brother, Jasper, and three sisters: April, May and Baby June. Each of them is physically or psychologically maimed: April is stone deaf, obsessed with her own appearance, and appears to have had a lurid marriage to a sex-crazed husband; May has a deformed hand and is a competent shop-lifter; Baby June is stunted in growth, uneducated (the money had run out) and 'in thrall' to the farmhand responsible for her horses. Jasper, the only brother, has lost an eye and appears incapable of forging a close personal relationship with anyone. In terms of the conjunction of the personal and historical which characterises the Big House novel, their emotional defects are ascribed to the overpowering impact of their late mother: 'She crippled them all with awful old love' (152), but obviously refer more broadly to a society maimed by its past, unable to come to terms with an alien present. The lasting negative effects of 'Mummie's' love even after her death, equates the paralysing hold of the past on the present life of that society. The decline of fortunes on the estate is always described with reference to objects or actions denoting the more gracious past and often associated with 'Mummie'. This conjunction of present decline and past glory suggests the unwillingness of the Swifts to exorcise the past and come to terms with the radical alteration in their (and their Society's) fortunes:

> Mummie had chosen the stuff for his tweed coat too. She had purred suggestions to the tailor during the fittings and the resulting coat still moved in a flow of perfection, giving grace with austerity. Perhaps the cuffs, grafted and integrated with their sleeves and serving no more useful purpose than that of pleasing the eye, were it most touching and elegant feature. An ageless antique and needing care, it could fall to bits on him any day now … [He] shuddered: three hundred pounds for anything proper today. Forget it. Horrible. Horrible times. (152)

Threadbare elegance disguises present horror.

The agent that rips up all the disguises and pretences, revealing both the fraudulence of their present existence and the horrors of the past, is their long-lost cousin Leda. She manages to ferret out all the deepest secrets of their aberrant behaviour, and in a climactic scene reveals each one's moral disabilities to the others over the breakfast table. She maliciously tears open the wounds of the past but ironically, the operation actually has salutary results. The tissue of lies, the house of cards of their displaced and denatured lifestyle is destroyed and the glamorous but corrupt past is exorcised. This is symbolised by the burning of all 'Mummie's desecrated clothes', hitherto carefully preserved as part of the cult of the past, in the orchard. Released from their obsolete aristocratic inheritance, the four siblings regain their vitality, embarking on new enterprises, 'grace gone, age apparent in all its inadequacies' (234). They deal with the graceless, inadequate, unglamorous present on its own terms, liberated from 'a long sustained dream, and empowered [for the] practical decision for tomorrow' (232). Far from the adjustment painful, the now mature Swifts rejoice in their new-found autonomy. Each one devises his or her own modest and distinctly unaristocratic *modus vivendi* in a new Republican Ireland: April retires to a convent, May is engaged to work for a shop-keeper, Baby June comes to terms with the limitations of her job as a farmer, and Jasper reaches an agreement with the neighbouring monastery to keep his garden going. Significantly, the Catholic Church features prominently in the adjustments made by April and Jasper, suggesting the displacement of the Protestant Ascendancy by a Catholic establishment. The resolution suggests not only a symbolic laying to rest of the Ascendancy's glamorous but now inappropriate past cultural identity, but the achievement of personal autonomy on an immediate level for the individual characters.

The vital achievement of autonomy by individual members of the Ascendancy is even more clearly demonstrated in *Treasure Hunt*. Phillip and Veronica cannot afford to run an estate in lordly fashion, but have to run a farm in an economic way: settling down in the mire to assist a harrowing sow or spending a night in a stable with a colic horse. Faced with a choice between internal exile in the land of their birth and a harsh adjustment to the culture of the new Ireland, these people have the courage to 'emigrate' psychologically from the Old to the New Ireland, resolving the claims of a glamorous but debilitating history and embracing an unglamorous but self-determined present.

It therefore appears that while some of Keane's work endorses the view that the Anglo-Irish Protestant Ascendancy is enervated by the hold of past history, she does posit in some of her novels the potential for members of her class to move beyond the paralysing hand of history into an empowered, active present in the new Ireland. It is of course dangerous to read these novels too simplistically as fables of Irish history as the cultural and historical are consistently dealt with in terms of the personal and individual. It becomes clear, however, that Keane postulates divestment of a mythic past as a first prerequisite for what is ultimately for the individual the investment of a mature, energetic self.

Riding for a fall: Molly Keane and the equestrian sublime

RACHAEL SEALY LYNCH

'To excel as a horsewoman was the ambition of most of us. Even without achieving that object, our horses were a source of unparalleled interest and enjoyment' (*Knight of Cheerful Countenance* Intro. 10). Thus speaks Molly Keane. She warms further to the subject of horses in an interview with Polly Devlin (Introduction to *Conversation Piece;* unpaginated): 'The only thing I thought about writing was that it would give me some money so that I could go on having lots of fun and going to horse shows and hunting ... I had my hunting and my hunting friends ... the hunting was tremendous.' In *A Portrait of the Artist as a Young Girl,* she reiterates: 'Hunting mattered more than anything else' (75). Race meetings, fox-hunting, and the good company of horses and those who loved them are as central to Keane's early books as they were to the young woman who wrote them. Even Keane's early *nom de plume* M.J. Farrell was dreamed up 'from a pub, as I rode home', she tells us, so that her dubious status as an author would have no impact upon her social life. Of *The Knight of Cheerful Countenance* she says: 'I did have it published on my own initiative but I would not have admitted that I was writing at that time. It would have been considered a rather anti-social thing to do in that hunting society – a society in which I wanted to get on jolly well' (*Portrait of the Artist as a Young Girl* 76). It is clear that Molly Keane participated enthusiastically in Ascendancy social life, particularly as a young woman. What changed as she aged was the degree of acerbity, and indeed ambivalence, with which she portrayed that life.

A comparative study of Keane's novels in the order in which they were written will bring to light subtle changes in subject and tone as early as *Conversation Piece.* Her treatment of her characters, their caste, and their preoccupations – and in particular their obsession with all things equine – becomes more nuanced and layered with every new publication. However, Molly Keane scholars cannot but engage with the apparent chasm separating her early and mature work. How and where can we discern the Keane of *Good Behaviour, Time after Time,* and *Loving and Giving* in earlier M.J. Farrell novels like *The Knight of Cheerful Countenance* or *Conversation Piece*? The startling differences in tone, mood, and point of view mask what in fact are significant similarities in subject matter and thematic content. Keane's three later novels are the product of a harshly realistic authorial gaze, while her earlier works appear, superficially at least, to be far more effervescent and untroubled. While there is no doubt that Keane's fiction undergoes drastic changes, particularly in tone, when she returns to writing in 1981 after a twenty-year break,[1] her subjects and their pastimes actually show a remarkable consistency throughout her *oeuvre*.

Keane's critics have employed various means to discuss her increasingly acerbic portrayals of life in the crumbling world of the Anglo-Irish Ascendancy, and to connect her eleven earlier novels to the final three. To take a notable example, Keane's fascination and increasing disillusionment with the emblematic Big House and its inhabitants have been well documented by her critics. Vera Kreilkamp, Paul Deane, Rüdiger Imhof, Ellen O'Brien, and others have focused on Keane through the lens of Big House fiction, discussing several of her novels in relation to other Big House fiction. In *The Anglo-Irish Novel and the Big House* Kreilkamp argues, rightly I think, that Keane views the nostalgia of the Big House and its inhabitants as dependent upon 'carefully constructed patterns of delusion, on wilful misinterpretation of the past in order to construct self-protecting illusions of stability' (182). More recently, Moira Casey[2] and others have been working on the Queering of Keane, noting the many homosexual characters populating her novels, and tracing the increasing complexity of their treatment as we move from *Devoted Ladies* through *Good Behaviour* to *Time after Time*. Yet, despite the centrality of the horse to Keane and to her work, her critics typically mention this animal in passing and then move on.

I would like instead to focus upon the enormous importance of horses to this woman whose caste bears, in the colloquial appellation 'Horse Protestant', witness to the obsession. Keane's early novels were highly popular when they first appeared; as Polly Devlin recounts, a 'devoted' following gloried in what Devlin terms their 'horsy habitat' (Introduction to *Devoted Ladies*, v). In addition, I would like to propose that we can perhaps deploy Keane's treatment of horses as a way to try to understand the transition from her Young Entries into the field of fiction to her later work. I will here examine Keane's staging of the Ascendancy as 'Horse Protestants' riding to their doom. Using

1 While Keane was devastated after the unexpected death of her husband Bobby in 1946, she continued to write, enjoying considerable success on the London stage. *Treasure Hunt* was produced in 1949, and the widowed Keane, mother of two young daughters, was glad of the income. Her daughter Sally Phipps stresses that it was not grief, but rather the failure of *Dazzling Prospect* in 1961, and the vicious reviews it received, that caused Keane to put down her pen. When Keane began writing for an audience again, with *Good Behaviour* in 1981, Phipps believes that 'the time was right for her to be herself; being seventy-seven, she felt freer; she could speak'.   2 Casey is currently completing a book entitled *The lesbian in the house*. In a chapter on the Irish lesbian character pre-1960 in which she focuses on Keane and Kate O'Brien, she argues that 'the movement into Ireland in *Devoted Ladies* brings about the violent suppression of lesbian desire, while the movement out of Ireland in *Mary Lavelle* exposes a greater degree of sexual alternatives for women even if lesbianism is still not a real possibility'.

selected novels, two early and two late, I explore Keane's focus on matters equestrian, showing how we can chart in the chronological progression of her work the last hurrah, decline, and fall(s) of the Anglo-Irish mastery of the horse. We can also investigate the possibility of reinvigoration, thanks to a surprising 'assist' from a Traveller. The possibility that Ireland's humbled and repositioned Ascendancy may be able to re-establish themselves in a form more adaptable to current conditions is hinted at in Keane's penultimate novel *Time after Time*. Keane's treatment of her equestrians and their increasingly visible discontents allows us a fascinating insight into her fictional evaluation of the caste into which she was born. It functions as a bright thread running through a tapestry depicting a vanishing dynasty.

Unlike earlier Ascendancy writers, Keane, who was born in 1904, bore personal witness to the social and political upheavals that marked the violent birth of the Irish Republic and the steep decline of her own caste. In her novels she is increasingly clear-eyed about the end of the world she knew, if not without regrets. As she says herself in her Introduction to the 1993 Virago edition of *The Knight of Cheerful Countenance*, 'Re-reading it now, some seventy years later, I am forced to accept that the world of my youth has vanished and that, for the modern reader, there may be some explaining to do' (5). Like Canon Claude Chavasse, she realises that 'the class [she] belonged to simply failed to survive'. As he put it, 'We thought we would go on forever. Now we've pretty well died out' (Kevin Myers). As Keane brings us across a span of fifty-two years from 1926 to 1988, moving from houses full of servants to Jasper Swift reigning alone in his cavernous kitchen, we can chart a continuum, and horses ride all the apparent fences. A focus on horses in her fiction affords us a ringside seat at her exploration of this continuum.

Keane is of course not the only writer to honour the vast and nuanced importance of the horse to the Anglo-Irish, or the only devotee of the hunt. Keane's writing on hunting in her early fiction is as knowledgeable and enthusiastic as any we encounter in *The Irish R.M.*, and many of the same issues appear in both Keane and Somerville and Ross. For example, we encounter the pleasures of the hunt and the evils of fox-poaching in both *Conversation Piece* and 'Great-Uncle McCarthy.' Furthermore, as Bi-Ling Chen has argued, Somerville and Ross use fox hunting as a metaphor for Irish cultural identity: 'In as much as the English gentry enjoyed fox hunting, and saw it as a part of their tradition, Somerville and Ross's manipulation of the sport to distinguish between the English and the Irish was certainly a distortion of historical reality. But such a distortion allows the novelists some space to view the Irish from an insider's angle,' and 'to locate the Irishness shared by the Anglo-Irish and the native Irish' (39). As I will show, in *Conversation Piece* we see Keane deploying the hunt in a similar fashion, and in *Time after Time* she notably uses horses a locator of shared Irishness. However, in her treatment of matters equine, Keane moves forward in a direction no earlier Anglo-Irish writer could have taken. In her earliest novels, the hunt is portrayed relatively unambiguously, with very little, if any, ironic distance. When Keane resumed writing after her silent years, hunting is no longer a key focus of her narratives. Horses and the people who ride them remain central to her concerns, but after 1981 their portrayal is fraught with layers of irony, implied meaning, ambiguity, and metaphorical resonance. Keane does not so much subvert traditions of Ascendancy writing on hunting as move beyond them, while retaining the horse as a metaphor for Anglo-Irish, native Irish, and shared Irish cultural identity in post-colonial Ireland.[3]

A useful text from which to begin this enquiry is Keane's very first novel. *The Knight of Cheerful Countenance* is a hunting Romance, written as she recovered from an illness at the age of seventeen. Her own review of her adolescent debut is withering. She calls it 'an awful little hunting romance. It really was dreadful, but I suppose it was all the things I wanted to be and all the things I wanted to happen; a terribly attractive girl and smashing young men riding like mad to hounds ...' (*Portrait: POA* 76).

However, despite Keane's own dismissal of her work of apprenticeship, and despite its undeniable superficiality, lack of ironic distance, grammatical turgidity, and overabundance of sophomoric dog jokes,[4] it is a fascinating document for several reasons. First, its very artlessness ensures a clearer 'take' on her world than appears in her later, far more finely crafted work. It was first published, interestingly, by Mills and Boon, in 1926, and references to the recent Civil War are abundantly in evidence, although not central to Keane's youthful concerns. After all, Keane was 17 in 1921 and Ballyrankin, her childhood home, was, she explains, 'burned down (by Sinn Fein) as a reprisal for some Black and Tan atrocity' (*POA* 74). Her father sat on a haystack and watched. English-born himself, he mouthed 'one singular oath', Russell Harty tells us, as he sat and watched his property burn. 'I'd rather die in Ireland than live in England!' (Introduction to *Loving without Tears* vii). So not surprisingly, *The Knight of Cheerful Countenance* contains references to house burnings, Republican kidnappings, and the continual and pervasive threat of violence. While the 'district round Bungarvin' is hardly the centre of the 'almost daily' 'deeds of unbelievable foulness and treachery' recorded in the newspapers, still, the narrator notes solemnly, 'wrecked police-barracks and court-houses, country houses standing empty, and the charred

3 Sally Phipps emphasises that Keane considered herself to be Irish, but did not question the dubious nature of her Irishness. 4 Keane emphasises her abundant affection for her canine companions, rivalled only by her feelings for horses, in many ways and in many places. Most of her key protagonists, like the three sisters in *Time after Time*, are complemented by their beloved dogs, and her *Book of Nursery Cooking* ends with a 'Tailpiece', replete with recipes suitable for dogs and suggestions for their optimum maintenance and feeding as they age.

walls of what had been country houses, all went to show how little of a myth was the state of civil war in Ireland' (29) at the time of English Cousin Allan's arrival at Ballinrath House.

Against this backdrop we are presented with cover-to-cover horses, hounds, hunts, races, and thoroughly equine encounters and occasions. The only time the characters in this novel are parted from their beloved horses is when they are in bed. The narrative opens with Miss Ann Hillingdon dividing her attention equally between Captain Dennys St Lawrence, the human love of her life, and 'the good-looking chestnut mare,' her beloved Pet Girl (14). It closes with Miss Ann's younger sister Sybil cementing her romance with cousin Allan by sharing her plans concerning a wonderful horse named Sailor. 'She ran her hand under the sheet to get the comfortable feel of Sailor's warm shoulder ... "I don't know now what he thinks about it, but *I* should say he'd look very nice in print as 'the gift of the bride' – don't you?" Allan, of course, "thought so too"' (272), and the future union of this happy couple and their equine companion is assured. Note that even as young love blooms it is the horse, not the man, that Sybil is caressing. In this novel, as in much of Keane's early work, horses genuinely do seem to be more desirable than humans, and hunting a more erotic activity than any other. The predominant mode of Keane's early narratives is not ironic. While the Black Friday Yearling functions in *Good Behaviour* as a steamy signifier of hidden homosexual desire, the eroticisation of the horse in early narratives like *The Knight of Cheerful Countenance* perhaps relocates the expression of desire in a society that placed great value on decorum and frowned upon abandon, allowing the characters to give vent, in an appropriate setting, to displays of emotion and affection. In other words, horses function as genuine objects of desire, or at most as substitutes, not symbols, in these early works.

In *The Knight of Cheerful Countenance* the young Keane is still apparently under the influence of certain potent myths of Empire. She establishes the terms of an idyllic equine dialectic, an equestrian sublime,[5] in which the English and

5 I coined this term to identify and describe the single-minded absorption and the intensity of emotion we observe in Molly Keane's horse-obsessed characters. I had two sources in mind when I did so. First, and most obviously, was Keats' reference to Wordsworth's 'egotistical sublime' in his letter to Richard Woodhouse, 27 October 1818 (*Letters* 387). Second, I wished to suggest that in their passionate devotion to equestrian pursuits, including the danger, art, and ritual of the hunt, Keane's characters are granted access to an aesthetics of sorts, poetry in motion for a philistine society. Edmund Burke speaks, in his *Philosophical enquiry into the origin of our ideas of the sublime and beautiful,* to the knife-edge of fear, horror, and enthrallment inherent in an activity like fox hunting. He comments suggestively that 'Whatever is fitted in any sort to excite the ideas of pain, and danger ... is a source of the sublime' (39), and that 'the angry tones of wild beasts are ... capable of causing a great and awful sensation' (84). Through their horses, Keane's characters experience what Burke calls 'the great power of the sublime', the effects of which are 'astonishment ... admiration, reverence, and respect' (57).

the Anglo-Irish gentry, and certain key family servants, function as sporting men and gentlemen, winners even when they occasionally lose. Honourable men and women of all classes can be identified and are connected, within this ide-alised mythic world, by their dealings with their horses. Meanwhile, cads and bounders appear within the ranks of the locals and also as a result of the unfor-tunate mixing of blood that occurs when a Horse Protestant lady runs away with her social inferior. In her Introduction to the novel, Keane comments that 'Marriage beneath one's social status was looked on as a disaster and almost never occurred, no matter how scarce the contemporary and social equals of the young ladies of the time' (8). The novel's gentlemen and bounders fall neatly and comfortingly into place as they do in comic books, obeying the dictates of caste and nationality so important to the Ascendancy frame of mind.

The nuances of caste in the novel, while rigidly deployed, are fascinating. At one end of the spectrum is Cousin Allan. Rich, handsome, well-educated, English Allan is sent to Ireland to stay with his cousins the Hillingdons by his aunt, Lady Semple-Maugham, because she considers him to be beneath her own daughter Dillys, who has fallen violently in love with him. Yet he would be, she thinks, a 'splendid chance for one of those Irish girls' (31). Allan is a sporting gentleman through and through, socially acceptable and extremely fond of dogs and of course horses. He is an experienced civilised Colonial boy; he had lived 'as a subaltern in a cavalry regiment' (30) in India, so is likely to adapt to Irish living with ease. The Hillingdons are all they should be socially, although a hint of the gathering clouds can perhaps be seen in Major Hillingdon's funk. '... his nerve was gone. It was cruelly hard, he who had been the best man to hounds in the country, and now – well the very sight of a plunging horse made him feel cold and sick' (129). Luckily the hunting and shooting gene re-emerges triumphant in the Major's three children, Ann, Sybil, and Rickard. Yet, because of the Major's funk, he can no longer function as Master of Foxhounds, and the honoured position passes to the character rep-resenting the bounder, the socially inferior Mr. St. Lawrence. While also an Anglo-Irishman, he belongs to the sub-caste of 'buckeen' (39), distinctly below the 'county' Hillingdons. As Ann explains to Allan, despite their knowledge of horses, Buckeens are non-U, as Nancy Mitford would have put it.[6] 'Oh ... you know ... they're different, somehow. They pronounce castle to rhyme with tassle and dance with pants' (39). His son Dennys, while frowned upon by the

---

6 Mitford cites a system developed by Professor Alan Ross of Birmingham University in sup-port of her contention that upper class English usage is clearly distinguishable by virtue of is 'hundreds of small but significant landmarks'. Not wishing to be accused of snobbery herself, she writes that 'The Professor, pointing out that it is solely by their language that the upper classes nowadays are distinguished (since they are neither cleaner, richer, nor better-educated than anybody else), has invented a useful formula: U (for upper class) -speaker versus non-U speaker' (25).

Major, is tolerated only because his mother was an Ascendancy lady who married beneath her and subsequently died of grief. Mr St. Lawrence does not actually abuse his hounds, and he is a good horseman, but he is a swindler, cad, and cheat. Even worse, his swindling revolves around horses; he is a 'horse-coper' who will stoop so low as to trick his own son into acquiring a horse from a disadvantaged local family with a worthless check. He symbolically taints the mythic world he enters; perhaps the decline of the Ascendancy is foreshadowed by his promotion to a key equestrian position as a direct consequence of a prominent insider's inadequacy.

Dennys, however, is straight and honourable. He has his mother's pure blood coursing through his veins, and also, a crucial point, his maternal grandfather left money in his will for Dennys, his only grandson, to be educated in the manner appropriate for an Anglo-Irish gentleman, at a 'great' English public school. Winchester (172) performs its metropolitan magic, ensuring that Dennys will grow up to be a gentleman. 'There he learnt many things outside the curriculum, things which made him sick when he thought of his father's shady methods of horse-coping ... the great public school had him for her own, and continued to exercise an ever-increasing influence over him ...' (60). He becomes, in Joseph Bristow's words, an Empire Boy.[7]

Thanks to his education, Dennys, while not 'of her own caste' (63) does constitute a fitting mate for Ann Hillingdon. However, first he must prove to her that he is not a cheat, despite the evidence against him – it is Dennys who unknowingly tenders the bad cheque for the horse. Ann, after all, only backs winners. Even after his innocence is proven, he and Ann can marry and find happiness only through the Victorian ending of emigration, such is the taint of miscegenation overshadowing their union. So Dennys and his new wife export their knowledge of horses to the new World, where Dennys can oversee a ranch in Texas and make a new beginning away from the stifling social order boxing in the inhabitants of Bungarvin. Even in this early novel, Keane is clearly aware of the cracks in the myth

In *Conversation Piece*, written a decade later and appearing in 1932, the cracks widen. In this novel the equestrian idyll with its embodied myths of Empire is subject to intense scrutiny, and it does not emerge intact. Again the novel opens with an English visitor, Oliver, arriving at Pullinstown to stay with his Anglo-Irish cousins, Sir Richard and his children Dick and Willow. Again, the narrative is unabashedly horsey, and its equine focus is central to

7 Bristow explores the potent formative effects of English public school life, and of narratives portraying that life, on both upper- and middle-class boys in the late nineteenth and early twentieth centuries. He cites the 'special value' placed on such an education, demonstrating its importance as an incubator of a 'philosophy of Christian manliness' (53) in a race of future servants of Empire. Exposure to a public school education supposedly ensured an enhanced physical and moral development.

Keane's agenda. Oliver, the novel's likeable and reliable first-person narrator, leaves us in no doubt on this key point:

> Horses, many horses; horses past, present, and to come; horses good and bad; hunters, point-to-point horses and race-horses ... all these bright, dangerous horses, never one forgotten, forge a chain of memory, speculation and future event which holds these three, Sir Richard and his son and daughter, to one another; or, contrarily, drags them each to a point of passionate difference that must, one would think, cause them to forgo for ever any illusion of family unity or kindness. (206)

Oliver comes 'for the Springwell Harriers' point-to-point meeting' (1) and stays on, the willing participant in multiple equestrian events and endeavours. Oliver himself is wholesome, gentlemanly, and of course an excellent rider. The joys of the hunt are celebrated in loving detail; indeed, the eroticisation of the hunting experience, and the devotion of its participants, that are hallmarks of Keane's work are much in evidence in this novel. It is important to emphasise that in Keane's early work, the hunt does not receive identifiably nuanced or ironic treatment. Yet clearly the language of passion, of physical excitement, of poetry, of yearning, or of intense feeling of any kind, discouraged in any other context in the rigid decorum of Keane's Anglo-Irish world,[8] finds a legitimate outlet in the context of the hunt. Sexual love, even when heterosexual and sanctioned by the Church of Ireland, is apparently unable to speak its name. However, a mounting breathless excitement can find expression through the language of the hunt. It is through the equestrian sublime, here in the form of the art of hunting, that these characters experience an approximation of both physical consummation and cathartic release. Consider, for example, Oliver's ecstatic description of these high points from a hunt, early in the narrative, featuring the West Common hounds:

> A useful, active-looking sort, the West common hounds ... I would love them in their work, I knew ... The bloom on the hounds spoke a real psalm in praise of their kennel huntsman ... My heart shot up to the last pounding notch of excitement. That almost insane shock of courage, which the view of a good fox leaving a covert gives one, rose choking me in its intensity ... [Anthony's hounds] ran well together, their voices a tearing ecstasy in the evening ... The exalta-

8 Consider, for example, Richard's parents' horror upon discovering that he was consuming 'unhealthy-sounding' poetry in his tree-house (*GB* 31) or Aroon's mother's insistence upon 'quiet, well-behaved sorrow' after Papa's death (*GB* 240).

tion of effort fulfilled mounted within us ... None of us listened to
one another, but almost we loved one another. (87–102)

Yet several distinct changes, even at this early point in Keane's career,
should be noted. The villain of the piece is a parson named Mr Fox whose
infamy is such that he breaks 'the greatest rule of fox-hunting, "thou shalt not
draw another man's coverts"' (85). He is not a buckeen but an insider, a high-
caste younger son. The suffering of the hunted fox is dwelt on perhaps a little much for comfort, while simultaneously softened through reference to his
'quick and gallant death' (101).[9] A visiting English girl, a 'fascinating beauty'
with whom Dick is initially much taken, is portrayed as a terrifying avatar of
Empire. Despite being embedded in a romantic plot, she hunts and kills with
a blood-lust that has little to do with notions of good sportsmanship. She lies
and steals to further her ends; 'all strife and effort this girl's spirit to her,'
Oliver says of this girl who 'resolved [her] unrequited passions in the desperate pursuit of BIG GAME' (191). She plays to win, and, in her own words,
'can't bear to be defeated about anything' (187). Portrayed as 'hard and acquis-
itive' (182), she employs 'systemized endeavour in the pursuit of game' (202).
Unlike Dick, Willow, and Oliver, who thrill to the chase, the girl is driven by
the desire to amass a bloodied heap of trophies. Wide-eyed, she recalls a 'wonderful' day: 'I caught two fish before luncheon. I rushed home and got my
gun and shot a brace of grouse; rushed home and got my rifle and shot a stag
before dinner' (177). This 'pretty sneak ... no fit partner for crime or for love'
(203) leaves without the repelled Dick in her bag. This Empire Girl, with her
lust for trophies, allows Keane to 'distinguish between the English and the
Irish' (Chen 39), as do Somerville and Ross. The contrast between the girl
and her hosts (and Oliver, who appears to be granted immunity from
Englishness in this regard, perhaps because of his blood ties to his cousins)
suggests that the Anglo-Irish notion of the ritual of hunting as an art form,
pursued for its own sake and for the emotions it engenders rather than for
material reward, is far superior to the English notion of hunting.

However, not even a love of hunting in its purest form can save the
Anglo-Irish from themselves. Most indicative of the beginning of the end so
unsparingly portrayed in Keane's later novels is the self-destructive inter-fam-
ily skirmishing that takes place between Sir Richard and his aged cousins, the
ironically named Honour and Beauty. Templeshambo, the cousins' family

9 It is difficult to guess Keane's intent here with any degree of accuracy. The hunt is presented
in glowingly positive terms, Keane herself adored and excelled at the sport, and there is no
other evidence in the novel identifying the uncomplicated, forthright Oliver as an ironic narrator. Yet the suffering and death of the anthropomorphised fox suggests the presence of an ironic,
critical authorial distance. Perhaps the savagery inherent in the hunt portends the vicious inter-
family fighting that speeds the decline of the Ascendancy.

seat, offers a preview of the decay of the Big Houses in Keane's later novels: 'The roof's falling in on them … [they are] the last of that lot, and they're broke' (109). Their fights are bitter and nasty, fuelled by the lingering passions of 'Romance forgotten, but with a nip to it still as though it had wilfully been put from them, not out-worn and sick from sentiment' (125). As Oliver observes, Sir Richard and Lady Honour 'can't let each other *alone*' (214; emphasis Oliver's). The central ongoing battle consuming this ageing pair is waged, at its most intense, with nothing less than Willow's love and esteem as the prize, and both parties routinely deploy horses as their weapons of choice as they appal the ever-decent Oliver with their 'evil sport of bandying Willow and Willow's favour back and forth between them' (223). Sir Richard foiling Honour's attempts to cheat in a point-to-point (164–5); Honour taking Willow to a choice horse show behind Sir Richard's back; Sir Richard buying back his daughter's loyalty, for now at least, at the end of the narrative with the purchase of 'the horse she rode today … He's not to sell him till the end of the hunting season' (272): in these repeated scenes of internecine bargaining, bribery, and double-crossing we are afforded a terrifying preview of the family feuds of the later novels, and of the dissolution of the Ascendancy. The apparition of the fairy Duke, a resident long-term ghost at Templeshambo and avatar of the family fortunes, neatly symbolises approaching doom for the Horse Protestants.[10] He appears, of course, on horseback. Lady Eveleen ('Beauty') tells Oliver the story of the Duke: 'He rides up those stairs on a little chestnut horse and *out* with him through that window … That little horse is silver-shod, and the luck of this family goes up and down with the thickness or thinness of those shoes' (126). In his most recent apparition, the fairy Duke's silver shoes were worn 'thin as paper' (132).

Upon her return to published writing after the silent years, Keane no longer hesitates to portray her declining caste in an obviously critical, caustic manner. It is perhaps in *Good Behaviour* that the symbolic decline of the Equestrian Sublime and all it denotes is deployed to the greatest effect. Aroon St Charles is, notably, Keane's first unreliable narrator,[11] and Keane portrays her as an example of pathetic self-deception, an abused child who herself abuses her inherited power. Aroon displays on the walls and chimneypiece of Gull's Cry a sort of shrine to her father and the patriarchal power now in her hands, thanks to the terms of his will. Imported from Temple Alice are rows of silver cups, 'not to mention the model of a seven-pound sea trout and sev-

---

10 The Fairy Duke is a mysterious figure; the narrative does not explain exactly who he was. He functions in the narrative as a sort of equestrian male banshee. 11 Sally Phipps stresses the significance of Aroon's unreliability, suggesting that it affords Keane an opportunity to expose the dark side of her crumbling Ascendancy world from a position once removed. Phipps confirms that Keane suffered from feelings of guilt for betraying her caste and felt ambivalent about so doing, so Aroon functions importantly as an enabling narrative device.

eral rather misty snapshots of bags of grouse laid out on the steps' (4). And, accompanying the cups, in further homage to Papa's equestrian prowess, are 'pictures and photographs of him riding winners' (4). His equestrian success is here linked with his patriarchal potency at its zenith.

But while Aroon has inherited what is left of the family fortune, she is not portrayed as a winner in anything other than the most literal sense. Her murdering of Mummy in a gruesome death by rabbit is anything but sporting. The foxes destined for execution in *Conversation Piece* are offered far fairer chance of escape. Persecution is one thing; unfair trickery quite another. 'Rabbit – rabbit chokes her, rabbit sickens her, and rabbit killed her ... if it was a smothering you couldn't have done it better ... We're all killed from you,' charges the old family servant Rose across Mummy's corpse. Rose, we remember, also accuses Aroon of tricking her mother out of Temple Alice, the ancestral home, and of hastening the deaths of the previous inhabitants of Gull's Cry: 'I heard the roaring and the crying when you parted Mister Hamish from Miss Enid and put the two of them in hospital wards, male and female, to die on their own alone' (8).

So what does the state of horsemanship in the novel have to do Miss Aroon's reprehensibly bad behaviour? Everything, I would argue. A focus on matters equine enhances our understanding of both family dynamics and Ascendancy decline in the narrative, indicating clearly first that the power and status passed on to Aroon by her father are both corrupt and waning, and second that Aroon is an unfitting recipient for what is left of her family's potency.

Papa was in his heyday indeed a winner, both in the field and in bed with his countless mistresses. Yet his attempts to breed were, as we see, a sorry failure. His line ends with Hubert; even had Aroon's only brother lived, his homosexuality would have virtually guaranteed the end of the male bloodline. The hinted pregnancies resulting from his illicit unions (with Mrs Brock and Blink Crowhurst) are blighted from the start, and are cut short and denied by Mrs Brock's suicide and Blink's departure for England. Symbolically, Papa, himself so centaur-like, is lamed in the Great War and thereafter unable to ride. Horses and their handling in this novel, rather than representing the sportsmanship, courage, and decency of the Anglo-Irish at the height of their powers, become instead emblematic of the potency that is no longer within their grasp, and also of their uncontrollable, unmanageable desires. Aroon experiences great fear and difficulty atop a horse throughout the book. Even Hubert, whose equestrian prowess as an adult made his father proud, struggled as a child to gain mastery. As the siblings enter adulthood, their horses function as symbols of smouldering, uncontainable, forbidden sexuality. Hubert may wish to compel his horse, Arch Deacon, to 'good manners' (89), but after Hubert's death Aroon's attempts to ride him render her world 'a fearful place' (117). Richard and Hubert's union sizzles around the Black Friday Yearling they buy together at the Dublin Horse Show. In a sexually charged scene, 'As he took a last look at the yearling, Hubert gave a tingling kind of shudder'. (87)

Later, after Hubert's death, Richard gives the yearling to Aroon – a potent symbol of secrecy, repression, and all that she cannot manage, control, or understand. Keane's use of the horse in *Good Behaviour* as a metaphor for the secret, the shameful, the unmanageable, is in marked contrast to Keane's earlier, joyous eroticisation of the hunt. As readers we appreciate the depth of complexity of Keane's later work, as we note how she moved from apparently simple equations and substitutions (hunting as sexual experience; the horse as an art form) to a masterly layering of multiple meanings[12] We remember that this equine gift is made in a missive from Africa, filled with rhapsodic accounts of a bull elephant and other specimens of wildlife, that Aroon ridiculously misinterprets as a love letter, and Keane's own words about the novel echo in our ears: 'wouldn't it be funny to have a fool who doesn't see what is happening' (Introduction to *CP*; unpaginated). Horses are integral to this agenda, as Aroon falls off her mounts, struggles for control, and misses the point repeatedly, until, flush with her hereditary winnings, she politely brutalises her family as her mother brutalised her, as Papa astride his steeds looks down from the wall. Power of the type Papa enjoyed is no longer an option; Aroon is, in contrast, a petty tyrant.

Keane's evaluation of her equestrian kind is, however, not unremittingly cynical. In *Time after Time* she offers up a fascinating possibility of productive future co-operation between two groups usually placed at opposite ends of the socio-economic spectrum, but linked nonetheless by their obsession with horses and their increasing marginalisation in post-independence Ireland – the Horse Protestants and the Travellers. In this novel the four Swift siblings struggle to cope with and make sense of a world in which their caste is becoming increasingly marginalised and dispossessed. Two of the siblings face down the future (we leave April in stasis and Jasper failing to take seriously the looming threat of disestablishment and unwilling to exert himself to make the compromises that he understands, at least in theory, to be necessary for economic survival). May's is the smoothest transition; she emerges as a tough, adaptable survivor, redefining her 'place' – and power dynamics between her and Jasper – by legitimising her talents. She remakes herself, moving from shoplifting to antique restoration, and finding in the process economic independence outside the walls of Durraghglass, her crumbling fortress. However, more pertinent to our focus here is 'slow' (46) Baby June's fragile reconstruction of the equestrian sublime. June had been an excellent horsewoman in her youth. When we meet her she has lost her nerve, but she passes on much of her vast store of knowledge to

---

12 Of relevance here, I think, is Sally Phipps' comment that 'the hunting world is a philistine world.' Phipps believes that Keane's theatrical experience in the Thirties and Forties 'made her gradually understand she was an artist'.

her stable boy, Christy Lucey. Christy deserts her, however. Tempted away by neighbours of the Swifts, he decides against continued service in a decaying Ascendancy establishment. He opts instead for a bourgeois Catholic marriage to his pregnant girlfriend, a job with a house in possession of decent indoor plumbing and 'a ride in Dublin show' (200) included, and the pleasing of his mother. While June does feel terribly betrayed, she nevertheless then climbs tremulously back in the saddle again, and survives a potentially devastating riding accident to hire and train Christy's successor, a Traveller boy who shares her equestrian passions. June, the outsider within the Swift family, themselves outsiders in the new Ireland, here forges a symbolic alliance with another marginalised group, the Travellers. Does this new alliance allow for a cautious optimism, suggesting as it does a breaking down of the mistrust that so divides Irish social classes?[13] June even makes an effort to understand Christy's choices from his perspective: 'she glimpsed a little of his predicament, entailed between his mother, his pregnant girlfriend, and the strictures of his religion. All considered, he could be granted ... perhaps not forgiveness, but a last indulgence' (244). June's willingness to make allowances, and to embrace a restructuring of the rigid social order that has governed her entire life, are in marked contrast to the genteel isolation and destructive internal feuding so prevalent in Keane's earlier novels. Significantly, June is more connected to her environment than are her siblings; she 'was the only Swift who spoke like the people. There had been no English school for her. No one could teach her to read' (9). Furthermore, a 'peasant ancestress, the regretted dairy-maid' (243) besmirches the Swift siblings' bloodline; can this supposed taint in June in fact take partial credit for her reinvigoration, allowing her to escape the confines of her moribund caste and its past, moving instead towards a new beginning? It is certainly in keeping with Keane's sense of what is important that she offers us this tailpiece, a hint, if you will, of a vision of the future, through the evolution of a new, more fluid and vibrant, 'horsy habitat'. June and her new acolyte may never be winners, but at least they are in with a chance.

---

13 Sally Phipps brought to my attention V.S. Pritchett's comments on the unifying powers of the horse in Irish society in his 1963 essay on 'The Irish Character' – sentiments with which, she said, her mother wholeheartedly agreed: 'The Horse has always been the heroic solvent of Irish evils, and I half believe that any Irish man or woman would as soon be a horse as a human being' (196).

Narrating Anglo-Ireland:
Molly Keane's *Time after Time*

ELLEN M. WOLFF

Communities are to be distinguished not by
their falsity/genuineness,
but by the style in which they are imagined.

– Benedict Anderson, *Imagined Communities*

The real consciousness is the chaos, a grey
commotion of mind, with no premises or conclusions or problems or solutions or cases or
judgments.

– Samuel Beckett, letter to Thomas MacGreevy

Since the mid-1970s, many working in the field of Irish Studies have been
spurred by what cultural historian Terence Brown has labeled 'a steadily
increasing urge toward an informed Irish self-understanding' (1985, 247). As
F.S.L. Lyons announced in the first of his Ford Lectures, delivered at
Oxford in 1978, 'the roots of difference within Irish society are being explored
with much greater sensitivity and thoroughness than ever before' (1979, 2).
This attention to the diversity of Ireland's cultural and religious traditions
has stemmed in part from an urge to rescue the representation of Irish identity from the essentialism which, as Clifford Geertz has argued, typically
characterises the discourse of new states (234–5). This trend was also, its
practitioners made clear, a response to the 1969 outbreak of violence in
Northern Ireland and to the violence that continued to plague the politics of
the North. The aim, in Brown's words, has been to answer sectarian violence by studying 'acts and artifacts of human beings in their Irish setting'
in such a way as to reveal 'a complicated mosaic of cultures and social forces'
(1985, 248). The preface to a collection of pamphlets published by Ireland's
Field Day Theatre Company (which, with the discontinued Dublin journal,
The Crane Bag, formed the vanguard of the literary branch of this interdis-
ciplinary effort) describes the project as an attempt to redress 'the present
[political] crisis by producing analyses of the established opinions, myths and
stereotypes which have become both a symptom and a cause of the current
situation.' Seamus Deane elaborates:

The communities have become stereotyped into their roles of oppres-
sor and victim to such an extent that the notion of a Protestant or a
Catholic sensibility is now assumed to be a fact of nature rather than
a product of these very special and ferocious conditions ... It is about
time we put aside the idea of essence – the hungry Hegelian ghost
looking for a stereotype to live in. As Irishness or as Northernness
he stimulates the provincial unhappiness we create and fly from ...
Everything, including our politics and our literature, has to be rewrit-
ten – i.e. re-read. That will enable new writing, new politics. ('Heroic
Styles' 1986, 57)

The present essay is part of a larger study that re-reads what has come
to be called 'Big House fiction' in the context of this anti-essentialist project.[1] As I argue more fully there, novels by writers such as Molly Keane,
Elizabeth Bowen, and Samuel Beckett forcefully challenge 'the established
opinions, myths and stereotypes' of Anglo-Irishness that have retained cur-
rency in Irish cultural discourse,[2] making important contributions to the ongoing effort to '*detribalise* those myths' that have fueled Irish troubles past and
present (Kearney 1984, 65, italics Kearney's). Keane's *Time after Time*,
Bowen's *The Last September*, and Beckett's *Watt*, among other texts, give form
to a set of topics that together constitute what might be called the Anglo-Irish
problematic[3] – topics including land, property, work, servitude, Irishness,
Anglo-Irishness, hierarchy, and authority. These novels are driven by their
authors' pressing, even anguished, interrogations of these topics. How shall I
assess Anglo-Ireland's systems of value and belief? How shall I account for
its relationship to Irish land? How shall I portray its relation to Ireland
'proper'? In attempting to answer such questions, Keane and others produce
narratives that record Anglo-Irish writers' ongoing debates with their own
visions and revisions of history and culture.

---

1 See '*An anarchy in the mind and in the heart': Narrating Anglo-Ireland*, forthcoming from
Bucknell University Press. There and in this essay I use the problematic terms 'Big House fiction' and 'Anglo-Irish fiction' interchangeably.   2 Seamus Deane's influential early assessment
of Big House fiction, in 'The literary myths of the revival,' provides a case in point: 'The Big
House surrounded by the unruly tenantry, Culture besieged by barbarity, a refined aristocracy
beset by a vulgar middle class – all of these are recurring images in twentieth-century Irish fiction which draws heavily on Yeats's poetry for them ... The survival of the Big House novel,
with all its implicit assumptions, is a tribute to Yeats and a criticism of the poverty of the Irish
novelistic tradition' (1985, 31–2). And the shadow of identity politics still looms. Writing in
1998, Vera Kreilkamp comments: 'To some extent, of course, Anglo-Irish country house novels inevitably create a discomfort that emerges largely from extratextual sources' (1998, 12) –
from Anglo-Ireland's storied role in Irish history.   3 Like Fekete, I use the term 'problematic'
to refer to a 'social, ideological, or theoretical framework within which complexes of problems
are structured and single problems acquire density, meaning and significance' (217–18).

In *Criticism and Ideology* Terry Eagleton describes literary texts in terms that illuminate the ways in which Anglo-Irish novels register their topics' powerful charge. He calls the text a 'problem-solving process': 'The text is thus never at one with itself, for if it were it would have nothing to say. It is, rather, a process of becoming at one with itself – an attempt to overcome the problem of itself' (1976, 88–9). This is an excellent description of much Big House fiction.[4] Given the unsettling topics they confront, the fraught cultural context in which they confront them, and the divided readership before which they do, these writers produce a strikingly dynamic and self-divided fiction. They answer their driving questions one way and then another, producing increasingly self-reflexive narrative structures that register varying degrees of scepticism as to their own viability. And in the process, they posit an anti-essentialist redefinition of one Irish identity. They cast Anglo-Irishness as an inconclusive attempt to narrate itself, an unfinished quest for a discursive home.

The work of Homi Bhabha and others on 'nation as narration' provides another frame for re-reading Anglo-Irish fiction. Bhabha affirms the 'conceptual indeterminacy' of 'the ambivalent figure of the nation' (1990, 2). His practice is to investigate 'the nation-space as the *process* of the articulation of elements, where meanings may be partial because they are *in medias res*, and history may be half-made because it is in the process of being made, and the image of cultural authority may be ambivalent because it is caught uncertainly, in the act of "composing" its powerful image' (1990, 3, italics Bhabha's). Bhabha's nation, like the Anglo-Ireland these novels posit, 'is neither unified nor unitary in relation to itself, nor must it be seen simply as "other" in relation to what is outside or beyond it' (1990, 4). Rather, it is characterised by an 'interruptive interiority' (1990, 5).

Though in some ways unrepresentative of novels in this putative tradition (it was written very late, from long retrospect, about long decline), *Time after Time* is a paradigmatic instance of the narrative tendencies that I have suggested characterise much Anglo-Irish fiction. Multivocal and multivalent, it constitutes a dynamic and indeterminate attempt to represent those topics at the core of the Anglo-Irish problematic. It is not, as some would argue, mere satire or pure critique.[5] And it certainly isn't nostalgic celebration. The

4 I disagree, however, with Eagleton and like-minded ideology critics regarding the relation of ideology and literature as theorised, for instance, in Eagleton's 1991 *Ideology: an introduction.* In practice, ideology theory provides an inadequate model of political consciousness as Anglo-Irish novels represent it.   **5** Working from feminist theories of women's humour, for example, Rachael Jane Lynch has asserted that Keane 'displays and ridicules' Anglo-Ireland by way of 'merciless' satire: 'Laughter wins, because the world of Keane's fiction does not deserve to survive; we sense that Keane herself is bringing down her house, killing and burying a decaying microcosm with an overwhelming sense of relief' (1996, 74, 77). Vera Kreilkamp argues that 'Keane's great achievement as a novelist was to reject the nostalgia that is a major cultural production of a declining imperial state' (1998, 174).

novel both vindicates and incriminates Anglo-Ireland, and evokes a broad
swath of attitudes in between.

Time after Time is brimming with the standard Anglo-Irish literary motifs.
It centres on a decaying estate, the ramshackle Durraghglass, and on its eccentric, insular occupants, the ageing Swifts. It indicts many of Anglo-Ireland's
time-honoured habits of mind: the habit of euphemism and evasion, for
instance, and the constricting code of 'good behaviour'. The novel denaturalises
the myth of innate Anglo-Irish grace, civility and 'traditional sanctity and love-
liness' by displaying the hard labour that the myth denies. It rubs readers' noses
in what propriety would repress, revealing dire economic realities and, as Ellen
O'Brien has shown, the abject body and its functions. Indeed, as O'Brien argues,
Keane's insistent representation of the body and its functions implicates Anglo-
Ireland in Bakhtin's grotesque, Kristeva's abject 'that which disturbs identity,
system, order. What does not respect borders, positions, rules' (Kristeva 1982,
4). Keane's bodies manifest Lacan's 'Real,' which (in the words of Slavoj Žižek)
constitutes 'corporeal contingency' and 'logical contingency', providing 'a shock
of a contingent encounter ...; a traumatic encounter which ruins the balance
of the symbolic universe of the subject' (1989, 171). In 'present[ing] the Anglo-
Irish ideal beset by bodily abjection', O'Brien concludes, 'Keane revises the Big
House genre so that the fall transpires not because of outside forces or new
ideologies, but because the Anglo-Irish, despite their facade of rituals and props,
embodied the Real all along' (1999, 44, 40).

Time after Time thus imparts an exposé of Anglo-Ireland that is both
broad and biting. But this is just part of Keane's story. If the novel evokes
Keane's rejection of Anglo-Ireland, it suggests, too, her continued and complicated bond. One of the primary vehicles for communicating this tension is
character.[6] Keane's portraits of the Swifts are disconcertingly mixed, elicit-
ing conspicuously varied reader responses. Hopelessly divided by old jeal-
ousies and hurts, grotesquely devoted to their pets, absorbed in activities that
can seem petty distractions from past pains and present anxieties, the Swifts
are not an appealing bunch. But Keane plants seeds of compassion that prevent us from viewing them as merely contemptible or absurd. We learn that
all of them were subject to wrenching rejections and betrayals when they were
children. We see that their pastimes function as hedges against the vacuum
left by the disappearance of the world in which they were reared. In Ann
Hurlbert's view, these 'brittle caricatures are still capable of surprising them-

---

6 This tension is analogous to the disconcerting generic and tonal tensions that characterise Keane's
novels. Mary Breen asserts: 'The most difficult task when discussing Keane is to find a genre
into which she can fit comfortably' (1997, 206). Ann Owens Weekes observes, Keane's novels
'jolt the reader with their mix of the mundane and the shocking, the comic and the tragic' (1990,
151). Of *Time after Time* in particular James Lasdun writes: 'part of the charm of the novel is
that just when you think you have the measure of it you find you've been outwitted' (1984, 73).

selves, Keane convinces us – and curiosity thus roused can lead unexpectedly to sympathy' (40).

The novel's structure augments the instability of Keane's characterisations. The novel has a contrapuntal structure, which gives us the Swifts alone, the Swifts with cousin Leda, and then again the Swifts alone. This structure modulates reader response. If we were initially repelled by the Swifts, if they struck us as laughable when going about their business alone, we find ourselves siding with them when they're besieged by the Machiavellian Leda. Under Leda's onslaught they appear vulnerable, even comparatively noble, and their good behaviour, so evasive in other contexts, seems a sign of admirable self-possession.

The novel offers similarly open-ended representations of habits of mind and systems of value historically central to Anglo-Irish mythology. Take, for instance, Keane's handling of a stock feature of Big House fiction: the nostalgic comparison of Anglo-Ireland's current decline to its former (ostensible) grandeur. At its most typical, the convention generates a sombre reflection on some aspect of a run-down estate – the shabby drawing room, the untended demesne. At the beginning of *Time after Time*'s second chapter, Keane plays mischievously with this literary cliché:

> Late in the evening there came a civilised pause before dinner. Servantless and silent, the house waited for the proper ceremony it had always expected and still, in a measure, experienced. The utter cold of the spring light shrank away from the high paned windows. A steep distance below the house the river gave up an evening daze of fog. A lavatory clattered and shushed. Obedient to its plug and chain the contents went down the perpendicular drain to the open water ... Once there had been an open, not a covert, drain. Every morning housemaids lifted a grille and sluiced buckets into a sloped stone spout from which the doings of the night flowed down their paved way to the river. Not any more, of course. Those were the days of tin baths in front of bedroom fires, of mahogany commodes containing pos or bidets, commodes with three steps for the ascent to bed – the days of lots of money. (22)

Keane yokes the conventional perspective to anomalous content, subverting the elegiac contrast in parody.

Elsewhere, as in May's extended recollection of her mother's garden, Keane's distance from the conventional point of view is less certain and less complete. For much of this long passage, the narrative seems to join in May's nostalgia, to celebrate Violet Swift's refusal of 'the present snobbish form of gardening, of balancing and landscaping even a small area. She planted exactly where her plants would do best.' May's impassioned recollection is also Keane's. Yet towards the passage's end, Keane dispels the elegiac mood. She names the time that May evokes 'Better Days', objectifying the nostalgic cast of mind. But she then goes on to recall, from within the nostalgic point of view once more:

> There was little or no planting of shrubs round a country house. Instead there were acres of mown grass; a pony, shod in leather, for their mowing; wide dappling of tree shadows smooth on their surfaces. The gravel sweeps were weedless and stone pineapples had not toppled off the pillars of the steps going down to the river. It was definite as any photograph to May. (119–20)

And it is, by way of Keane's narrative, now definite to us. This passage rescues the mythological Anglo-Ireland from time and loss, inviting the reader into the nostalgic point of view.

Keane sometimes writes with what seems undiluted elegiac feeling. Just three pages before her cheeky comparison of past and present plumbing, Keane describes June's daily walks up and down the Durraghglass drive:

> June walked the distance, back and forwards several times a day. She was familiar with its potholes and long, stony depths and she ignored the riot of briars and nettles on its once orderly verges. Close to the back of the house, a different and more precise archway from that of the farmyard led to the stableyard; a now derelict clock in the archway's face had once told the time. It still looked pretty. The stableyard was built round rather a grand semi-circle. Loose-boxes, weedy cobblestones to their doors, were empty – all but one, June's brown hens scratched about on the wide central circle of grass round which horses had been ridden and led and walked and jogged, or made to stand as they should, to be admired by afternoon luncheon guests on Sundays. (19–20)

The juxtaposition makes for a striking tonal disjunction.[7] Or does it? As in other passages in the novel, point of view is ultimately indeterminate. Does the passage transcribe June's train of thought? Is it authorial? Is Keane crit-

---

[7] Providing the kind of intertextual disjunctions that characterise the work of many Anglo-Irish writers, Elizabeth Bowen in particular, Keane's essays and interviews contain passages in which she appears to do this literary convention straight. Consider this description, taken from the introduction to an anthology she compiled with her daughter, in which she records what could be called the Platonic Form of the decayed Big House: 'Sometimes the remnants of a stableyard, a half-circle of elegant Georgian architecture, heartbreakingly unspoilt, fanlights over every loose-box door, will cling to the ruin of a house. Wild birds fly in and out through the windowless and doorless spaces to circle the linked drawing-rooms and morning-rooms where, less than a hundred years ago, aunts mended sheets with darns finer than *petit point*, unaware in

ically dramatising a frame of mind? Is she enacting it herself? Such questions
thwart a reader's conclusive assessment of the passage, preventing one from
determining the text's precise relation to this literary convention and, by extension, the culture from which it grows. Such textual indeterminacy plays a
crucial role in keeping the text beyond the binary logic of ideology critique.

A comparable unsettledness characterises Keane's handling of landscape.
At times, Keane represents the land with brutal realism, challenging the touris-
tic view embodied in May's tweed pictures of pretty cottages and ruined tow-
ers. Consider this wry description of the farmyard: 'The mountainy fields
rose quietly outside it towards gorse and heather. Below its nearly slateless
cow-sheds and tumbling iron-gated piggeries, a steep slope drained liquids
from all ordure down to the pretty river' (18). But Keane also composes
Romantic portraits of the countryside, the farmyard, and the work done there,
calling to mind some of the most saccharine failings of the Celtic Twilight.
Often the farmyard is less a vivid reality than a quiet refuge from the 'frac-
tious living' of the house (29). So Keane's representations oscillate. Sometimes
the farmyard is a site of stinking labour. Sometimes it is a site of primal peace.

This tension reflects more than the debatable aesthetics of landscape. It
registers the historical Anglo-Irish relation to Irish land. Representing the land
is a charged project for the Anglo-Irish writer. Metaphorise, romanticise, or
idealise the land and the writer risks enacting a colonialist's hopeless alienation
from it, or whitewashing the harsh material realities of it, or co-opting what
has been cast as the native Irish relation to it. Write realistically, and she risks
estrangement from an Anglo-Ireland that, as *Time after Time* shows, did not
typically acknowledge harsh realities, and often represented place as a metaphor
for political power. Caught between the rock and the hard place bequeathed it
by history, Keane's narrative does not finish the business of formulating a unified and coherent representation of landscape. It remains in search of one.

Note that I write that Keane's *narrative* does not finish this business. As
one reads this novel one inevitably wonders: Was Keane aware of her text's
oscillations? If pressed, I might say that Keane was intermittently aware. But
one cannot know. Bakhtin reminds us of the limits of any reader's interpretive claims: 'one often does not know where the direct authorial word ends
and where a parodic or stylized playing ... begins' (77). And to assert an opinion regarding the degree of authorial self-awareness would seem tantamount
to asserting an opinion regarding authorial intent. If, as David Lloyd has written, 'history is written from the perspective of and with the aim of producing a non-contradictory subject' (17), fiction is not. Again and again *Time
after Time* asks us to forego the false comfort of the final word. In the end,
'the narrative tells itself' (Barthes 213).

their elderly innocence of the merry tales such sheets could tell. Grey tweed skirts from Donegal
fell to their ankles, long and undisturbed as fluted pillars' (*Molly Keane's Ireland* ix).

In addition to such novel wide tensions, *Time after Time* contains more discrete sites at which the difficulties involved in narrating Anglo-Ireland reveal themselves at their most intense. The figure of May Swift is one.

May seems closely associated with Anglo-Ireland in Keane's mind. Like Anglo-Ireland, she is precariously placed. Her rights of residence at Durraghglass are more tenuous than the others', since she contributes less to the estate's upkeep than her brother and sisters do. May's kitschy tweed pictures call to mind a distorted understanding of a conquered land. Made not just of tweed, but of bits and pieces of the countryside itself (heather, bird feathers, snail shells), these pictures entail not just an erroneous imaginative appropriation of the landscape but a trivialising physical appropriation as well. May is the most willful of all the Swifts: the most insistent on order, obedience, discipline and control. And we are reminded throughout the novel that May's brave shows of confidence mask a fundamental lack of it, not unlike Georgian Dublin and the totemic Big House itself – structures that R.F. Foster reads as performative gestures, built to help their owners 'convince themselves not only that they had arrived, but that they would remain' (1989, 194). As Keane writes, 'Only May could guess at the cringing second self she must defend so long as they both should live' (70).

May's kleptomania constitutes the novel's bluntest indicator of her association with Anglo-Ireland. The genesis of May's kleptomania is significant. May starts stealing at age seven, when feeling excluded from Leda's and April's 'giggling best-friendship'. Hidden in a laurel grove that Keane calls May's 'secret house', she longs 'to belong to the group so near and so divided from her'. So she rushes out of the bushes where she's gone for 'a quick out-of-doors pee' – without pulling up her underwear. The others see her and laugh. 'Trembling in a hot brew of embarrassment, May went back again to hide in her dark house … Hidden and comfortless, she watched them through the laurel leaves, heads together, talking, talking.' As the other girls leave the lawn, May sees something fall to the ground. Later, she discovers it is a small toy fox, 'Leda's mascot and treasure.' May buries the fox in her kitchen garden. Then 'she felt better, stronger … [S]he had yielded nothing' (40–2). The career of petty thievery launched by this furtive plantation garners May what Keane calls 'a colony' of china rabbits (27).

The scene is rich in historical undertones. Coloniser-like, May feels an outcast in her own home. She experiences her alienation from the distant group as alienation from their talk, evoking the linguistic divide between native- and Anglo-Irish.[8] She emerges from and returns to what Keane calls

---

8 Keane expresses difference in linguistic terms elsewhere in the novel, contrasting Irish women's 'sweet Irish voices' to 'Lady Alys's voice, from a different Irish world' (76). In her introduction to *Molly Keane's Ireland*, Keane elaborates: 'language helped to maintain a class difference

a dark and secret house, evoking the ostensibly protective Big House and the archetypal pattern of departure and anxious return. Later, as if burying Leda's fox there somehow marked it as hers, the kitchen garden becomes May's one sovereign realm:

> [May] resented the present overgrowth and hated the ash saplings taking over the tennis courts – like letting in the tinkers, she thought.
>
> The kitchen garden was a different matter – it was enclosed. Ivy might cloak and drag at its walls, docks and nettles invade its distances, but those parts maintained by her vigilance were May's thrust into a conceit of happiness. Every foot of the walled wilderness that could be kept under cultivation was of vital importance to May. It was her province. She fought for its maintenance with all the strength of her immense will. The rotations of peas, beans, spinach; the triumphant hatchings in battered frames of new potatoes for Easter; the continual supplies of parsley, chives, mints (in choice varieties), thymes, oregano and basil were the successes May brought to birth, properly in their seasons or their perpetuities.
>
> … The lock on the wooden door had a big smooth keyhole and the easily turned key made its own possessive sound as May turned it and went in, like a robin or a fox, to possess her territory. (120–1)

May fights the apparent disorder beyond the Pale-like walls. She subdues her territory to what she considers civilised use.

What are we to make of May here? What are we to make of what Keane makes of May? As Sally Phipps and Virginia Brownlow have made clear earlier in this collection, Keane loved gardening. She must have relished the passage's long list of vegetables and herbs. The repetition of the affirmative trope of birth, like the comparison of May to bird and beast, naturalises May's cultivation of her territory. Thus read, this passage competes with the image of Ireland as Anglo-Ireland's tweed picture, giving us Ireland as Anglo-Ireland's fertile garden. But certainly Keane's appreciation of May's produce is countered by her authorial distaste for 'her immense will'. And interpretability attenuates one's reading of the passage. If the images of robin and fox naturalise May's relation to this land, the image of the fox also implies a rapacity that one might argue carries imperial overtones. But then, in another turn of the interpretive screw, the fox figured chiefly as the hunted prey in Keane's milieu. And recall that Keane has imagined the genesis of May's thievery,

down the years. The settled ascendancy spoke English between themselves … Only the beautiful languages of fox hunting, racing, shooting and fishing were shared and broke the silence between the classes in that great union of sport that is careless of politics and innocent of terrorism' (xv–xvi).

back on the lawn, in terms of a painful childhood hurt with which the reader is hard pressed not to empathise. Indeed, that scene sympathetically reenacts a timeworn conception of Anglo-Ireland's identity as the wronged and wounded outsider. Keane's portrait of May as Anglo-Ireland remains unsettled, a trace of Keane's dynamic interrogation of Anglo-Ireland.

Keane's representation of May's final theft is crucial in communicating the complexity and instability of her attitude towards May and, by extension, Anglo-Ireland. As the climactic theft approaches, the narrative seems to move beyond explaining the psychological functions of May's kleptomania to justifying it. What had been cast earlier in the novel as May's 'ultimate protest and defence against her infirmity' (132) becomes 'an adventurous travesty of dull morals', a function of May's aesthetic sense, of 'her feeling for all pretty things and the importance of their preservation'. The narrative may go so far as to justify May's failure to regret her thefts: 'who repents adventure?' (223).

Perhaps explanations verge toward justifications here because it is here that May gets caught. Perhaps they do so because it is here that the text identifies the issue that is at stake in May's kleptomania, despite its sometime identification as a 'small private guilt.' Through a two-way mirror, shop owner Ulick Uniacke sees May steal a porcelain rabbit. He insists on searching her bag. '"Let go", she ordered, "at once. Everything in this basket is my own private property."' Ulick then names the issue to which May's kleptomania alludes: '"Our ideas on private property don't quite match up"' (229).

Ulick's frankness is refreshing. It can seem initially as if May is finally getting what she deserves, but May's subsequent vulnerability is painful to behold:

> May loosed her grip on the bag. She bent her head. Her need for a cigarette was beyond endurance. And, at this moment of her greatest need, her hand failed her. Her thumb and finger were shaking so shamefully they were past any obedience; they could not open her cigarette case; it was as if their life was ending. She laid her cramped hand on the edge of the table and stared at it, and touched it with her left hand, inattentive to what Ulick meant to do to her, or say to her. Or say to others. (230)

When, after this passage, Ulick's politeness turns to glib mockery, May appears his victim. For her misdeeds we may condemn May, but for what she suffers 'at this moment of her greatest need,' as Keane represents it, we sympathise. At May's most dramatically guilty moment, Keane tempers condemnation with sympathy.

But this is not *Time after Time*'s final word on May, either. One might read the remainder of May's career as an allegory of Anglo-Irish redemption.

In the end, Ulick offers and May accepts a job in his restoration business. May's employment is part of a broader trend in the novel, which gives all the Swifts new companions and occupations. But in May's case the change has a reformative dimension: the thief becomes a legitimate wage earner. The non-contributing resident of Durraghglass finds the means to pay her way.

May's last appearance in the novel complicates this happy allegory. Having, as she puts it, 'undertaken such a full-time job in the Antique World', May is, suddenly, preternaturally aware of business opportunities. The new May is not just a legitimate wage earner; she is an ardent capitalist. On her way home from work one evening, she enters a Travellers' caravan to retrieve her dog, the errant Gripper:

> May climbed the steps leading to the squalor that she expected and deplored. As the door shut behind her, she was surprised to find herself in a smugglers' cave of old lamps ... May swallowed a gasp of wonder and delight at the prospect of such an exchange and mart at her gate. Near to dreaming, she considered how, one by one, these peerless objects might be bought, re-conditioned and re-sold, by her to Ulick. (241)

After deciding to haggle for the lamps, she goes outside and tells Jasper, '"They've got some pretty things. Stolen property, obviously"' (242).

Keane's response to May's hypocrisy is swift and harsh: 'Jasper stared at her. How, after Leda's revelations [of May's thefts], could she pronounce the word "stolen" in a way suggesting that it was only tinkers who stole?' (242–3). Having replaced May's bald thievery with what resembles a neocolonialist's capitalist aggression, the narrative here rebukes May's impulse to project her dark side onto the Other, reinvigorating our impulse to condemn May, requiring us to revise our understanding yet again.

May is not the only site of such contestation and debate in the novel. The June – Christy dyad is another at which Keane's effort to narrate Anglo-Ireland unfolds with particular intensity and struggle. These and other shifting representations of elements of the Anglo-Irish problematic record a play of attraction and repulsion that elicits from readers a similarly shifting and at least double response, so that *Time after Time* ultimately stands as an open-ended and equivocal narration of Anglo-Ireland.

Keane's comparatively stable representation of *Time after Time*'s most conspicuous storyteller figure sheds additional light on her relationship to the project of narrating Anglo-Ireland. Keane explicitly aligns Leda, the novel's abhorrent traitor, with the novelist generally and a Keane-like novelist more specifically. Having learned about May's thefts Leda exults, 'Such a good story – who should she tell it to?' (165). Commenting on Leda's malicious accumulation of the Swifts' guilty secrets, Keane remarks, 'Leda might have been wanting to write a book about her cousins' (145). If Keane generates a narrative that manipulates and misleads (leading us to worry toward the end of the novel, for instance, that June is dead) so does Leda, though her mischief is decidedly more treacherous.[9] Moreover, Leda, like Keane, tells 'tales of terror and filth' (109), dramatically defying prevailing constructions of civility.[10]

The consequences of Leda's tales are dire. We witness firsthand their devastating impact on the Swifts, particularly on May. But the outcomes of narratives that Leda told long ago, in the past that precedes the text's present, were even more grave. Her apparently exaggerated accounts of her long-ago affair with the Swift's father, Leda's Uncle Valentine, helped precipitate his suicide. 'A man had died on her account,' Keane's narrator puns (130). And as we learn late in the novel, the tales Leda told as a Nazi collaborator, like those she continues to tell to authorities about her Nazi ex-lover, are similarly fatal.

Perhaps the figure of the story-telling Leda evokes Keane's anxiety about the project of narrating home culture, revealing her sometime conception of the terrible power of her own tale.[11] Certainly textual tensions and reversals such as those I've described here connote strenuous moral and intellectual struggles. The representation of these struggles carries enormous affective power. If, like other Big House novels, *Time after Time* calls out intermittent sympathy for the Anglo-Ireland it seeks to represent, in the end it generates perhaps more sustained sympathy for its author's efforts to narrate Anglo-Ireland. The moral and intellectual anguish these novels embody, the anarchy in the mind and in the heart to which they attest, corroborate the story that Irish history tells us: that despite the substantial and long-standing rewards Anglo-Ireland reaped from its status as Empire's accomplice, in the end, it can be numbered among Empire's casualties, if not the most severely wounded.

---

9 Ann Hurlbert also notes this similarity: 'Keane depends on curiosity to spin out her old-fashioned fiction. So does cousin Leda to ensnare the Swifts. In fact, Keane seems to mirror in Leda the manipulative imagination that is at work in her own art' (40). 10 O'Brien observes: 'Leda's use of excrement as a signifying practice, coded as the undeniable subversion of ritualized civility, mimics Keane's use of abjection ..., for clearly Keane uses excessive "nasty stuff" to concentrate our attention on the delicacy and descendancy of Anglo-Irish culture' (49). 11 Keane was aware of the legendary power of the ancient Irish poets: 'Courts and kings dared not refuse them hospitality, although they were sometimes boisterous and troublesome, because their satire was much feared' (*Molly Keane's Ireland* xi). And Leda's name, which evokes so many readings, suggests her power to unleash catastrophe.

Untimeliness and the Big House novel: Molly Keane's *Full House*

CAROLYN LESNICK

Explorations of untimeliness, and the wide range of its forms and meanings, figure prominently in Anglo-Irish Big House novels.[1] The representations in these novels of the Big House and its inhabitants as untimely have largely been viewed as reflecting the prolonged decline of the historical institution of the Big House. It is certainly the case that by the late nineteenth and early twentieth centuries, the Anglo-Irish Ascendancy class had lost most of its political, economic, and social power in Ireland. However, it is important to remember that any historical or temporal narrative is a construction that creates relationships between, and gives meaning to, historical events. As literary and historical scholars know well, historical narratives – and especially those narratives that acquire a wide applicability, like the narrative of decline – function by excluding events or perspectives that do not conform to the larger arc of the narrative. I want to draw a distinction between historical events in Ireland and what Eviatar Zerubavel describes as the 'highly formulaic plot structures' of historical narratives, because the compelling and very powerful decline narrative can eclipse, or render critically illegible, other historical and temporal narratives at work in the Big House novel (2003, 4).[2]

It is important to mark this distinction between historical events and the 'plot structures' of historical narratives in the context of Big House novel studies because historical and temporal narratives play a crucial role in the construction of cultural and national identity formations. These narratives do not merely describe changes in political, social, or economic structures, but rather contribute to the production and naturalisation of these structures. In

---

1 In this essay, I use the term 'untimeliness' to refer to a general sense of being not-timely – that is, as being out of sync with normative or 'natural' models of temporality. However, I also want to evoke the use of 'untimely' to denote a condition of prematurity (*Oxford English Dictionary*, 2nd edition, 'untimely' *a*. def. 1 and *adv*. def. 2). As I will suggest in what follows, the powerful image of the Big House as being in the final, twilit stages of a long decline has tended to obscure the ways in which some twentieth-century Big House novels suggest that the 'end' of the Big House – and, later, the Big House novel – had been prematurely announced.
2 It is equally important, of course, to remember this distinction when considering the representations of decline in Big House novels. Allusions to decline in these novels are most productively viewed not simply as an aspect of the Big House novel's social realism or an indicator of its transparent historical referentiality, but also as the site of a self-conscious engagement with a generic cultural narrative.

the case of the Big House novel, temporal and historical narratives have been deployed as part of an effort to marginalise and exclude these novels from a 'canon' of Irish literature that reflects a specific conception of Irish cultural and national identity. We see the strategic use of such narratives in Seamus Deane's 1977 essay, 'The Literary Myths of the Revival: A Case for their Abandonment'. Here, Deane criticises the 're-emergence' of the Big House novel in the late twentieth-century as being out of sync with a natural temporal model that is meant to coincide with the temporality of the Irish nation: 'The Big House novel, one would think, died in the nineteenth century or thereabouts, when the Big House, as an important political feature of the Irish landscape also died' (1977, 321). Such politicisation of these temporal models makes it especially important to attend to the alternative – 'unnatural' or 'untimely' – temporal and historical narratives in the work of an Anglo-Irish Big House novelist like Molly Keane.

In this essay, I examine one aspect of the Big House novel's untimeliness that has been eclipsed by the identification of the Big House novel with a 'natural' narrative of decline. In the middle decades of the twentieth century, the Big House novel engaged in an effort to identify a temporal narrative that was appropriate to the historical, contemporary, *and future* position of the Anglo-Irish Big House in Ireland. From the perspective of the late twentieth and early twenty-first centuries, perhaps nothing seems more untimely than the suggestion of a future for the mid-twentieth century Big House. However, the question of what future role the Anglo-Irish minority might play within the Free State – and, later, under de Valera's Fianna Fáil government – and what contribution the Big House might make to twentieth-century Irish culture and society was one that the literature of the Big House was actively negotiating during this period. We see, for example, Lennox Robinson concluding his 1926 play, *The Big House*, with the rebuilding of a Big House that had been burned. This question of the future of the Big House persisted well beyond the immediate post-Treaty period of Robinson's play, as we see in Elizabeth Bowen's 1940 essay, 'The Big House', which looks to the architectural structure of the Big House to develop a vision of how it might contribute to a contemporary and future Ireland. This is not to say that the future of the Anglo-Irish Big House appeared certain, or that its shape was clear to these and other writers; it was not, and that is why Big House novelists of the 1920s, 1930s, and 1940s were actively seeking temporal models that could posit a future for Anglo-Ireland and the Big House.

Big House novelists of this period would thus have been looking to a set of historical, temporal, and evolutionary narratives that were prevalent both within and outside of Ireland. In addition to the narrative of decline, and its close relative the narrative of degeneration, these would include: a progressionist narrative of modernisation and democratisation; a model of cyclical time that is assumed to derive from the natural world; and a model of historical time that Zerubavel characterises as a 'recurrence narrative' – a model which informs the narratives of revival that are so significant for Irish national and cultural histories (2003, 25). However, none of these narratives could posit a future for the Big House in the mid-twentieth century: even when the narrative does not culminate in the end of the Big House, as in models of degeneration or decline, the Big House is denied or written out of the future posited by these narratives. Thus, for example, in a progressionist narrative of modernisation, the Big House figures an institutionalised social order and economic system that is viewed as anterior to modern socio-economic relations and as destined to be superceded and replaced by them.

This irreconcilability of the twentieth-century Big House with any forward-looking temporal narrative is a factor that informs many of Molly Keane's Big House novels, and her response to this irreconcilability varies over the course of her long career. In Keane's early novel *Young Entry* (1928), any suggestion of either a future for, or an imminent end to, the Big House is markedly absent – accordingly, the novel closes before its heroine comes of age. In the late 1930s and early 1940s, Keane's novels such as *The Rising Tide* (1937) and *Two Days in Aragon* (1941) explore the grotesque distortions produced by this irreconcilability of the Big House with forward-looking historical and temporal narratives. The 1935 novel *Full House* might be considered a transitional text within her work: in this novel, Keane directly addresses the positioning of the Big House within historical and temporal narratives by staging a Big House family's struggle to identify itself with a future. In *Full House*, Keane makes historical and temporal narratives the subject of a critique within, rather than an assumed condition or climate for, her novel.

Full House opens with the arrival of a British woman, Eliza Blundel, at Silverue, the Anglo-Irish Big House of Lady Olivia and Sir Julian Bird and their three children, John, Sheena, and Markie. Eliza is a painter who lives primarily in London; she is a longstanding family friend of the Birds. From the first moments of her arrival, Eliza is identified with a 'natural' temporal model against which the Birds appear, in different ways, unnatural and untimely. This natural model with which Eliza identifies herself is characterised by a cycle of growth and decay; at thirty-five years of age, Eliza views herself as being at the midpoint of this cycle.

In one important respect, however, Eliza already identifies herself as being in the latter stages of this cycle. Eliza has long been in love with Olivia's husband Julian, and she interprets her desire, which she knows is not mutual, through the lens of this natural model: looking back on her 'years of barren loving for Julian', Eliza views herself as a 'screeching old baggery' – that is, as already beyond a time of growth and fertility (230, 207). Eliza's unrequited love for Julian thus functions as both the cause and effect of her identification with a narrative self-positioning that drastically circumscribes her future. In response, Eliza turns her attention to Julian's children, who serve as an indirect channel – what Eliza herself refers to as a 'side-road' – for her feelings for Julian, and as the embodiment of a surrogate future for herself (209). Eliza's highly charged investment in the lives of the two eldest Bird children, John and Sheena, gives the novel its shape and structure. Divided almost exactly in half, with the midpoint marked by Olivia's extravagant annual garden party, the novel focuses first on Eliza's relationship to John, and then to Sheena.

Eliza's arrival at Silverue coincides with John's return home. John had been under a doctor's care as the result of a psychiatric illness, and the first half of the novel depicts his struggle to readjust to life at Silverue and to reintegrate himself into the larger Anglo-Irish Big House community. Aware of his son's difficulties in this process, Julian asks Eliza to prolong her stay and to help restore John to his former, pre-institutionalised self. Eliza agrees to stay, and while she clearly desires to help John, the means to accomplish this only become apparent to her on the evening after Olivia's party. On this night, John finds Eliza alone and saddened (by an encounter with Julian) after the party, and realises suddenly that he is in love with her. Eliza, not unaccustomed to these 'sexual surprises that life so often holds in store for the most determinedly platonic friends', begins an affair with John (212). Well aware of the more than ten-year age difference between them – Eliza is, after all, his parents' friend – Eliza views this affair as part of John's recovery, and as futureless: in and through this transitional affair, John will be restored to the person he had been before his illness.

In the hours before John's sudden declaration of love, events are set in motion that will soon shift Eliza's attention from an increasingly well-adjusted John to Sheena. When Eliza arrived at Silverue, Sheena had been very happily engaged to Rupert, the son of another prominent Anglo-Irish Big House family. At Olivia's party, however, Sheena is approached by Rupert's sister, who confronts Sheena with the fact that Rupert's family has a history of insanity. Pointing out that Sheena's family also has a history of hereditary insanity – John's illness is traced back to the blood of his paternal great-great-grandfather, 'Mad Harry Bird' (141) – Rupert's sister convinces Sheena to call off the engagement, on the grounds that a marriage between the two would yield a child that 'might throw back to something most awkward' (113). Against Rupert's wishes, Sheena breaks off the engagement, but is destroyed by her loss.

Initially, Eliza views her role as helping Sheena to overcome and adjust to her loss. In this capacity, Eliza takes Sheena and John to stay with her in Brittany – during which time the narrative of the novel remains focused on events at Silverue. The narrative resumes its focus on Sheena's circumstances when Eliza returns to Silverue some months later. In the intervening period, Eliza had learned that Sheena was not in fact Julian's daughter, but rather the daughter of a man with whom Olivia had an affair early in her marriage. The hereditary insanity in the Birds' ancestry had been in Julian's line, and as such, there could be no objection to a marriage between Sheena and Rupert. Eliza returns to Silverue in order to confront Olivia with this knowledge, and ultimately obtains Olivia's consent – not without some difficulty – to tell Sheena of her true parentage. The ending of the novel seems at first to confirm Eliza's own perception of her role in the Birds' affairs as one defined by restoration: John has been restored to himself, Sheena has been restored to herself and to Rupert, and the pattern of life at Silverue has been restored to what it had been before Eliza's first visit. However, Keane not only undermines this specific narrative of restoration, with its nostalgic positioning of Silverue, but situates it within a broader critique of the ways in which these historical and temporal narratives can circumscribe, delimit, or foreclose the future.

This critique begins with a contrast, which will ultimately become a conflict, between two temporal models: the first, embodied by Lady Olivia Bird, is that of an unnaturally prolonged youth; the second, identified with the British visitor Eliza, is that of a 'natural' timeliness. Olivia is introduced in the novel as being 'still so beautiful, so unbelievably young for all those forty-eight years,' and as 'terrifyingly', 'oppressively and astonishingly young' (7, 29, 10). This is no Dorian Gray scenario, however: Olivia's 'shockingly youthful appearance' is the product of what Eliza characterises as a 'terrific sustaining effort' that includes Olivia's religious and masochistic observance of a 'thousand and one rules of health' (71). Over the course of the novel, Olivia's 'eternal girlishness' acquires a more disturbing cast: she sees herself as her children's contemporary. As Olivia explains to Eliza at the end of the novel, '... it's being Big Sister to my children that keeps *me* so young' (310). Olivia's prolonged youth, then, is not limited to the span of her own generation: she desires to become a part of the generation to which she has given birth.

The disturbing and untimely quality of Olivia's youthfulness is, of course, the product of her resistance to a particular temporal narrative of ageing. This narrative is implicitly present in the reference to Olivia's numerical age, but it is more explicitly presented in the model of the 'natural' cycle of growth and decay embodied in Eliza. Eliza is represented in terms of a timeliness that reflects, and is perceived to derive from, the processes of the natural world. She is described as having '[a] little face nearly the shape of a beech leaf, lined and rather dry, brown and curling. Hydrangea eyes and dark hair. She was not old. She was not oppressively and astonishingly young, like Lady Bird. She was her own age, which was between thirty and forty' (10).

Thus, at the beginning of the novel, Eliza's synchronicity with the natural world functions as a privileged narrative, against which Olivia's prolonged youthfulness is judged to be unnatural and untimely. By the end of the novel, however, this narrative has been thoroughly undermined and divested of its privileged status: Eliza's self-identification with a narrative of 'natural' time-liness can only be sustained in opposition to the untimeliness of the Big House. Eliza's investment in perpetuating – or more accurately, producing – the untimeliness of the Birds is made visible on the first evening of Eliza's arrival at Silverue. On this night, Eliza's bedtime reading is taken from Shakespeare's Sonnets, and the following lines of Sonnet 18 – 'Shall I com-pare thee to a summer's day' – are reproduced in the text.

> But thy eternal summer shall not fade,
> Nor lose possession of that fair thou owest,
> Nor shall death boast thou wanderest in his shade,
> When in eternal lines to time thou growest. (65)

Eliza's response to these lines is to ask, 'Was that Sheena?' (65). The narra-tor almost immediately criticises this way of reading and perceiving Sheena by interjecting with the comment that 'Eliza was too romantic, and forever deceived herself as to the depth and meanings of other people's passions or tragedies' (65). Throughout the novel, Sheena is characterised by her 'faith-fulness to the present'; here, the novel exposes Eliza's projection of a time-less, unchanging vision of youth onto Sheena as a mis-reading of Sheena's investment in the present (95).

Eliza's nostalgic desire shapes her relationship not only to Sheena, but to the entire household of Silverue – a point that Keane makes by returning to the Sonnets later in the novel. When John, lying by the sea with Eliza, asks Eliza how long she will be staying at Silverue, she replies with a reference to Sonnet 87: '"Quite a time. Until I can bear it no more and then I go back to my whoring life in London saying, 'Farewell, thou art too dear for my pos-sessing.' Do you ever read the Sonnets?"' (145). As in the case of Eliza's read-ing of Sheena, this reading of Silverue into the Sonnets' 'eternal lines' is chal-lenged by the text. Immediately following her quotation of the Sonnet, Eliza insists that she and John return to the house so that – significantly – they will not be late for dinner. John replies with an accusation that Eliza is being a 'true country house visitor' (145). Keane thus links Eliza's perception of Silverue to the nostalgic cultural fantasy of the country house: in this fantasy the country house, as an embodiment of tradition, remains unaltered by the forces of mod-ernisation and democratisation. Eliza casts the Big House as a similarly untimely, because timeless, culture against which she can construct and sustain her own timeliness and her identification with a process of natural change.

By thus exposing the privileged narrative of a natural timeliness to be as culturally constructed as any other narrative, Keane opens up a space in which to consider the larger cultural implications of the narrative positioning of the Big House as untimely. Throughout her novels, Molly Keane addresses political and cultural concerns by locating them within, and at the level of, individual, inter-personal relations. In *Full House*, these broader cultural resonances are present within Keane's representation of the conflict between the two temporal models represented by Eliza and Olivia. When Eliza returns to Silverue at the end of the novel, she confronts Olivia with her knowledge that Julian is not Sheena's father, and attempts to convince Olivia to make this fact known to Sheena. While Olivia readily acknowledges her affair with Sheena's father, she initially refuses to tell Sheena of this fact, fearing the effects that this revelation would have on her own life. Eliza responds to this concern with the argument that '"... compared to Sheena and John, our lives – yours and mine and Julian's – are over. They don't count"' (300). Olivia replies, '"They're not over. Mine's not over"' (300).

Eliza's logic should sound familiar to scholars of the Big House novel: it is the same as that which subtends both political attitudes toward the Big House in the early twentieth century and literary-critical attitudes toward the Big House novel in the later twentieth century. In the political register, this logic suggests that the remnants of the Anglo-Irish Big House culture that were not eliminated by either the Land Acts or the violence of the Troubles and Civil War should efface themselves, thereby making way for the emergence of an independent Irish nation that would define itself through new progressionist narratives – in which, needless to say, the Big House would not figure.

In this context of an Ireland actively developing new national and historical narratives, Olivia's refusal to relinquish her future, along with her desire to be a vital part of the next generation, resonates with the position of the Anglo-Irish Big House in the post-Treaty era. This is not to suggest that Keane is arguing for the perpetuation of the kind of Anglo-Irish culture that the Birds represent. Indeed, I would argue that Keane is deliberately not proposing any specific narrative or model for the Big House; rather, she is making visible and challenging the uncritical identification, of both individuals and cultures, with received historical and temporal narratives – especially, as in this case, narratives that literally posit one's own extinction.

In this respect, Keane's representation of the largely unrecognised and often unconscious functioning of these historical and temporal narratives recalls a critique that Nietzsche makes in his early essay, 'On the Uses and Disadvantages of History for Life' (1874). This essay is directed at a culture that Nietzsche believes has identified itself with historical narratives that foreclose the possibility of a vital and robust future. For Nietzsche, one of the primary effects of this damaging self-identification – and one that is particularly relevant when considering the Big House novel – is that it 'implants the belief, harmful at any time, in the old age of mankind, the belief that one is a latecomer and epigone' (1997, 83). A crucial component of the 'antidote' that Nietzsche prescribes to counteract this condition is the development of forward-looking narratives; he enjoins his contemporaries to '[f]orm within yourself an image to which the future shall correspond, and forget the superstition that you are epigones' (120, 94). In this way, he claims, his contemporaries will become like the 'great fighters *against history*', and not the willing victims of historical narratives that delimit and foreclose the future: 'Not to bear their race to the grave, but to found a new generation of this race – that is what impels them ceaselessly forward: and even if they themselves are late-born – there is a way of living which will make them forget it – coming generations will know them only as first-born' (106–7). This is a point that Nietzsche will make repeatedly throughout the essay: historical and temporal narratives are cultural constructions that derive their power from acts of self-identification; the 'antidote' to this 'malady of history' is found in the ability of individuals and cultures to change the way that they conceive of, and position themselves within, these narrative structures (120).

Like Nietzsche, Keane focuses on the way that an uncritical identification with these historical and temporal narratives can delimit – or altogether eliminate – the future. This recognition is the basis for the conflict between Eliza and Olivia, and it also informs the narrative and novelistic contexts within which Keane situates this conflict. There is a well-established set of tropes, common throughout Big House novels, by which the Big House is read as being in the end stages of a prolonged decline, and by which its inhabitants are viewed as, in Nietzsche's terms, latecomers and epigones. These tropes include the decay of the physical structure of the Big House, a loss of income and socio-political status for its owners, and a quality of enervation, effeteness, or sterility that pervades the Big House and the lives of its inhabitants. What is remarkable about *Full House*, however, is that this novel is devoid of any such tropes or signifiers of decline in the Big House's political, economic, or cultural status.

By refusing to figure the Birds and Silverue in terms of a narrative of decline and decay, Keane shifts the focus of the novel onto the ways in which Eliza and the Birds identify with and resist historical and temporal narratives – and further, gives real credence and significance to these negotiations. It is useful to envision the alternative: if Keane had staged the conflict between the temporal models embodied by Olivia and Eliza in a Big House that was – like so many literary Big Houses – literally falling down around them, Olivia's claim to a future would have been sharply ironised. Instead, these historical and temporal narratives become the site of a critique within this Big House novel.

Juxtaposing Nietzsche's essay and Keane's novel allows us to situate Keane's treatment of the Anglo-Irish Big House within a much broader context of philosophical and cultural critique. Nietzsche's essay is also useful in that it makes visible Keane's radical resistance to the privileging of any historical or temporal narrative in this novel. While both Keane's novel and Nietzsche's essay expose a temporal model that is perceived to be natural as being in fact a construction and projection of culture, the natural returns to dominate the conclusion of Nietzsche's essay. Properly administered, Nietzsche's 'antidote' to the 'malady of history' would result in a culture that is defined by its 'robust health' and above all its 'youth' – a youth, moreover, with a 'more natural nature' than the latecomer, the epigone, or the '"greybeard" of the present' (120–1).[3] In the concluding pages of his essay, Nietzsche effectively replaces the historical narratives he had criticised with a redefined 'natural' model as the basis for a forward-looking historical and temporal narrative. In the concluding pages of *Full House*, Keane initially seems to perform a similar re-inscription of a privileged narrative. The narrative to which Keane turns in this concluding section of the novel is not a 'natural' model of timeliness, but rather a progressionist historical narrative of modernisation. However, Keane introduces this highly influential narrative only to subject it to the kind of critical reconsideration that has informed her representation of historical and temporal narratives throughout the novel.

The novel closes with Eliza's second, and likely her last, departure from Silverue. Olivia and Markie drive Eliza to the train station, where they wait with her despite the 'shower of rain' that 'came down with sudden definite venom', and the fact that Eliza's train is late (314). While they are waiting, Markie 'produced chocolate and match-boxes from his pockets,' but when Eliza asks him for a match-box, he refuses to give her one, explaining that he 'had bought these for Julian. And the chocolate was for himself' (314). This provokes a scolding from Olivia, in the midst of which Eliza's train arrives. From her window on the train, Eliza watches as the figure of an apparently regretful Markie, his hands 'full of match-boxes and pieces of chocolate,' runs 'frantically down the length of the train ... Wildly it ran, and wildly called: "Eliza! Eliza!"' (315). The tone of this scene seems to be building rapidly toward tragedy, or melodrama; the conclusion is represented from Eliza's position on the train.

---

3 I do not want to misrepresent the complexity of Nietzsche's argument. The 'natural' model that Nietzsche posits at the end of this essay can only be achieved when two conditions are met. First, as I have already described, his contemporaries must recognise that the historical models they view as 'natural' are in fact culturally constructed or anthropomorphic narratives – and thus not 'natural' at all in the way that Nietzsche seeks to define this term. Secondly, this 'natural' model will be the product of a selective self-positioning *vis-à-vis* three different attitudes toward history – a history which is further subdivided into three types, or in Nietzsche's terminology, 'species', each of which must also be selectively employed (72).

> Struggling with her window, Eliza cried to him to be careful (that futile cry to Ardour). A porter caught him by the long skirts of his coat. Match-boxes and chocolate were scattered on the wet platform. The train moved out. Markie was late. He too, was defeated. Eliza leaning from her window could not tell whether rain or tears were on his face. He stood very still now, waving and waving to her. (315)

The fact that 'Markie was late' is both the dramatic climax of this scene and the final event in the novel. This narrative positioning in the concluding moments of the novel, together with the fact that Markie's lateness is produced by the arrival of the train, invites a reading of this scene that attends to its cultural resonances. Historically a symbol of the inexorable progress of modernity and the implementation of a standardised, uniform temporal system, the train passes by Markie, rushing its passengers to the modern, urban spaces of Dublin and cities beyond. In this respect, the scene evokes the narrative positioning of the Anglo-Irish Big House as culturally belated: having failed to adapt to and identify with a progressionist narrative of modernisation, the Big House now lies outside and beyond the mainstream of modern national and historical narratives.[4] The irrelevant and untimely position of the Big House within this narrative is underscored in the text: '[t]he great train of the day could not waste a minute in such a small place. It must instantly be off' (314). Markie's 'defeat' thus signals his internalisation of, and inscription into, a temporal order that defines him as belated in two senses: first, as a member of a culture that has outstayed its historical moment; and secondly, as an individual who – despite his youthful speed and energy – has arrived too late to participate in the culture of the modern.

This reading, however, is problematised by the text in two ways. First, the assertion that 'Markie was late' is presented from the perspective of Eliza, whose attempt to impose a particular temporal narrative onto the Birds has been exposed and criticised in the novel. Keane further calls into question Eliza's estimation of the significance of Markie's lateness by rendering Markie's response to the fact of his lateness ambiguous: 'Eliza leaning from her window could not tell whether rain or tears were on his face' (315). Secondly, Markie and the culture of the Big House are not the only belated figures in this scene: The imagery that evokes this reading is also 'late'. By the mid-1930s, in which the novel is both published and set, the use of the train to symbolise modernity and progress no longer has the contemporary resonance and impact that it would have had in the late nineteenth century and in the

---

4 Even within Big House novels, the reasons given for this failure to modernise are complex and diverse. See, for example, the representations of abortive and abandoned efforts to modernise or 'improve' agricultural production in Somerville and Ross's *An Enthusiast* (1921) and in the figure of Cousin Francis in Elizabeth Bowen's *The Heat of the Day* (1949).

early years of the twentieth century. The belatedness of this metaphor is signalled in the text: the train itself is late. By using a culturally belated image
to evoke this narrative, Keane disrupts the straightforward metaphorical reading of Markie and the Big House as being outside or beyond a trajectory of
modernisation. Further, this handling of the narrative of modernisation makes
visible one aspect of the entirely contemporary relevance of this Big House
novel. In the 1930s, Ireland was actively questioning what form 'modern'
socio-economic relations would take in this largely rural and agricultural
nation. Keane's resistance to identifying either Markie, or the 'small place'
where he lives, as 'belated' intersects with this contemporary negotiation of
Ireland's position within a narrative of modernisation.[5] The significance of
the challenge that Keane poses to her readers – to attend to the ways that
temporal and historical narratives are uncritically imposed and adopted – thus
extends well beyond the Big House and its demesne.

I would like to conclude by returning to my suggestion earlier in this
essay that the logic Eliza deploys in her conflict with Olivia is the same logic
as that which has subtended not only political attitudes toward the Big House
in the early twentieth century, but also an influential strain of late twentieth-
century literary criticism on the Big House novel. In the literary-critical register, this logic runs as follows: the 'natural' end of the Big House novel was,
or should have been, coterminous with the end of Ascendancy power and
privilege. The persistence – and even coalescence – of the Big House novel
long after this 'natual' endpoint is untimely and anachronistic. The Big House
novel should thus relinquish its claim on the present, so that more politically appropriate and representative generalisations of Irish writing can
emerge.[6] The ideological assumptions and bias on which this and similar

---

5 Keane's engagement with this narrative of modernisation should encourage us to reconsider
the very general, but influential, formulation of that narrative that I described above. Joe Cleary's
recent essay, 'Toward a materialist-formalist history of twentieth-century Irish literature', provides just such a reconsideration of this narrative that has important implications for reading
the twentieth-century Big House novel. Cleary writes: 'To think beyond current orthodoxy in
Irish social and cultural history – which usually construes Ireland as only badly and belatedly
catching up with a model of modernization immaculately completed much earlier in Europe –
we need to work toward a less linear and more global and conjunctural mode of analysis that
starts from the assumptions that Irish modernity comprises a particular configuration of wider
global processes, and that its modernity is therefore directly coeval with other modernities. But
coeval here suggests a contemporaneity that recognizes the possibility of difference' (2004,
210–11). From this perspective, Cleary argues that the fact that Ireland 'produced no extended
modernist culture' was 'not because Ireland was a premodern or traditional backwater too isolated from the rapids of twentieth-century modernity to do so, but because it was in one broad
sociohistorical sense *too modern*, since it had been, via colonialism, catapulted directly into modernity without ever having passed through the feudal stage and hence had so little of the ver-
nacular "high culture" that many of its European neighbors had to work on' (2004, 225).   6
This logic is most directly stated in Seamus Deane's 'The literary myths of the revival: a case

arguments are based have been ably exposed and criticised.⁷ I would like to emphasise here that Keane pre-empts this logic by making the historical and temporal narratives that produce the untimeliness of the Big House both the focus of a critique in *Full House* and the site of the novel's full engagement with the contemporary cultural moment. As Keane demonstrates in her staging of the conflict between Eliza and Olivia, to assert a 'natural' end, or the inevitability of decline, is to deploy a specific, culturally constructed narrative of history and temporality. Ultimately, by insisting on the need to recognise, confront, and challenge the workings and effects of these narratives, Keane lays the groundwork for her own and others' continuation of the Big House novel as a vital and vibrant generic form into and beyond the late twentieth century.

for their abandonment' (1977). Deane's essay can be seen to rely upon this logic both in the section I quoted above, and in the following passage: 'The re-emergence of the Big House novel, with all its implicit assumptions, demonstrates the comparative poverty of the Irish novelistic tradition and the power of Yeats's presence even now. But the anachronism which bedevils so much Irish fiction of this kind surely relates to the fact that the Big House is more concerned with tourism and tax concessions, the preservation of the artifacts of "Culture", rather than with power or value. It has about as much pressure on contemporary Irish life as the Norman ruins of the South-East. The extension of a myth into this kind of social literalism has finally led both to its vulgarization and to a failure in the fictional tradition itself. It is surely time to abandon such a myth and find intellectual allegiances elsewhere' (321–2). Significantly, in the version of Deane's essay that is published in *Celtic Revivals* (1985), Deane revises the section addressing the Big House novel, focusing more directly on his claim that the Big House novel perpetuates a Yeatsian mythologisation of the Ascendancy, and downplaying his problematic use of a narrative that seeks to naturalise the 'death' of the Big House novel. 7 See, for example, Neil Corcoran's *After Yeats and Joyce: reading modern Irish literature* (especially pages 34–6), and the Introduction to Vera Kreilkamp's *The Anglo-Irish novel and the Big House*, in which Kreilkamp criticises a 'nationalist criticism that has minimized the importance of Big House novels in the canon of Irish writing', but at the same time resists an alignment of her work with the 'revised interpretation of Anglo-Irish society underway in current historiography' (1998, 10).

Comparative contexts

Colonial Ireland in retrospect in Somerville & Ross's *The Big House of Inver* and Molly Keane's *Two Days in Aragon*

SILVIA DÍEZ FABRE

This essay discusses fictive rationalisations of Ascendancy failure to achieve hegemony in colonial Ireland, with particular reference to Somerville & Ross's *The Big House of Inver* and Molly Keane's *Two Days in Aragon*. *The Big House of Inver* was produced in 1925, after the Irish War of Independence and the subsequent Civil War. In this novel, the last published under the names of Somerville and Ross, Edith Somerville acknowledges the end of Anglo-Irish political Ascendancy and provides a historical perspective on its decadence and subsequent decline. This perspective thus offers a much more perceptive view on the question of leadership in a colonised territory than any of her previous novels. Although not actually set during the Troubles, *The Big House of Inver* explores a long period of colonial misrule and suggests Anglo-Irish improvidence as the cause of the eventual downfall of colonial Ireland. Some twenty years later, in the reality of a new Irish Republic, Molly Keane's novel *Two Days in Aragon* (1941) appears to be a retelling of *The Big House of Inver*. In this, her most political novel, Keane attempts an understanding of the Anglo-Irish colonial experience by placing her Big House narrative into the immediate situation of the Troubles, and by depicting the evils of colonialism in terms of class oppression and sectarian conflict. Molly Keane distances herself from a sentimental view of the tragedy of the Anglo-Irish on the verge of extinction. Instead, her interest is in exploring the ideological foundations of this social world, laying bare the cultural formation of a colonial discourse that helped the Anglo-Irish political Ascendancy to sustain itself. It should be highlighted that both Edith Somerville and Molly Keane use the same central figure of an illegitimate daughter of the Big House, intent on saving the Anglo-Irish heritage, as a metaphor for the failure of the Ascendancy to impose moral authority on Ireland. These strong powerful women, in spite of their humiliating illegitimacy, are determined to defend the cause of the Ascendancy's status and preserve the gentry house and lineage. By making a comparative analysis between Shibby Pindy in *The Big House of Inver* and Nan O'Neill in *Two Days in Aragon*, I point out the ways in which these two characters differ as both victims and agents of domination, arguing that, while Edith Somerville sympathises with the values of colonial leadership, Molly Keane offers a harsh indictment of a system based on colonial victimisation.

The background to the story of the female protagonists, Shibby in *The Big House of Inver* and Nan in *Two Days in Aragon* is linked, I argue, with the Irish cultural representation of hegemony. This hegemony originally identified the land as a woman married to the ruler of the country, a colonial counterpart to the union of the dominant male authority of England with the feminine quality of subordinate Ireland. Yet the Anglo-Irish and Gaelic origins that Shibby Pindy and Nan O'Neill share – an Ascendancy father and a peasant mother – are not legitimated by marriage, but are the result of an illegitimate union between English colonial power and Gaelic Ireland. These two characters bear the debasing imprint of colonial Ireland that is implicit in the burden of an unlawful relationship between the coloniser and the colonised. It is important to observe that, although unrecognised daughters of the Big House because of their inferior Gaelic origin, Shibby and Nan are resident Big House housekeepers and feel a blind devotion to the superior lineage of the house and family. In these Big Houses the unacknowledged daughters try to exert influence, however devoid of moral authority. Their struggle for self-affirmation is complicated by their illegitimacy, which denies them a rightful place in leadership. Shibby and Nan's problematic status is emblematic of the Ascendancy's vulnerable position in the face of hegemony. As Terry Eagleton suggests: 'The real test of hegemony is whether a ruling class is able to impose its spiritual authority on its underlings, lend them moral and political leadership and persuade them of its own vision of the world. And on all these accounts, when the record is taken as a whole, the Anglo-Irish must be reckoned an egregious failure' (1995, 30). Both Edith Somerville and Molly Keane's texts illustrate this notion of hegemony by giving the central figures of their respective novels a 'half-recognized' identity. As a result, it is to Anglo-Ireland's myth of itself that Shibby and Nan turn in their search for self-definition. I would argue that Molly Keane's novel condemns the colonial system's unlawful power relation, a relation established between the coloniser and the colonised on the grounds of the superiority of the former. In Edith Somerville's novel, the power relation that lies at the heart of the colonial system is sealed by the feudal bonds that derive from the rights of conquest. The conquering principle conveys aristocratic leadership and asserts the lawful superiority of the coloniser. Therefore, the unlawfulness of the position does not involve abuse of power, as it does in Molly Keane's novel, but rather the recognition of the coloniser's misuse of power. In Edith Somerville's novel, the failure of the Ascendancy to achieve hegemony is due to misgovernment rather than to any doubts about the aristocratic authority of this class. Conversely, in Molly Keane's novel, the oppressive basis of the colonial system invalidates the moral authority of a class created out of an inherent wrong. There is a sharp contrast between Edith Somerville and Molly Keane's main characters, with Shibby

Pindy embodying the waste of Anglo-Irish aristocratic values, while Nan O'Neill incarnates the destructive myth of Anglo-Irish superiority.

Edith Somerville's *Irish Memories* (1917), written before her novel *The Big House of Inver*, provides a context for the story of her heroine, Shibby Pindy. Edith Somerville indicates in *Irish Memories* that 'an ideal of art rose for [them]' when they decided to write about the 'half-acknowledged, half-witted, wholly horrifying' representatives of the fall of the Big House, a subject which, from the time of *An Irish Cousin*, remained 'far and faint as the half-moon, and often, like her, hidden in clouds, yet never quite lost or forgotten' (131). This ideal of art was supposedly prompted by Somerville and Ross's visit to a ruined Big House inhabited by a distant relative, a woman 'of an old stock, isolated from the world at large, wearing itself out in those excesses that are a protest of human nature against unnatural conditions' (130–1). Through this event, which made them aware of the shame of misalliance, they perceived the moral decline of their own class. As a result of this visit, Somerville considers the collapse of the Anglo-Irish world in terms of genetic degeneration and from the standpoint of *noblesse oblige*. Yet, perhaps because Somerville and Ross 'had been warned of certain subjects not to be approached' (130), the disempowerment of the Anglo-Irish, presented in earlier novels such as *An Irish Cousin* and *The Real Charlotte*, relies on the trope of misalliance to reflect the degeneration of a landed class while ignoring its political and colonial context and background (Kreilkamp 1998, 115–23; Diez Fabre 101–8). Although *The Big House of Inver* has the same allegorical strain pervasive in other Anglo-Irish fictions (MacCormack 1985, 104), the issue of misalliance – as represented by the character of Shibby Pindy – comes to the fore in the novel in order to tackle the problem of hegemony in colonial Ireland. In this novel Edith Somerville takes the analysis of Anglo-Irish social disorder a step further and goes into the depths of the moral decline of a colonialist class. *The Big House of Inver* mirrors the actual story of misalliance of the St George family of Tyrone House, in Co. Galway, which was pointed out by Martin as a fitting subject for literary inspiration in a letter written to Edith in 1912 (*The Big House of Inver* 313; Lewis 294). Thirteen years later Edith's fictional account fulfills Martin's suggestion but she is aware, as she later notes, that 'this is the history of one of those minor dinasties [whose] names are sunk in squalor, mis-spelt, mispronounced, surviving only illegitimately' (*The Real Charlotte* xii). The reality of Irish independence made Somerville more overtly political in *The Big House of Inver* than in previous novels. Instead of dealing with the problems derived from land tenure, there is a fundamental preoccupation here with the failings of the Ascendancy as a social entity. Somerville sees the Anglo-Irish as born with the coloniser's status, and therefore endowed with the privilege of leadership, yet unable to live up to its aristocratic role. In the light of this failure, Shibby Pindy's efforts to redress her Big House family's errors are futile.

Shibby Pindy is presented as a handsome woman, who derives her physical beauty from her Anglo-Irish origins and her wily character from her
Gaelic peasant heritage. Edith Somerville's emphasis on 'the invisible, invin-
cible webs of heredity' throughout the novel is directed towards the idea of
Shibby's polluted lineage (32). The mark of her illegitimacy is powerfully
evoked as a critical reminder of the disastrous effects of misgovernment –
though Shibby shows aristocratic pride she lacks the refinement and taste of
a Big House lady. She lives in the Anglo-Irish family household, to her
father's shame, and although she has been there since her early childhood,
she still cannot be considered a rightful member of the family. The absence
of moral authority and the lack of taste in her behaviour bespeak the con-
tamination of the feudal ethic and the civilised ethos proper to Big House
status. Shibby personifies the pollution of an aristocratic class made degenerate by colonial misgovernment.

The novel gives the historical context that accounts for Shibby's disgraced
situation through the ups and downs of the Prendeville family. The right of
conquest, embodied in 'the family motto "Je Prends"' (9), has been asserted
through a landowning tradition of centuries, dating back to a 'Norman ancestor' (7). With Mr Robert Prendeville, 'a man of taste' (7), the building of the
Big House of Inver attests to the fact that the family enjoyed class privilege,
as expressed by its architecture 'which still stand[s] to justify Ireland's claim
to be considered a civilised country' (8). The Prendevilles are renowned for
arrogance, since they have maintained their position in circumstances of suspicion and defensiveness. The splendid isolation apparently enjoyed by the
Prendevilles is reflected by the Big House of Inver itself which, 'stood high
on the central ridge of the promontory of Ross Inver, and faced unflinching
the western ocean' (7). 'Its builder's reason for traversing the usual practice
of his country, and sacrificing shelter and bodily comfort, to scenery' is mis-
leading, for he 'had not much thought for the beauty that lay, almost literally, at his feet' (7). The need for self-assertion finds dramatic expression at
the beginning of the novel when the proud Lady Isabella Prenderville, married to Beauty Kit Prenderville and herself of 'the noble house of Breffny'
(9), endeavours to assert a sense of colonial Ascendancy for the beleaguered
Prendervilles, which alienates her from the 'people'. In response to this alienation, she closes ranks around her privileged home and family, 'refusing, in
arrogance, to know, or to let her children know, her neighbours, freezing herself into, as it were, an iceberg of pride, living to see, at last, her only son,
Nicholas, marry the daughter of one of the Inver gamekeepers, and her two
daughters, Isabella and Nesta, go off with two of her own grooms' (10). Lady
Isabella's illegitimate descendant, Shibby Pindy appears as the inevitable result
of 'successive generations of mainly half-bred and wholly profligate
Prendevilles [who] rioted out their short lives in the Big House, living with

country women, fighting, drinking, gambling' (10–11). As Lady Isabella's cor-
roded namesake by 'tavern usage' (38), Shibby is a living memory of the
Ascendancy's improvidence, but also the successor of a class under pressure
to assert its authority.

At the same time, the need to enforce dominance remains a most important drawback for the Anglo-Irish when they come to face the responsibility
of feudal leadership. The Prendevilles' feudal legacy, exemplified by Shibby's
half-recognised identity, demonstrates an unlawful relationship between the
ruling elite and the country people, offering them little opportunity for achieving hegemony as an aristocratic class. Shibby's father, Jas Prendeville, justifies his position of superiority on the family principle: 'They should take who
have the power' (24), but weakness lies behind his apparent strength and this
is made evident by his misbehaviour. Shibby is in fact born out of her father's
'sufficiently mediaeval' practice of the '*Droit de Seigneur* that was, as a rule,
based rather on might than on right' (23).

By the time the novel reaches the late 1880s, a vivid picture of decay is
conveyed through the irresponsibility of old Jas. The Big House is uninhab-
ited, the family having been confined to the old Norman Tower for the last
two generations, and the demesne now belongs to the land-agent, the
Protestant middle-class Weldons. In this context, the debasing conditions of
Shibby's supposed shameful parentage seem to be totally out of proportion.
She becomes her half-brother's 'slave', (39) and 'the servant of her father,
making no claim on him, her single protest a proud refusal to take wages'
(38). But her acceptance of such a servile role in the family is ambivalent,
since 'as Shibby Pindy, Isabella Prendeville went through life, silently, without complaint' (38). She is indeed fighting back in order to achieve the recognition of her Big House identity. Shibby's apparent self-denial emphasises
her humiliating position as a colonial victim. However, at the same time her
rights as a member of the aristocratic family become increasingly evident. By
championing her family's aristocratic status, this 'faithful, though unacknowledged daughter of the old house' finds moral strength 'to renew her
energies, and to enforce her inspiration' in her otherwise barren life (50).

The story involving Shibby's efforts to reunite the Big House and the
demesne begins in 1912. Enthralled by the aristocratic ideal, she tries to refur-
bish the Big House at her own personal cost. She also embraces the role of
a surrogate mother devoted to her half-brother Kit, a full member of the gentry, though inevitably affected by the family weakness of arrogance. By scheming to arrange a match between Kit and Peggy Weldon, and by casting off
Kit's peasant mistress, Maggie O'Connor, who has become pregnant, Shibby
intends to save the symbols of class privilege and erase the sins that derive
from a colonially rooted past. However, Shibby gets trapped in the historical
forces of social mobility, and Anglo-Irish improvidence is fatally brought to

resolution by English intervention. In the end, the Big House is sold to the English parvenu, Burgrave, and Kit's sexual affair with Maggie O'Connor frightens off Peggy Weldon, who chooses her more respectable English suitor and forgets her love for Kit.

The Big House of Inver intertwines the tragic story of Shibby Pindy with Somerville's own purpose of defending the aristocratic cause of the Anglo-Irish against the charge of questionable leadership. Although there is abundant evidence of Anglo-Irish misrule, Somerville justifies it from the standpoint of a victimised class that is unable to assert its aristocratic authority because of the stigma of a colonial Ascendancy. Shibby's insightfulness is revealing when she mourns the loss of the Big House: 'I'm beat! I done my best. There never was luck in it! There was too much pride and wickedness long ago' (309). However, haunted by the accusing ghost of the Irish peasant girl Maggie O'Connor, Shibby says, 'Let her follow me if she likes! I'd do the same thing again tomorrow!' (308). Violently opposed to Maggie's unlawful relationship with Kit, Shibby disapproves of the same type of colonial union that resulted in her own birth, but only because Maggie disrupts her plans for the restoration of the Big House. Shibby's Gaelic identity is effaced of necessity, since she feels compelled to favour the superiority of the Ascendancy. Her ambiguous position is echoed in the position of Somerville herself. Reflecting Albert Memmi's concept of the 'colonizer who refuses'(39), Somerville is the colonial writer who won't consider the situation of the colonised, despite her rejection of the politics of subjection on which the colonial system is founded. This refusal is important in a novel written soon after the independence of Ireland and is reminiscent of the Anglo-Irish re-definition of identity after the Union which reflected 'the possibility that the moves of the colonizers towards the politics and culture of the colonized are motivated by the desire to achieve influence through an act of association and appropriation rather than identification and (self)absorption' (Cairns and Richards 1990, 25).

In contrast to Edith Somerville, Molly Keane dissociates herself from any sentimental consideration of the failure of Anglo-Irish leadership. Instead, Keane looks on the superiority ascribed to the Ascendancy with a cold eye. In *Two Days in Aragon*, the mark of illegitimacy looming large in the historical memory of Ireland reveals that the imperial system sustains itself on exploitation. Thus, the leading role conferred on the colonial elite is that of subjugators of the people-nation. It may be appropriate to remember here R.M. Foster's observation that the Ascendancy 'evolved an idea of the 'Irish nation' that was [...] visionary', and 'the fact that it depended on a sectarian definition of citizenship as mercilessly reductionist as the purest classical facade was taken for granted: so much so that the Ascendancy easily ignored the exclusive and oppressive basis of their power' (1988, 194). Molly Keane does not ignore the exclusive and oppressive basis of Anglo-Irish power. Her novel demonstrates her conscious rejection of the assumptions of superiority to which the Anglo-Irish turned in order to justify their abuse of power and their lack of hegemony. In *Two Days in Aragon*, Nan O'Neill, an illegitimate daughter of the Big House, collaborates happily with the oppressive and sectarian ideology of the colonial relationship that brought her into being. By acknowledging the exploitative role implicit in the superiority of the Ascendancy, Nan's belief in the authority of the Big House forces our realisation that the whole Anglo-Irish position is morally indefensible. Molly Keane's novels have been critically appreciated for their subversive quality, for the outstanding contribution of a novelist of the Big House genre who 'was to reject the nostalgia that is a major cultural production of a declining imperial state' (Kreilkamp 1998, 174). Her description of Anglo-Irish political demise in this novel shows her insight into a dismembered world, structured in dominance and power. Tamsin Hargreaves' apt remark that 'the basic psychological premise of [Molly Keane's] novels is that psychological wholeness, emotional integrity, no longer exists' points towards the idea of alienation as characteristic of a decadent world where power is materially a void (297). Relationships between the Anglo Irish and Irish in the frame of Big House society or domestic life are exposed as destructive. In this respect it has been highlighted that there is a prominent focus on sexual desire in her novels, an element that supports Keane's clear distinction between 'they who have the power to hurt and those who, lacking this power are hurt' (Breen 208). In spite of its irrelevance in the social and political arena of independent Ireland, the Big House cocoon in Molly Keane's novels seems to be burdened by a need for domination that propels the Anglo-Irish world toward cruelty and accounts for 'the Ugliness in the Big House' (Keane, *Young Entry* 280). In *Two Days in Aragon*, Anglo-Irish power is implicated in the struggle for hegemony during the Irish War of Independence, and the end of the Big House is marked by the politics of abuse. Consequently, Nan O'Neill bears the mark of the colonial experience through which the historical and political implications of 'the Ugliness in the Big House' can be seen.

It could be argued that Nan O'Neill's good looks, embodying the best elements of her 'father's quality and mother's beauty' (111), confirm the success of the colonial enterprise, insofar as it endorses the dominant role of the coloniser. Yet the fact of Nan's illegitimacy is in itself a threat to the lawful dominance of the coloniser. It should be remembered that, according to English colonising discourse, assimilation with the Irish was forbidden in order to enforce the colonial relationship of English supremacy over Irish inferiority. The sectarian measures taken to maintain this colonial relationship, far from allowing the coloniser to legitimise his leadership, merely reinforced the colonised subjects' continued opposition to oppression. In this sense, the dom-

inant position of the Anglo-Irish remains under threat, unable to assert hegemony. Nan's attempts to fashion her own identity are influenced by the different responses of her Anglo-Irish and Gaelic-Irish background to her illegitimacy. Although Nan had lived in the country with her peasant mother
and foster-father without ever seeing or visiting Aragon, it is through her
mother, who 'had been slave' to the duties and the passions that the Big
House demanded (108), that she learns about life 'somewhere between hell
and heaven, a glorious and dramatic purgatory' (107). Nan perceives her birth
as tainted, especially when her mother condemns the sexual attack by the
master of Aragon that led to pregnancy and exile from Aragon: 'Ah, child,
never do what I did. Never get yourself caught like that' (109). It is in her
Irish environment that Nan learns to see herself as the product of an unnatural, abusive relationship. Yet, it is precisely as a daughter of the Big House
that she is at least half-recognised. She is the exception among all her father's
illegitimate children, the only one saved from the fate allotted to the illegitimate infants of the servant girls of Aragon whose 'babies' bones were little
and green scattered skeletons on the river bottom' (122). Nan's purpose is to
legitimise her Anglo-Irish identity by reacting against her Irish family's inferiority and subordination. Nan despises her mother, 'a stupid loquacious slat-
tern' (107), and becomes a servant in Aragon by her own wish, consciously
aware of her devoted service to the superior Foxes; 'for how could her love
for Aragon ever be admitted, or her share in the Fox family ever be allowed
– the vanity and reverence for her own blood were the first to deny its admission' (112). Yet the sacrifice of her life to the glory of Aragon is expressed in
disquieting terms which make her an ominous figure of ruthless devotion to
the Big House status: 'All her life was as clear to her as if she opened an atlas
and looked at a map. It would be a map of Aragon with the blood of her life
and the strength of her mind and her body marked on it in strong visible
ways' (106).

Although Nan cannot be insensible to the beauty and splendour of
Aragon, it is its hegemonic power that makes the house 'the dream in her life'
(107). Behind the myth of superiority that the Big House promulgates, lies
the reality: the abuse of power, the terror and tyranny that are the fabric of
Aragon: 'There were noddings and whisperings and tales of childbeds in far
corners of the Big House, and pale heavy-breasted girls dragging themselves
again about their work' (108). It is revealing that Nan worships the superiority of the Fox family, while endorsing the politics of fear behind the regime
at Aragon. Her commitment to Aragon as an illegitimate daughter and social
inferior reflects her total compliance with the ethos of the Big House, an ethos
that has formed the basis of her colonial identity. This duality is expressed
in her double role as a victim/victimiser; it comes as no surprise that Nan
should feel her position in the family legitimised when she is alone in the

house with all the dead that haunt Aragon. The ghosts of the past, her Fox ancestors, the servant girls of Aragon and their babies, are the means by which Nan's sense of belonging to Aragon is fully realised. She is, thus, legitimated by both the victimisers and the victims that coexist inextricably in her Anglo-Irish world: 'The ghosts at Aragon were only seen and heard by the Fox's, and the Fox's [*sic*] were usually afraid of them and denied their presence. [...] But for Nan it was another thing, and a glorious thing. She went towards the hauntings, the shadows, the fullness in empty rooms, with a great embracement of spirit. To her this proof of her Fox blood was a wonder and a satisfaction beyond price' (121).

The haunting images of skeletons, bones and bodily remains pervades the narrative of the novel. Nan's implacable determination and purpose as a servant to the Big House spirit is seen in 'the bones round her eyes', which 'were of that full exciting shape which age makes more true and regular' (12). In sharp contrast to Aragon's illegitimate children, whose bones lie scattered at the bottom of the river, the physical beauty of the two legitimate daughters is dwelt on in detail with references to Grania Fox's 'pretty bones', which attest to her mercenary sensuality (6), and descriptions of the 'cool and charming' Sylvia Fox, wearing 'a string of river pearls round her neck' (19). It is precisely in order to help Mrs Fox with the upbringing of her two daughters – and also to look after dotty Aunt Pigeon – that Nan goes into service in Aragon. She performs her duties with the aim of strengthening the family's Big House status and she keeps a watchful eye on the behaviour of the daughters of Aragon. In contrast with the pride that Nan feels for Sylvia and Grania, she despises Aunt Pigeon's weakness and treats this 'small old woman, the flesh all fallen from her elegant bones,' (9) with great cruelty. Nan's subordinate role in Aragon and her function as an agent of domination is embedded in the ideological skeleton of the Big House.

Nan's attempt to legitimise colonial leadership means that she must assume both the role of victim and of victimiser. Her acceptance of her Irish subordination involves defending Anglo-Irish discrimination and tyranny, and results in the formation of an identity which is divided. This duality is the reason for her eventual failure, made worse by the opposition she encounters from her own son, Foley, who has become a member of the IRA. Foley's involvement in the Irish War of Independence not only puts Nan in an awkward position with the British forces and with the Foxes (whom she continues to serve devotedly) but also reflects her estrangement from her son and country. Thus, Nan's Anglo-Irish position is exposed, caught between the two sides of the colonial divide. It is little wonder then that both the British army and the Irish revolutionary forces should collaborate in bringing about her violent and undignified end. In an ironic twist, Nan meets her death when she is knocked down by a lorry carrying British soldiers who are on their way to save Aragon, which has been torched by the IRA. Nan's death demonstrates that the colonial relationship is untenable when confronted with the struggle for hegemony of the Troubles.

There is, on the whole, the ironic realisation that the colonial apparatus is self-defeating: the Anglo-Irish are victimised by their lack of moral authority against which they enforce victimisation and, consequently, effectively invalidate their right of existence. The Anglo-Irish relationship cannot therefore be justified. Its colonial pattern is as unjustifiable as the intricate design that shapes the very architecture of Aragon: 'A magnolia's horned and flowerless bones were crucified against a shallow alcove in a wall alcoved for no reason but to complete an alcove at the house's farther extreme' (227). In the face of hegemony, the burning of Aragon brings the symbol of colonising power to an end. The disappearance of the Big House and Nan's death imply the downfall of the colonial foundations and this is conveyed by the colonised's refusal to consent to unlawful power. Nan's death operates as a mocking metaphor for the failure of the Ascendancy to move towards identification with the people-nation, thereby demonstrating that a dominant class 'must "nationalise" itself in a certain sense' in order to be hegemonic (Cairns and Richards 15).

The Anglo-Irish Big House under pressure: Elizabeth Bowen's *The Last September* and Molly Keane's *Two Days in Aragon*

DEREK HAND

There is much to link Molly Keane's *Two Days in Aragon* (1941) with Elizabeth Bowen's *The Last September* (1929). They both fit the general trajectory and tropes of the Big House novel: the delineation of a fading Ascendancy, cut off from the world about the Big House demesne, clinging to an enervated culture that has been reduced to the colonial performances of 'dressing' properly for dinner at eight and playing endless games of tennis. Bowen famously said of *The Last September* that it was her only novel to be set back in time, published as it was in 1929 and set during the Irish War of Independence in 1920 (*The Mulberry Tree*, 122). Keane's novel is also set back in time, during that particular period of turmoil and upheaval. Thus, both novels deliberately open up a fictional space that allows for a consideration of the conflict between Irish, Anglo-Irish and British. Questions surrounding loyalty and belonging are brought to the fore as the pages are filled with IRA soldiers, British soldiers and the seemingly hapless Anglo-Irish caught impossibly in between these two poles. And, of course, both novels end with an enduring image of conflagration, emphasising the precariousness and the real threat to continued Anglo-Irish life in post-independence Ireland.

It can be argued that Molly Keane's *Two Days in Aragon* is a reimagining of Elizabeth Bowen's earlier novel. They were, after all, lifelong friends (Glendinning 206) and perhaps this connection – even on the level of the unconscious – implies that Keane's work is a response to Bowen's *The Last September*. Both writers quite knowingly register their concerns about Anglo-Ireland in terms of issues surrounding gender and sexuality. In turn, for both writers, these questions about gender and sexuality are mediated through images and perspectives of the Irish landscape, in a way uniting and making palpable the threat to property and familial continuity for the Anglo-Irish. As will be seen, in many ways Keane's response is to consider the subterranean, to hone in on that which is beneath the surface and hidden in Elizabeth Bowen's novel. One result is that she sees the real threat to the Anglo-Irish Big House coming from within the house itself, whereas for Bowen the threat comes from outside the demesne walls. In the analysis that follows, I will examine *The Last September*'s negotiations of issues of sexuality and gender, thus providing a context for Keane's explorations of the same issues in *Two Days in Aragon*.

In *The Last September* Lois Farquar's position as a woman becomes a means of gauging Britain's colonial relationship to Ireland. Gerald, representing the English perspective, likes things 'square and facty'(84), a situation where there is a place for everything and everything in its place. This directness and confidence has a wide arc of influence for him:

> He sought and was satisfied with a few – he thought final – repositories for his emotions: his mother, country, dog, school, a friend or two, now – crowningly – Lois. Of these he asked only that they should be quiet and positive, not impinged upon, not breaking boundaries from their generous allotment. (41)

Gerald brings this imperialistic poise to his relationship with Lois. At one stage Lois equates Ireland with being a woman, saying 'no wonder this country gets irritated' and then going on to claim that she does not know why women should not be hit or saved from wrecks 'when everybody complains they're superfluous (49).' Gerald replies that it would be 'ghastly' if these things were lost. Lois says she does not understand his attitude and she is a woman. This reply leaves Gerald pondering:

> Which was ... exactly why it wasn't expected or desired she should understand ... She had one limitation ... she couldn't look at her own eyes, had no idea what she was, resented almost his attention being so constantly fixed on something she wasn't aware of. A fellow did not expect to be to a girl what a girl was to a fellow ... so that the girl must be excused for a possible failure in harmony ... When he said: 'You will never know what you mean to me,' he made plain his belief in her perfection as a woman. She wasn't made to know, she was not fit for it. (49–50)

Here is an example of the 'male gaze', of the masculine imagination producing an image of the female that has no input from the female side whatsoever. At one point Gerald picks up a newspaper and reads an article on 'Unrest', which makes him think of Empire:

> He looked ahead to the time when it all should be accurately, finally fenced about and raked over. Then there should be a fixed leisured glow ... as on coming in to tea ... with his mother ... He turned in thought to confident English country, days like the look in a dog's eyes, rooms small in the scope of firelight, neighbourly lights through trees. (87–8)

What at first might seem a benign, indeed ineffectually romantic view of Lois in particular and women in general can be seen to be linked to the view of the world that aggressively imposes its own value systems upon other people and other cultures. Even a cursory glance at the language shows us that Gerald's world is a rigid one: a place where ideas are fixed and immutable; where progress inevitably will lead to an 'end', when finally everything will be 'fenced about and raked over.' Empire's function is to bring order: that is its ultimate goal. Gerald sees this 'end' in terms of a homely garden image, of a space with its boundaries firmly in place, and within this garden all aspects are finally arranged and completed.

Increasingly Lois's, and the wider Anglo-Irish community's, marginal and indistinct position is understood through this linkage with landscape. Travelling back to the Danielstown estate, Lois' perspective of the demesne is one of clear-cut separation from the surrounding countryside:

> To the south ... the demesne trees of Danielstown made a dark formal square like a rag on the green country ... Looking down, it seemed to Lois they lived in a forest; space of lawns blotted out in the pressure and dusk of trees. She wondered they were not smothered ... Their isolation became apparent. The house seemed to be pressing down low in apprehension, hiding its face, as though it has her vision of where it was. It seemed to gather its trees close in fright and amazement at the wide, light, lovely, unloving country, the unwilling bosom whereon it was set. (66)

Earlier a 'furtive lorry' disrupts the silence of the evening at Danielstown as it crawled 'with such a menace along the boundary, marking the scope of peace of this silly island, undermining solitude' (31). The limits of the demesne are identified – there is a clear and unambiguous sense of what is 'inside' and what is 'outside' this space. This lorry has another function in that it simultaneously highlights the permeability of this barrier, showing how it can be easily crossed over. Directly after this, Lois encounters an Irish soldier making his way through the estate:

> there passed within reach of her hand ... a resolute profile, powerful as a thought. In gratitude for its fleshiness, she felt prompted to make some contact. (34)

Lois, however, does not make contact and the soldier passes on. To do so would suggest the possibility of connection between Irish and Anglo-Irish and nothing in the novel allows for such a meeting. Indeed, the end of the novel emphasises Lois's apartness: her leaving is merely told to us and not dramatised in the text itself. For a character that has basically been the main focus throughout the novel her absence at the close – and the manner of her exit – must be considered significant. It leaves open the possibility that Lois can indeed escape the debilitating difficulties possessed by the Anglo-Irish. Another way of considering this exit is that it is typical of Lois: she misses out on one of the most important and exciting events to have occurred in or around Danielstown for quite some time. Quite simply, she's not there to witness it. This too could be construed as a comment upon the Anglo-Irish in general: that, ultimately, because they have failed to change or re-imagine themselves, events pass them by.

That the IRA man can so easily infiltrate the boundary of the demesne says much about the lack of power wielded by the Anglo-Irish. The sexual undertones in the above encounter with the IRA man are obvious. His 'fleshiness' – his palpability – is in contrast to the absence of vitality and the general air of stasis and sterility surrounding the Anglo-Irish. That he is linked to the landscape, seems almost a part of it, is in contrast to the Anglo Irish Big House which imposes its alien presence upon the landscape. These encroachments are not made solely by the Irish but are also made by the English. Gerald drops into lunch unannounced and uninvited while Mrs Vermont and Mrs Rolfe comically arrive one morning to a very frosty reception from the entire household. All of these intrusions serve to show the Anglo-Irish inability to sustain the integrity of the Big House boundary, their inability to keep chaos and violence at bay.

In the face of Anglo-Irish ineffectiveness, Lois needs to assert herself, to take control of her own future. Thus Lois's various dalliances throughout the novel can be viewed as attempts at self-definition. Early on in the novel she toys with the idea that she may be in love with Hugo Montmorency, a former, unsuccessful, suitor of her dead mother, Laura. With this brief attachment, Lois is considering continuing on in the Anglo-Irish 'tradition', following in the footsteps of the previous generation. In doing so, she brings nothing of herself, her youth, or her generation to bear upon that tradition and the attachment soon ends. Hugo's attraction to Lois highlights his generation's shortcomings, revealing a tendency towards fantasy on his part and hinting at the moral bankruptcy of his generation.

As has been noted, Lois's relationship with Gerald offers her no future. Gerald's vision of her in his imagined landscape offers her no actively creative part in its construction or maintenance. It might also be said that Lois wants to achieve a proper perspective of the Irish landscape, one where her own individual place is secure within that landscape. She imagines that:

> There must be perfect towns where shadows were strong like buildings, towns secret without coldness, unaware without indifference. She liked mountains, but she did not care for views. (99)

She imagines a Utopia – a no place – somewhere where she can exist and 'be' herself. Lois's hoped-for place is presented in very uncertain terms. Indeed, in comparison to the 'square and facty' nature of Gerald's vision of peace, for instance, Lois's dream appears somewhat inadequate. Lois's 'utopia' could be said to be an attempt by her to move away from the rigidness of masculine constructions, to offer a feminine counterpoint to Gerald's patriarchal imagination. Thus, her dream place does not conform to the strictures and conventions of masculine language and imagination: it challenges these conventions and tries to move beyond them and imagine something 'other'. Her 'utopia', then, is a rejection of the male/imperialist culture she is forced to inhabit.

Events at the mill mark the turning point for Lois. She and Marda are transformed by an encounter with the Irish soldier where Marda is shot at and slightly grazed. Lois finds the experience both frighteningly 'real' but also thoroughly liberating. As a result, she is no longer enslaved to someone else's narrative. This liberation is evident when Lois muses on her future selfhood:

> 'Funny,' said Lois. 'Queer.' Her heart thumped, she looked at her watch. 'Half-past six,' she said. 'It's harder, for some reason, to imagine what I'll be doing or where I shall be.' (128–9)

Suddenly the unknown potential and possibility of the future challenges Lois and she has no need now for 'the escape into other people's clothes!' (76). She is now master of her own destiny because of the very fact that she does not exactly know what that destiny might be. She is, in other words, free now to choose her own role to play, imagine her own future, no matter how uncertain it may be, instead of having other roles thrust upon her. Lois confronts and begins to transcend the patriarchal narrative of Gerald and others. In terms of the wider relationship between Anglo-Ireland and Ireland, however, she can be seen to ultimately retreat from this conflict because of her departure at the end of the novel. Clearly her personal survival is at the cost of communal survival.

The challenges to authority experienced by Lois are not unique; the Anglo-Irish in general also have the power of authority wrested from their grasp. They become a part – insignificant as it turns out – of someone else's story. The encroaching threat of the Irish landscape upon the orderly gardens of the Big House signals this shift in power and authority:

> A sense of exposure, of being offered without resistance to some ironic un-curiosity, made Laurence look up at the mountain over the roof of the house. In some gaze – of a man's up there hiding, watching among the clefts and ridges – they seemed held, included and to have their only being. The sense of a watcher, reserve of energy and intention, abashed Laurence, who turned from the mountain. But the

> unavoidable and containing stare impinged to the point of a trans-
> formation upon the social figures with their orderly, knitted shadows,
> the well-groomed grass and the beds, worked out in this pattern. (119)

They are no longer in control of their own destiny and their presence in this landscape is mediated by the watching Irish. Authority has been passed, like a torch, to others. The Anglo-Irish are thus powerless, helpless and doomed.

Keane's rendering of these same issues of authority and identity in *Two Days in Aragon* is at once more complicated and simplistic. Whereas Lois is the main focus in *The Last September*, the combination of the question of gender and nation in Molly Keane's novel is presented through two characters, Grania and her sister Sylvia Fox. Grania is having an affair with Foley, a horsey Irish native, while her sister Sylvia is having a relationship with an English soldier, Captain Purvis. Obviously, the pull of differing loyalties is made manifest in these relationships. However, it would be a mistake to think that the relationships being played out resolve themselves neatly or can be understood in a straightforward/stereotypical 'either/or' fashion. Clear lines and national demarcations are blurred by being made knotty and indistinct.

This is one of the major points at which easy comparisons of the novels diverge. The fault lines can also be observed at the level of technique. Whereas in *The Last September*, Bowen manages to exhibit her characters' uneasiness and anxieties in subtle, almost imperceptible and subterranean ways, Keane's method, in contrast, is to lay bare the unconscious undercurrents surrounding sexuality, nation and gender. Different writers, of course, will have differing perspectives and differing processes with which to render their artistic vision. Here, though, it could be argued that, while in their fiction and in their lives Bowen and Keane had much in common, their vision for the Big House is fundamentally at odds with one another. Possibly it is because Bowen inherited her family estate and thus felt the very real pressure of attempting to continue on with Big House life and tradition that alters her view of the Anglo-Irish in post-independent Ireland. Certainly much of her fictional writing is concerned with tracing the shift in power away from traditional aristocracy, and detailing the trauma for those dispossessed characters now inhabiting this fallen world. Indeed, the fate of Lois at the close of *The Last September* – her ambivalent exit – suggests that Bowen wavered between the desire to keep up Big House living and the impulse to escape that responsibility. Molly Keane, on the other hand, certainly with the evidence of *Two Days in Aragon*, seems more prepared to consider the Big House continuing – in perhaps a compromised form – in the new Ireland. As will be seen, she is prepared at least to acknowledge the presence of the Irish in her novels in a way that Bowen does not.

In *The Last September* much stress is made of Danielstown's apartness, it is cut off from the surrounding countryside. The implication is clear: it cannot continue in this hostile environment and it will eventually be swallowed up and destroyed. The final moment of violent conflagration is merely a material confirmation of the Big House's imaginative and cultural disconnection from Ireland. In contrast to Bowen's destruction of the Big House at the end of *The Last September*, Keane imagines a future for Aragon at the end of her novel. This difference, I think, opens up a more complex interconnection between the work of Keane and Bowen. The difference, I would argue, centres round variant ideas concerning sterility and fertility. Grania's relationship with Foley, for instance, is a physical one and, while not voyeuristically detailed in the novel, gets more attention than any such relationship in Elizabeth Bowen's work. There is, in short, an earthiness to this novel, an emphasis on lushness and fecundity that critiques – perhaps consciously – the kind of sterility at work in Bowen's *The Last September*. It is not just people that are described in this way, but crucially, the landscape as well.

The world of Aragon and its environs is constantly described in terms of lushness and abundance:

> The scent of azaleas caught in the back of her nose like a fog of honey and pepper. The harsh almost animal breath that is behind its scent was not here yet, only the wild pungent sweet of its earliest flowers. Great groups almost grown to the size of trees flowered along the wide grass borders of the avenue towards the house ... Above the house again, the hill climbed up nursing the sun in its hollows and elbows, sheltering the rare trees, and the rhododendrons, and tender magnolias, and camellias that flowered so freely along the side of the valley. (16)

Keane also stresses colour: almost every description of a place, and especially Aragon itself, has a mention of vibrant primary colours. There are no shades or half colours here, no creams or greys. Perhaps all this focus on colour can be thought of as lurid, in the sense of being sensational and excessive. Certainly, there is an impression generated within the novel of wildness and unrestraint being associated with the flowers and these stark colours. Untamed and uncultivated nature might be thought of as a place that may harbour danger if left unchecked. Also, perhaps the presence of colour is a technique employed to create the frisson associated with the Gothic genre: the colours acting as a signal to the reader to be aware, or beware, of the heightened and potentially overpowering emotions pulsating beneath the seemingly calm surface of decorum and rectitude.

While Bowen is concerned with detailing the predicament of Anglo-Ireland in terms of political conflict, using landscape to emphasise boundaries and differences, Keane, in the other hand, is more concerned with the world within the Big House estate, concentrating much of her focus on the Anglo-

Irish themselves. Consequently, Keane's eroticised landscape suggests that the Anglo-Irish predicament has as its source the inner world of the characters rather than the outer world of political and public controversy. The significance of Keane's description of landscape becomes clear when the reader is introduced to Nan Foley. She is a servant to the Fox family, the product of a sexual union between an aristocratic Fox and a common Irish native and is thus an illegitimate heir to the Big House of Aragon. Her marital home is Mountain Brig and Keane's description of it illustrates Nan's ambition, her desire to control the landscape:

> Nan had always hated the poor twist of mountainy farm she had married into. But when she lived there she had worked and striven on it with all her power, civilising it a little more every year. (7)

That it is Nan Foley who possesses this notion of civilisation is noteworthy, because of her position within the novel as a product of a union of mésalliance her status is marginal.

The emphasis on blood and mésalliance and the consequences for Anglo-Irish inheritance of the Big House recall Yeats's *Purgatory* and Somerville and Ross's *The Big House of Inver*. These texts were written after the fact of Irish independence and were withering in their denunciation of those Anglo-Irish who married outside their class and caste, implying that the blame for the current state of dispossession and cultural marginalisation was to be found in such moments of promiscuousness. Another point of textual reference is Maria Edgeworth's *Castle Rackrent* where the character of Thady Quirke, like Nan Foley, reverses the traditional master-servant dichotomy. As Robert Tracy's reading of *Castle Rackrent* argues, this reversal of the expected power structure has disturbing consequences for the colonial status quo, raising questions about legitimate authority and the role of the native Irish in constructing the Big House myth for their own ends. However, in Keane's representation of Nan, there is no sense in which she is consciously an image of the colonised subject who 'simultaneously feigns loyalty, manipulates his rulers, and subverts their control' (Tracy, 17). Nan does abuse her position, especially with the sadly unstable Aunt Pidgie, but her actions are not intended to destroy Aragon and Anglo-Irish rule. Rather, her ultimate hope is for Aragon to continue on and on indefinitely. She has internalised the colonial mindset, believing in the Ascendancy's relevance and its worth much longer, and to a greater extent, than the Anglo-Irish themselves. Her sole selfish motive is that she will continue to be at its centre.

It is Nan who possesses the real, hidden history of Aragon in the form of repulsive stories concerning the sexual exploits of various Foxes from the past and their many dalliances with their tenants and servants.

> In just such trouble as the poor country girls who worked in the house had been in with the bad Fox's of all times, and they had been despised and aborted, their babies, dead and dying thrown to the river, unless they were lucky like Nan's own mother and found some man to put shoes on a Fox's pleasure. All these things have happened, all these things were true and strong in the past. They have happened again and again. Cruelty and pain and tears and death had been common mates to childbirth at Aragon. The family had kept their horrid ministers for such times, women like old Anne. There had always been somebody like that old Anne, tolerant, understanding, skilled and merciless. (156)

Despite Nan's desire to forget or to remain neutral about this hidden past, she cannot disguise the hint of danger that is always present in these memories. She recalls some of the older servants' warnings to her and to other young women to always stay where there is light: 'You wouldn't know where you'd be in the dark' (109). Later, the reader learns of a sexual chamber deep in the basement of Aragon:

> The walls of this room has been papered over in blue and white, but where the paper has peeled in the damp from the air from the near river, you could see underneath one of the old chinese design, a most peculiar design, perhaps rightly hidden and in parts purposely defaced ... White and gold pelmets over the windows, an Italian decoration on the ceiling ..., a strange room to find in the basements of Aragon where the hordes of servants had slept in dirt and confusion. Once the room has been hung with mirrors. Other curious contrivances were set in the walls ... It was fifty years now since any one had opened it and closed it, sick and shuddering at a half-understanding of delicate ivory-headed cutting whips and other fine and very curious instruments. (193)

Again, the threats of very real danger and violence associated with Aragon are intimated here. Interestingly though, as with this basement room itself, the implications remain broodingly subterranean and concealed. This secret and repressed history, however, can be connected with the all-pervasive use of lurid colour in that an unbridled sexuality and lust pulsates throughout the entire Big House of Aragon, from both the man-made structure and from nature.

For the Anglo-Irish Big House the threat to its continued existence is multifaceted. As with *The Last September*, much can be made of how the descriptions of abundant nature presents the susceptibility of the Big House to being overwhelmed from without. However, the presence of this chamber of sexual perversion indicates that the real risk is from within. The fact of the construction and the use of this basement room suggest the absence of control and restraint that in turn is reflected in that world of bountiful nature surrounding the Big House. It is this manifestation of wild sexuality and unrestrained fertility that undermines Anglo-Irish dominance and inheritance. In other words, what the basement room signifies, as an image of unruly ascendancy, is a profound loss of authority, as a Fox ancestor decadently abuses his position and misdirects his energies and his desires. The traces of this abuse are found in the eroticised landscape of Aragon where order is thoroughly absent.

It is Nan, then, who is not only endowed with this knowledge and secret history, but possesses, too, an instinctual and intuitive relationship to her forebears. As with Elizabeth Bowen in *The Last September*, this is observed through the family portraits that line the walls. She is also, it is said, aware of the numerous Fox ghosts that haunt the passageways of Aragon, which are referred to throughout the novel. On one occasion, interestingly, we see that Nan knows her place, knows that she must always take the back stairs, that her true position must remain veiled and out of public view:

> For how could her love for Aragon ever be admitted, or her share in the Fox family ever be allowed – the vanity and reverence for her own blood were the first to deny its admission. (112)

Her role is not to wrest power and control but to silently uphold it. It is said of Nan that, 'She was the beginning and the end of Aragon' (127). It is curious that it is she who appears to be the sole heir to this concealed history. Although Aunt Pidgie might have a few stories to tell, it is Nan who has access to this past, which suggests that only an illegitimate and marginalised character can be the reservoir of a past that the Anglo-Irish themselves are incapable of understanding.

As in W.B. Yeats's *Purgatory*, the fact of mésalliance means that this 'fault' must be rectified, that it must be worked out if the Big House is to survive. The Old Man in that play misunderstands his own position in that he believes he is the cure when he is, in fact, the disease. It is a similar situation for Nan in *Two Days in Aragon*. Her tainted blood means that she is unable to 'save' Aragon, unable to avert the danger and threats to its continued existence, even though she thinks she is the single person capable of such action. Indeed, that Nan's son Foley has an affair with Grania is interesting in this reading of bloodlines and inheritance. Unlike his mother, Foley attempts to exist in a liminal space beyond the opposing poles of Irish and English. He helps both sides, or as the phrase has it in the novel, 'he runs with the hares and hunts with the hounds' (45). His position is an impossible one and, eventually, his playing of the both sides necessarily leads to his having to leave Ireland and go into exile. Alongside this, there is, of course, the reality of incest in his relationship with Grania; one more reason for it to end. That Foley is forced into exile, and that Nan is killed by the close of the novel, suggests that a purging of contaminated or tainted blood is necessary for the continued existence of the Big House. While this Yeatsian emphasis on blood and inheritance is undoubtedly a central element at work within the novel, it is also the transcendence of the past and history that is presented as essential to the continued existence of the Big House in a free Ireland.

Considering some of the possible implications of the names employed in the novel is useful in highlighting a self-reflexive commentary on the action within the novel. Aragon, for instance, suggests something exotic and definitely alien to the Irish countryside. Yet, the history of Aragon in the North of Spain, where in the fifteenth century Ferdinand of Aragon married Isabella of Castile, thus uniting the kingdoms of Aragon and Castile and forming the nucleus of modern Spain, suggests a potential narrative revolving round unity. The reader might make a link, too, with their daughter Catherine of Aragon and her inability to give Henry VIII a son, which led to the English break with Catholicism. This serves, perhaps, to indicate issues surrounding inheritance and fertility. The reader is also presented with the name Grania and its association in Gaelic mythology with illicit love and 'flight'. These names offer, perhaps, an ironic interpretation of the action within the novel, which seemingly offers the possibility of union: union between Foley and Grania, Anglo-Irish and Irish; union between Sylvia and her captain, Anglo-Irish and English. The novel makes these 'overtures' to unification through potential matrimony, only to have that potential dashed at the novel's close.

With the death of Nan, Grania and Sylvia are thrown onto their own resources. This is the key to understanding why Aragon will survive whereas Bowen's Danielstown does not. But before that final moment, both women acknowledge their apartness from others. Both women realise that they do not have to rely on others, especially men. Grania rejects Foley, having realised that he is incapable of loving her. The thought that she was pregnant with his child is proved mistaken and so the possible perpetuation of the mésalliance is halted. Sylvia, too, is observed making a stand on her own near the close of the book when she helps the IRA man to escape the British army:

> She had played traitor to them and in their betrayal she had known an hour of truth. For that hour she had been closer, more obedient to one from whom by every law of her nature she was divided, than she had ever been to any man or woman in her life. (250)

Though she will depart Aragon, she has recognised, even momentarily, the fundamental seeds of Aragon's rebirth with the removal of those whose connection is not truly Anglo-Irish. Thus, Nan has to die, Foley has to leave, in order that Grania can rebuild at Aragon:

> A house would be built here for happy Grania's children. Grania look-
> ing back to the lusty foolish child she had been ... would live here
> with her children, and the garden of Aragon flower after its desola-
> tion. (255)

As Nan imagines this, she is surrounded by all the ghosts of Aragon, who are happy too with this glimpse of the future. In the end, then, what is offered is a metaphorical 'wiping clean of the slate'. The past and that which is asso-ciated with it is transcended so that a new, not predestined, future can be experienced:

> But the house ... was to endure, purged by fire and rain and sun and
> frosts, of its evil and its ghosts, good and bad, until the day came for
> Aragon to be built again by the young Foxes. (228)

It is ironical that Nan dies after being hit by a lorry full of English sol-diers coming to the rescue of Aragon. The lorry, the reader is told, drives on 'the smooth well-kept avenue' (255). The menace of wild, uncultivated nature is brusquely checked with this seemingly insignificant description. The Big House of Aragon survives, it will not become a sign of failure, as so many ruins in Ireland did.

Molly Keane's conclusion is, then, in many ways different to that of Elizabeth Bowen. As Keane was writing *Two Days in Aragon*, Bowen was at work on her family history, *Bowen's Court*. For Bowen, this extended act of memory was absolutely necessary in a time of war:

> Yes, here is the picture of peace – in the house, in the country round.
> Like all pictures, it does not quite correspond with any reality. Or,
> you may call the country a magic mirror; reflecting something that
> could not really exist. This illusion – peace at its most ecstatic – I
> hold to, to sustain me throughout war. I suppose that everyone, fight-
> ing or just enduring, carries within him one private image, one peace-
> ful scene. Mine is Bowen's Court. War has made me this image out
> of a house built of anxious history. (339–40).

Keane's characters, in contrast, are not willing to apply such self-conscious scrutiny to the past of Aragon. Her solution is to have the Anglo-Irish engage in an act of forgetting, and engage in acts that will also get rid of those who might remember. The past is a Joycean nightmare, to be risen above and escaped, not to be painfully acknowledged and accepted. For both Bowen and Keane, then, landscape and sexuality are closely linked in their understanding of the Anglo-Irish Big House. Landscape is a reservoir of possible histories and repressed narratives. The land becomes an object to be possessed and controlled and it is the figure of women in both novels, and their relationship to various male characters, that manifests the tensions and anxieties of the Anglo-Irish community as a whole. It is only when these women – especially Grania – check their aggressive sexuality that the sentence of destruction that the house labours under is lifted. Thus a proper sense of sexuality and sexual decorum is recognised and embodied, making the future safe. Yet, as with the repression of history, this repression of sexuality is problematic. The descriptions of lush flowers and vegetation symbolise the continuance of this repressed sexuality, a sexuality that has the potential to rupture the calm surface at any time in the future.

Gender, abjection and sexuality

Abjection and Molly Keane's 'very nasty' novels

As Molly Keane's novels take their place in critical writing about Anglo-Irish literature and Big House fiction, her novels of the 1980s, *Good Behaviour* (1981), *Time after Time* (1983), and *Loving and Giving* (1988), merit attention not only as excursions into the Big House novel and its Anglo-Irish gentry but also as metacommentaries on the ideological and narrative structures of the genre. In proposing such a look, I offer a re-reading of her notorious use of excessive rot and decay, a quality which critics often characterise as a function of Keane's distinctly comic irony.[1] Is Keane funny? Yes. But if we situate her use of putrid excess within the category of abjection rather than comic irony, we can refocus our attention on the causes of the laughter that these representations elicit. The application of abjection theories foregrounds Keane's use of bodily decay rather than her oft-noted use of the decaying Big House, the big metonym of the Big House novel. For, in her attention to Anglo-Irish bodies, Keane recasts the Anglo-Irish role in the Big House by sidestepping the genre's fascination with the embattled structure of Anglo-Irish society (either by nature, land reform, or burnings) and placing the Anglo-Irish at the centre of their own decay. In fact, Keane's most telling contribution to and incisive commentary on the Big House genre lies not in her ability to fulfill the formula of the decaying architecture – though she skillfully deploys rotting structures – but in her relentless attention to the most improper material bodies of the Anglo-Irish. Presented as such, the Anglo-Irish are re-written within their own literary tradition; no longer poised as the 'embattled' ascendancy, they are physically and psychologically dismantled by a confrontation with their self-produced abjection.

An explanation of the term abjection can begin with a comment made by Jasper Swift of *Time after Time* about the urine and excrement that cousin Leda

---

This essay was first published in *LIT: Literature Interpretation Theory*, Volume 10, Number 1 *First Irish Literature Issue* and is republished here with the permission of the author and of LIT.
1 Many critics situate this excess in the realm of the comedic – often citing Vivian Mercier's theory of a satirising Irish humour in *The Irish comic tradition* (1962). Rüdiger Imhof argues that Keane's 'reliance on cranks and oddities' leads her into 'unwilful parodies of the Big-House novel' but adds that she might be 'establishing a particular variant of the Big-House novel, one that aligns the Big-House novel with the long-lived Irish comic tradition' (202). A comedic foundation leads such studies to understand her representations of rot and decay as comic moments with varying emphases: Rachael Lynch attributes it to a feminist/feminine comedic horror (74), Vera Kreilkamp suggests the 'cold eye' of 'comic detachment' (182), and Mary Breen sees the workings of 'black farce' (205).

deposits in his late mother's wardrobe: 'very nasty' (195). 'Abjection' describes
Keane's careful deployment of faeces, vomit, urine, spit, decay, excess, and/or
physical deformity in all three novels. A theoretical framework of abjection –
using the intersecting theories of Julia Kristeva, Mikhail Bakhtin, Jacques Lacan,
and Slavoj Žižek – highlights Keane's process of 'materializing the subject' (to
borrow a phrase from Linda Charnes) by which she investigates the Anglo-
Irish subject and the symbolic structures that produce and secure it. Kristeva's
theory of abjection in *Powers of Horror: An Essay on Abjection* (trans. 1982),
Bakhtin's ideas about the grotesque/abject in *Rabelais and his World* (trans.
1968) and Lacan's notion of the Real, especially as it is elaborated in Slavoj
Žižek's Lacanian studies, *The Sublime Object of Ideology* (1989) and *Enjoy Your
Symptom!* (1992), connect abjection to social, cultural, and psychological structures. Using these texts, we can interpret Keane's use of abjection and connect
that meaning to the literary/historical tradition of the Anglo-Irish Big House
novel. The proliferation of abjection in the lives of her characters allows Keane
to illustrate the relationship between the material body and the establishment
of subjectivity, class, and language and to challenge the way in which these
bodies have been previously represented.

Kristeva uses the term abjection to refer to decay, rot, excrement, and
corpses. She establishes two types of abjection: excremental, which I highlight here, and menstrual.[2] Excremental abjection – faeces, decay, infection,
disease, corpses – 'stand[s] for the danger to identity that comes from without: the ego threatened by the non-ego, society threatened by its outside, life
by death' (71). Kristeva offers the phrase 'to each ego its object, to each superego its abject' (2) to explain that abjection gives rise to subjective identity by
offering an opposition against which the symbolic order, as the system of
social constraints entered through language, can define itself. In other words,
symbolic law establishes taboos, the unrepresentable, and the 'other' through
categories of abjection. Because of this fact, abjection represents the frailty of
the symbolic order, a threat that must be but cannot always be contained:

> what is abject ... the jettisoned object, is radically excluded and draws
> me toward the place where meaning collapses. A certain 'ego' that
> merged with its master, a superego, has flatly driven it away. It lies
> outside, beyond the set, and does not seem to agree to the latter's

2 Menstrual abjection represents the danger issuing from within identity and obviously, has
specific ties to the feminine and the fear of sexual difference; Kristeva writes: 'Menstrual blood
... stands for the danger issuing from within the identity (social or sexual); it threatens the relationship between the sexes within a social aggregate and, through internalization, the identity
of each sex in the face of social difference' (71). Aroon of *Good Behaviour*, calls attention to the
abjectification of the menses when she notes its banishment from language and the social implications of complaint: 'those pains which I had been taught to disregard as slight monthly discomforts, not to be over-rated; to take them seriously was to be guilty of a social nuisance' (95).

rules of the game. And yet from its place of banishment, the abject does not cease challenging its master. (2)

Thus, according to Kristeva, the 'very nasty' functions in a cultural system of meaning, and the power of the system is continually contested by the challenging presence of abjection. In *Good Behaviour, Time after Time*, and *Loving and Giving*, this dynamic of banishment and challenge occurs repeatedly. Mummie of *Good Behaviour* banishes rabbit meat from her diet, but vomits and dies when it forcibly returns disguised as Aroon's 'delicious chicken mousse' (5). Jasper covers his 'filthy blind eye' (33) with a patch but must confront the 'dirty socket' each night (55). May employs gloves to hide her 'lopped hand' (72), which needs 'three and a half fingers to complete it' (15). Nicandra banishes the body through language as she refers to her stomach as her 'little insides' and her genitals as 'down there' (9).

Bakhtin's *Rabelais and his World*, in connecting the body to language and social practices, situates the disruptive powers of abjection, with its insistence on material existence, in the context of class structure and hierarchy. He argues that abjection disturbs because it 'ignores the impenetrable surface that closes and limits the body as separate and complete' (318). In defining grotesque realism, he explains that 'degradation' is 'the lowering of all that is high, spiritual, ideal, abstract; it is a transfer to the material level' (19) and that the grotesque is 'ugly, monstrous, hideous from the point of view of "classic" aesthetics' (25). The body is reinterpreted as symbolic structures change; of modern interpretations of the body, he writes:

> The new historic sense that penetrates them gives these images a new meaning but keeps intact their traditional contents: copulation, pregnancy, birth, growth, old age, disintegration, dismemberment. All these in their direct material aspect are the main element in the system of grotesque images. They are contrary to the classic images of the finished completed man, cleansed, as it were, of all the scoriae of birth and development. (25)

Bakhtin cites abjection's rejuvenating, comic properties and notes that the banishing of abjection arises with the onset of bourgeois ideology; the bourgeoisie's interest in individual subjectivity distances the body from existence through a mind/body dualism. The body, however, is originally tied to community: 'the material body principle is contained not in the biological individual, not in the bourgeois ego, but in the people' (19). Thus, the material exists in opposition to the individual and the private. In the 'modern canon' the body, he argues, is individualised, its popular functions severed and 'transferred to the private and psychological level where their connotation becomes narrow and specific' (321). Such privatisation leads to a disappearance of the 'lower strata' from representation. In this context, for example, Nicandra's stomach becomes a 'little inside' and her genitalia disappear 'down there'.

Bakhtin's theory can be applied to certain trends in Anglo-Irish development, especially if we connect his claim that the eighteenth-century aesthetic is most antithetical to the comic grotesque with the fact that the eighteenth century saw the economic and symbolic solidification of the Anglo-Irish gentry. As J.C. Beckett has noted:

> It was in the eighteenth century that the power of the Anglo-Irish reached its widest extension. Their dominance was now established in every part of the country and in all departments of life; and there did not seem to be any opposing force strong enough to make headway against them. It was in this century that they impressed their mark most deeply upon Ireland; and in this century, also, the arrogant self-confidence that was one of their characteristic traits showed itself most clearly. (149)

Elizabeth Bowen's capsule history of the Anglo-Irish establishment in 'The Big House' (1942) underscores the importance of the 'classic aesthetic.' Bowen notes that the Anglo-Irish of the eighteenth-century sought to instill nobility in positions that they felt to be 'ignobly gained' and that, accordingly, they 'began to feel and exert the European idea – to seek what was humanistic, classic, and disciplined' (197). She depicts their reluctant investment in a symbolic system:

> It is something to subscribe to an idea, even if one cannot live up to it. These country gentleman liked sport, drink, and card-playing very much better than they liked the arts – but they religiously stocked their libraries, set fine craftsman to work on their ceilings and mantle-pieces and interspersed their own family portraits with heroicized paintings of foreign scenes. (197)

This act of self-completion accomplishes the 'modern canon' of an Anglo-Irish aesthetic, the completion of an ego from which the abject will be severed or kept at bay with portraits, architecture and 'good behaviour' (Bowen 199).

The fact that the abjection of Keane's characters does not offer carniva-lesque rejuvenation but, rather, inspires the need for its banishment, suggests the importance of class ideology to which Bakhtin leads us with his emphasis on bourgeois devotion to private life and his insistence on the grotesque's threat to 'completed man.' Keane seizes upon these correspondent notions of the private individual and a transcendental subjectivity, and with her deployment of abjection she depicts the undoing of individual characters and an entire class. Lacanian studies allows us to approach the connections between subjectivity, class and bodily abjection in a more detailed way. In particular, by applying Lacan's ideas about 'the Real' to the body, we can sketch the symbolic structures of Keane's Anglo-Irish characters. In Lacan's Imaginary–Real–Symbolic triad (as in Kristeva's formulation), the Real is pre-symbolic. With respect to the body in particular, Bruce Fink explains the Real as follows:

> The real is, for example, an infant's body 'before' it comes under the sway of the symbolic order, before it is subjected to toilet training and instructed in the ways of the world. In the course of socialization, the body is progressively written or overwritten with signifiers; pleasure is located in certain zones, while other zones are neutralized by the word and coaxed into compliance with social, behavioral norms. (Fink 24)

In *The Sublime Object of Ideology*, Slavoj Žižek elaborates the vexed, dialectic tension between the Real and the symbolic:

> ... the Real is the rock upon which every attempt at symbolization stumbles, the hard core which remains the same in all possible worlds (symbolic universes); but at the same time its status is thoroughly precarious; it is something that persists only as failed, missed, in a shadow, and dissolves itself as soon as we try to grasp it in its positive nature. (169)

He adds, 'We have the Real as the starting point, the basis, the foundation of the process of symbolization' and notes that the Real 'in a sense *precedes* the symbolic order and is subsequently structured by it when it gets caught in its network' (169). The Real is, thus, 'neutralized by the word' and challenging that status simultaneously. For the purposes of investigating bodily abjection as an instance of the Real, its function as both material presence and symbolic disruption should be reiterated. Žižek reminds us that the 'status of the Real is at the same time that of corporeal contingency and that of logical contingency':

> In a first approach, the Real is a shock of a contingent encounter which disrupts the automatic circulation of the symbolic mechanism; a grain of sand preventing its smooth functioning; a traumatic encounter which ruins the balance of the symbolic universe of the subject. (171)

Given these qualities of the Real, abjection, as a 'kernel resisting symbolization,' presents itself to the characters of Keane's novels in its 'precarious' state – preceding, resisting, and caught in the symbolic order all at once. Her characters, confronting their own abjection, thus, hide it but deploy it when needed, banish it but attend to it, refuse to speak of it but allow it to speak for them as they struggle with encounters which threaten their symbolic order.

Together, the insights of Kristeva, Bakhtin, Lacan, and Žižek develop a highly nuanced definition of abjection capable of elucidating its role in Keane's novels. The assertive force of the material body both exists at and is inscribed at the intersection of symbolic language, class, and subjectivity, and there it maintains the ability to subvert the symbolic order, to resist being read, and to challenge its master. Because of these qualities, Keane's use of abjection should be interpreted as a structural aspect of the characters' lives and the novels in addition to its almost undisputed status as black comedy.[3] A representation of the Ascendancy in decline requires a look at its ideology, and the insertion of the 'very nasty' offers an efficient way to reveal the fragile limits of that symbolic network. In sending the abject to confront the Ascendancy, Keane revises the Big House genre so that the fall transpires not because of outside forces or new ideologies, but because the Anglo-Irish, despite their facade of rituals and props, embodied the Real all along.

In *Good Behaviour*, for example, the principles of good behavior and the bodies of the characters meet to enact the Kristevan dynamic of abjection: 'from its place of banishment, the abject does not cease challenging its master' (2). Iris Aroon St Charles, the centre of the novel as narrator and main character, relives such moments of banishment and challenge throughout the novel. One moment disgusted by her own material existence, and another consoling herself that she is 'no unwanted grotesque' because she has had a 'man in her bed' (142), Aroon seeks to contain her material excess within the symbolically-sanctioned role of 'fat woman in the fairground' (85) by openly devouring large quantities of food. Aroon's size defies the limits of the classically defined, 'closed,' aesthetic body; thus, in the nineteen-twenties world of Anglo-Irish womanhood, enforced by Mummie and others, Aroon's body exemplifies the Real. Narrating the novel at fifty-seven, Aroon can safely say 'bosoms are all right to have now,' but the twenties left her '[tying] them down with a type of binder' (4). Aroon's eagerness to eat is depicted in contrast to Mummie who 'had no enjoyment of food' (13); Mummie's distaste signifies a ritual rejection of her own material body. Because 'the size of anything appalled [Mummie]', Aroon's size can only be connected to the food

3 In turn, these theories of abjection help to define the disruptive point of contact between subject and symbolic meaning from which the humour erupts. Lynch, Breen and Imhof have situated the novels of Keane in the tradition of Vivian Mercier's Irish comic tradition. Lynch adds to this a reading of women's humour and the inherent confrontations with symbolic structure, i.e. patriarchal law, that it produces. Such a reading dovetails with theories of abjection and the feminine. My interest in this essay is to highlight the ways in which these examples enact a trauma of the Real which suggests another layer to the generally recognised 'black humour' of Keane's last three novels.

that disgusts her (180). Mummie's own vulnerability to abjection, no doubt, informs Aroon's decision to offer Mummie the rabbit mousse.

A cycle of food ingestion and a corresponding abjection, vomit, occurs throughout the novel. Kristeva explains the nature of vomit, both as a response to what is abject and the creation of abjection itself: 'Loathing an item of food, piece of filth, waste, or dung. The spasms and vomiting that protect me. The repugnance, the retching that thrusts me to the side and turns me away from defilement, sewage, muck' (2). A most telling example of the protective status of vomit is offered in Aroon's illness at the Hunt Ball. After glancing through the *Tatler* (in the process of appearing occupied rather than rejected, that is, abject), Aroon discovers the engagement announcement of her 'love', Richard, and the Honourable Alice Brownrigg. Here, Aroon loses the last illusion offering her symbolic identification, a man's love, the final protection from her abject status. The comfort that she is 'no unwanted grotesque' collapses, and she begins to make her way to the lavatory: 'Not tears but pain seized on me, my insides griping and loosening. The absolute need of getting to the lavatory possessed me. Even my terrible distress had to find this absurd necessity' (207–8). Thus, confronting herself as the Real, the unwanted grotesque, she turns away from her own self as banished object and (preceding, resisting, and caught in the symbolic order all at once) protects herself from her own defilement:

> ... pain was twisting in me again, and above it the dreadful childish call: I'm going to be sick – sick in the basin. Partly in the plate holding the Bromo, partly over my dress, into my shoes, on the floor, I was sick. I must escape before it was found, get myself into my coat and run, with this taste in my mouth, and the smell under my coat going with me. (208)

This scene constructs a near-repetition of one we have seen before in the novel. Aroon's vomit functions as the protective excrement of Mrs Brock does when she suffers a bout of diarrhoea upon being fired:

> Mrs Brock went straight to the schoolroom lavatory, where she was overtaken by a violent diarrhoea. When she got off the mahogany seat to lift the D-shaped hand-fitting which swirled out the blue-flowered basin, she sat down again at once 'in case,' that tiny euphemism that covered so much so usefully. The exhaustion of physical necessity calmed her. (35)

Among the props of symbolic containment, the ornamental facilities and the euphemism 'in case', Mrs Brock is consoled by this act. Like Mrs Brock,

Aroon is restored by the expelling of her own abjection. Aroon, dripping in vomit, does not identify with it; the abject is expelled, banished, and she is once again Aroon St Charles, the entitled member of an elite family. Travelling home with Mr Kiely, she assumes he has sensed the 'sour little smell creeping about under [her coat]' (210) as he lights cigarettes. But when he suggests that he could be the man to 'look after' her, she replies, 'You must be out of your mind,' and thinks, 'I was, after all, Aroon St Charles, and I felt it too' (211). Her name, finally, restores her symbolic identity by containing the material body that threatened her minutes earlier.

In the spectacular triumph of abjection with which Keane opens *Good Behaviour*, she reaches a pinnacle of abject representations; Mummie in her vomit carefully articulates the intricate connections between abjection and subjectivity and sets up a framework for the rest of the narrative. Here, Keane perfects the signifying power of vomit, one that Aroon apparently understands as she vengefully disguises the rabbit cream mousse as a 'delicious chicken mousse' (noting its fine preparation in the 'fine sieve' and 'Moulinex blender', the transformation of a vulgar food). What better way to end her mother's obsession with controlling the material body than to kill her in a confrontation with expulsion and excess? The nature of this confrontation is succinctly expressed in Mummie's final words, "The smell – I'm –," after which 'she g[ives] a trembling, tearing cry, vomit[s] dreadfully, and f[alls] back into the nest of pretty pillows' (6). This final tableau of remarkably 'bad behaviour,' the vomit amongst her 'pretty pillows' creating a pool from which Aroon must remove her mother's hand and 'put it down in a clean place' (6), resonates strongly within the context of class and the material. Recalling Bahktin's words, we could say that Mummie's 'degradation is the lowering of all that is high' and 'contrary to the images of the completed man, cleansed'. Of course, as a corpse lying in a nest of pretty pillows, she represents the ultimate contrast between abjection and its banishment. For, as Kristeva argues, the corpse, 'the most sickening of wastes, is the border that has encroached upon everything. It is no longer "I" who expel, "I" is expelled' (3–4). Here, Keane offers symbolic authority amongst her props killed by the assertive force of the Real; in her last act of banishment, vomiting, she renders her *self* the jettisoned abject.

Good Behaviour investigates more than excremental abjection. It also concerns itself with the regimens of the 'clean and proper body' – 'in the sense of incorporated and incorporable' (Kristeva 8). The tenuous state of the proper body is presented in the figure of Aroon's father who undergoes a slow process of bodily decay as the novel progresses. First injured in the war, he returns with an amputated leg, then suffers a stroke and remains bedridden until his death. His illness presents many difficulties to Aroon and her mother – including the unfathomable possibility of bed sores: 'Bed-sores,' [Mummie] mur-

mured. What disgusting thing will you think of next?' (180). Indeed, the necessities of the clean invalid are so contentious, that the task is handed to Rose, the Catholic employee who has served as housekeeper, cook, and now nurse to the ailing master of the house. Aroon considers Rose to be appropriate for the job because she is Catholic. Early in the novel, Aroon explains, '[Catholics] revel in death ... Keep the Last Rites going ... [Rose] can't wait to get her hands on Mummie, to get me out of the way while she helps Mrs Cleary in the nasty rituals' (7). Aroon's decision to interpret Catholic rituals of containment as abject highlights the class-based definitions of abjection to which she subscribes.

Rose, we are told, enthusiastically attends the dying and deceased Papa, and her attendance to 'nasty rituals' challenges Aroon's sensibility repeatedly. When Rose's status as caretaker is questioned by the hired nurse who accuses Rose of fulfilling Papa's sexual desires while rubbing his 'foot' under the bedclothes, language fails. The lower body strata must remain unspecified, contained in the word 'nasty.' 'Look,' Nurse says, 'you can't name it and I won't name it. It's a nasty name for a nasty thing' (169). The threat of abjection 'issues from the prohibitions that found the inner and outer borders in which and through which the speaking subject is constituted' (Kristeva 69), and as such, 'it is thus not a lack of cleanliness that causes abjection but that which disturbs identity, system, order. What does not respect borders, positions, rules' (Kristeva 4). Accordingly, the sexuality of an invalid becomes unnameable, just as Papa's sexual exploits, those that cross class lines and those that don't, remain unnamed throughout the novel. Nurse's accusation also borders on unthinkable for Aroon, for Papa's body has become abject, and Nurse's comments disturb the borders of the abject and the sexual, the living and the dying body. Not surprisingly, then, when the hired nurse leaves, Aroon senses a material remainder of what was not said: 'It was as if her body, clean and fresh as pine needles, had left a smell behind it on the air, a clinging smell, which I would rightly ignore' (169).

Papa's decline allows Keane to focus on his transformation from the 'clean and proper body' to the abject corpse. Aroon, standing with Rose and observing the process, reflects:

> He was breathing in a knotted, groaning rhythm. She stood and looked at him. She had been his nurse and washed and dressed him like a doll, and sat him up and laid him down. Now she stood apart from the difficulties of death, accepting all strife and pain he was in as necessary before death; nothing could ease him, so she stood apart looking on as though at the death of an animal. I felt the same. He was changed. Changing and lessening every moment from a person to a thing. (213–14)

In describing the death of her father in this way, Aroon highlights the abject nature of death – not the emotional or dramatic grief, but a clinical explanation of the corpse, as the 'I' itself is expelled and he treads in the realms of the animal. '[Her] grief for Papa' can only set in later when out in the corridor and away from the spectacle of the abject body, she sits down on the floor and waits for the 'weakness to pass away' (215).

The narrative of Iris Aroon St Charles presents the Anglo-Irish ideal beset by bodily abjection, which these Anglo-Irish characters produce and banish in a recurring cycle of traumatic confrontations. Yet the Real stubbornly returns, in the physicality of Aroon, in the bloated body of Mrs Brock, or in the vomit that ends Mummie's life, and as they try to maintain the symbolic balance, no character breaks out of this cycle. Aroon's mother, hitherto the symbolic enforcer, becomes the abject, but Aroon eagerly steps in as the enforcer upon inheriting Papa's wealth. This moment functions as a symbolic rebirth for Aroon; her new symbolic identity affords her power. Of course, characters – subjects – do not desire a breakdown of the symbolic network, for in being constituted by it, they are too heavily invested in its functioning. Because of this predicament, Aroon does not attempt to undermine a system. She simply ensures her own power by forcing Mummie to confront the subversive forces of the Real and then carries on exactly as Mummie did. In this framework, the abject material body repeatedly asserts itself against the 'good behaviour' of an Anglo-Irish gentry, and though the 'nasty name for a nasty thing' remains unspoken, the Real 'clinging smell' continues to resist neutralisation. Thus, Keane anatomises a class and an ideology and through relentless attention to the details of waste, asserts her critique.

This abject frame is reiterated in *Time after Time* where various regimens salute the symbolic order and banish bodily abjection. Indeed, we learn that these rituals were established by Mummie to counteract the abjection of her children who are 'all rather crippled'.[4] Now, old age adds another layer of decay. The siblings' marginal status, ensured by the society into which they were born, results in their remaining together in the halls of Durraghglass alternately inspiring morbid curiosity and repulsion in the community. For example, as a young woman, Leda, driven by curiosity, convinces Jasper to reveal what he considers the 'nastiness that went on behind his dark eye patch' (10) by expressing her desire to 'kiss it':

---

4 The position of mothers, here, as keepers of the abject coincides with Kristeva's argument that although patriarchy establishes the symbolic order, 'maternal authority is the trustee of the self's clean and proper body' (72): 'maternal authority is experienced first and above all, after the first essentially oral frustrations, as sphincteral training ... Through frustrations and prohibitions, this authority shapes the body into a territory having areas, orifices, points and lines, surfaces and hollows, where the archaic power of mastery and neglect, of the differentiation of proper-clean and improper-dirty, possible and impossible, is impressed and exerted' (71–2). We see such maternal authority in all three novels.

The luxury in her voice reached him in its absolute acceptance of his deformity. It held deliverance from all the hatred and disgust that possessed him, while washing his eye-socket, caring for it, covering it up. He freed his hand from hers and raised it uncertainly to his elegant black patch. Still delaying he bent down to meet her eyes – cold, rabidly curious eyes. Just for a look at his disfigurement she would have kissed. He pulled back from her, back into his own defended world. (55)

A 'defended world' exists for each sibling as they reenact Mummie's rituals after her death, but these rituals resonate as cultural rituals as well – not only the result of family deformity but the necessities of an arrogant class. The siblings continue to gather for the civilised evening meal. April, whose sole pleasure in life is to 'rule her body' (47), continues with her exercise routines, health foods, and anti-aging rituals. Horrified by Leda's obesity (excess), April is confident that even in a Nazi death camp, she would maintain herself: 'Even in a death camp April would have struggled to keep up her exercises, control her breathing. "Everybody eats too much, anyway," she would have said as she gnawed on a cabbage stalk' (99). Her rituals amount to a veritable rite of embalming as she prevents the ultimate state of abjection, the rotting corpse: 'she knew her looks to be miraculously unchanged, she willingly endured tortures in their preservation' (21). Likewise, the women's club members monitor and contain their bodies: 'every lady was on weight watchers,' except for May, who, because her containment rituals focus on her maimed hand, 'let[s] herself go on the chicken and ham paste' (75).

Despite the faithful repetition (time after time) of these regimens, the 'civilized policies' (16) of a greater era, the characters of *Time after Time* are constantly besieged by their own abjection. At Durraghglass, Keane establishes a general state of abjection. Anglo-Irish genes are implicated: the siblings of the Swift family are obvious examples of a genetic decay hiding in the Anglo-Irish line – in spite of the apparent perfection of their parents, Violet and Valentine. The sexuality of humans, skirting the abject according to Bakhtin's analysis of the 'modern canon', appears only in ways that defy the codes of decent Anglo-Irish society. Leda's attempts to seduce Jasper bring together two abject figures; she considers him 'monstrously embodied' (166) while he sees her as a 'blind earthworm' (164) as she makes her way to his bed. Allusions to April's late husband's interest in pornography introduce a form of 'love' falling fully outside the codes of Big House romance. Because of his pornographic tastes, April now '[knows] the value of her own bodily privacy' (47); his perversions inspire in her an interest in the closed aesthetic body. Human sexuality at Durraghglass remains abject and perverse, and is displaced by the characters' own preoccupation with animal sexuality. Gripper, May's dog, and Tiger, April's dog, compete for June's dog, Tiny, who is in heat throughout the novel.

The consummation of love – so common in Big House, marriage-market plots – descends into animality when it arises not between two people, but as the fortuitous union between Gripper and a local Tinker's dog.

Keane rounds out the general state of abjection with her narrator's attention to Big House sewage disposal and the lapse in its ability to deal with the production of Anglo-Irish waste:

> Late in the evening there came a civilized pause before dinner. Servantless and silent, the house waited for the proper ceremony it had always expected and still, in a measure, experienced. The utter cold of the spring light shrank away from the high paned windows. A steep distance below that house the river gave up an evening daze of fog. A lavatory clattered and slushed. Obedient to its plug and chain the contents went down the perpendicular drain to the open water. Faint pieces of paper floated among the starred weeds and iris leaves of flags. Very fat trout swam there. Once there had been an open, not a covert, drain. Every morning housemaids lifted a grill and sluiced buckets into a sloped stone spout from which the doings of the night flowed down their paved way to the river. Not any more, of course. Those were the days ... of lots of money. (20)

Keane offers this scene of 'proper ceremony', of raw sewage and its arrival in the river, to depict class decline as a confrontation with material debasement. Once again, the Big House in decline is not a collapsing architectural structure but an assertion of Anglo-Irish abjection, inefficiently banished and proclaiming its presence.

But the moments of abjection in these two novels are not simply moments of an omniscient narrator's glimpse at forbidden representations. On the contrary, the abject erupts out of moments of narrative tension and establishes turning points in the novel, and characters, constantly mired in their own bodily filth, deploy abjection to circumvent language and manipulate one another's vulnerability to it. Jasper, household chef and keeper of the kitchen, reveals his unspoken resentment through the abjectification of the family food. When May asks, 'Where's the beef I scraped all the blue mould off and left chopped up in their soup and brown bread?' (34), 'You've just eaten it,' Jasper replies, 'I put it in the pie' (34). Then, 'Delighting in May's screams and cries of protest and disgust, he stacked a tray with plates, dishes, spoons and glasses, put it in the lift and from there set off downstairs to the kitchen and the washing up, confident that no one would follow him' (35). Indeed, Jasper maintains his kitchen according to the strictest rules of rot and decay:

> in the big kitchen, where Jasper now ruled, nothing was ever tidied up, stored, or thrown away. Cats were the scavengers. Cardboard wine cases

that had carried more groceries than wine to the house were piled and heaped and thrown in corners. Cats had their kittens in them ... (2)

When not using abjection to offend his sisters (to challenge his masters), Jasper is '[u]nperturbed at the waste of disorder he had as though spewed and forgotten' (46).

In the character of Leda, Keane firmly establishes the challenge of the Real, articulated by Žižek as the 'grain of sand preventing [the symbolic mechanism's] smooth functioning' (*Sublime Object* 171). In *Enjoy Your Symptom!*, Žižek further defines the stain of the Real as 'a surplus, a material leftover circulating among the subject and staining its momentary possessor' (8). The narrative of Leda enacts this circulating stain of the Real. When, adding to the spit deposited upon her arrival, Leda defecates and urinates on the clothes of the late, beloved Mummie (whose wardrobe has become a shrine), May must literally and symbolically deal with this stain. Soap and water prove ineffective, so she dutifully packs the clothes away in suitcases to take them to the cleaners. Jasper agrees to pay the unaffordable prices if May will deal with explanations, but the defilement resists symbolisation:

> The phrases she rehearsed – '*Very* naughty little dog,' or, perhaps, 'some horrible cat,' – seemed every moment less convincing. Although sure, as ever, in the rightness of her actions, May felt almost overwhelmed by the flood of relief that swept through her when she saw that the cleaner's premises were shut, windows darkened for the night, her awful mission aborted. (232)

Thus, her final solution, equally if not more reverent and symbolically sound, is a ritual burning on a sacred pyre: 'every rag of Mummie's desecrated clothes would burn to ash on a funeral pyre of rosemary and lavender, apple-wood and sweet geranium' (232).

On another level, this stain of the Real is Leda herself, for circulating among the siblings and unsettling them, she signifies her unspeakable affair with Valentine Swift, which ended in his suicide and triggers imaginings of the horror of the concentration camps. These associations often flit across the minds of the Swift siblings but are always conveniently returned to the realm of the repressed, leaving only the disturbing feeling that 'There was still something untold and unforgotten about Leda' (91). Leda, thus, represents the repressed material leftover which they hitherto have been identifying as a properly disappeared and completely abject corpse: she is 'green bones in a grave now' (52). Accordingly, when the formerly beautiful Leda arrives, blind, obese, alcoholic, but alive, May responds, 'Leda? How embarrassing. Lead's dead' (107). May considers Leda's past a 'ring of horror' into which she does not want to step (116). Confronted by the living Leda, the sisters perceive her as both the physically abject and the unnameable:

> They realised together that Leda could have no idea of what she looked like now – an old, pitifully plain woman, blind and in need of their comfort. They found themselves, in their whole health and in their ability to give, in power over Leda, that legendary figure of glamour who had become a victim of a terror and a captivity they had steadily refused to envisage … They did not want to be disgusted and repelled by tales of terrors and filth they had so long ignored. (107)

When the narrator remarks, 'May made Leda alive seem like untidy business,' Keane presents us with an apt metaphor for considering Leda. As the circulating stain of the real, she is precisely that – the 'untidy' remainder of a symbolic network.

For Leda, her desecration of the wardrobe serves as the comforting expulsion of her own abjection as well as a reification of her own abject status, as one who was expelled from Durraghglass. For her first act of desecration, she rejects the wardrobe-shrine of the woman who expelled her: '… she stood from a stilled moment in reverent recollection before, gathering in her breath so that her body seemed to extend and exude power, she spat with virulent intention in to the padded breasts of a beaded evening dress …' (109). Leda's second desecration presents a commentary beyond the mitigating power of language, incapable of symbolisation; it is a last resort after she fails in her use of the power of language to embarrass, indict, and injure all the Swift siblings in one huge monologue. Jasper dismisses her accusations with the question 'But aren't we, all five of us, a bit old for these gambols' (109), and the whole episode is then interrupted by a dog fight and the arrival of Leda's daughter, who reveals that Leda collaborated during the war and puts an end to the siblings' death camp thoughts. As a result of her verbal failure, Leda, desperate before her return to the convent, spends her remaining time at Durraghglass exerting her only remaining power, her excrement, a force demanding acknowledgment when it is deposited in the last stronghold of symbolic law, Mummie's wardrobe.

Leda's use of excrement as a signifying practice, coded as the undeniable subversion of ritualised civility, mimics Keane's use of abjection as well, for clearly Keane uses excessive 'nasty stuff' to concentrate our attention on the delicacy and descendancy of Anglo-Irish culture. The sheer volume of filth, decay, and deformity in this novel sustains a commentary on the 'Real as the starting point' that constitutes and then menaces Anglo-Irish culture. The Swift siblings' fascination with and repulsion of abjection foregrounds the fragility of symbolic distinctions and replaces the individualised and transcendental Anglo-Irish subject with the material subject falling out of class ideology into the 'filth they had so long ignored'.

In *Loving and Giving*, Keane exchanges large volumes of abjection for the minutiae of one character's repeated confrontations with it. The symbol of the rotting Big House looms large in this novel; Nicandra Constance is killed by a fall through the rotted floors of Deer Forest. Economic instability is highlighted as the rotting structure undergoes repairs funded by Robert, a successful businessman, rather than by Anglo-Irish coiffers. However, Keane maintains her interest in the bodily presence of its inhabitants. Nicandra undergoes a series of abject trials while attempting to maintain the symbolic role of the Anglo-Irish lady. Repeated disruptions of this function, which reveal the existence of the Real, force Nicandra to regroup while memories of these traumatic encounters with the Real repeatedly assert themselves.

The first section of the book narrates the day in the life of Nicandra as a girl. This day, the day her mother deserts the family, constitutes a series of abject discoveries, discoveries which coincide with Bakhtin's description of the traditional contents of the grotesque: copulation, pregnancy, birth, growth, old age, disintegration, dismemberment. The sights tear holes in Nicandra's symbolic network, and return, unresolved, at the end of the novel. Among other things, she witnesses Anderson in the process of slaughtering a lamb, glimpses Patsy-Pudding 'writhing uncomfortably' as she gives birth to kittens, and watches the butler shaving his beard over 'last night's dinner dishes' which are 'still lying under the water into which flakes and soapsuds and hair were falling' (12).

The day is also filled with attempts to keep abjection in check. Aunt Tossie, for example, hides her hair combings: 'Hair combings from her brush went at once into hiding – a small stoup, designed for Holy Water, concealed their rather sordid swirls – in accordance with the unspoken law that anything ugly should be put out of sight, which applied to more things than hair combings' (8). Precautions are taken lest an inversion occur, in Bakhtin's sense of the term, in which the lower body register leads to subversion of the classical, ideal body. Accordingly, the undergarments drying on the line are located behind a hedge to protect the 'sensitive eyes of the gentry' (14). Similarly, language avoids references to non-classical, lower body orders: '"knickers" and "panties" were common words, not to be used. For the same reason, if you had a pain it was in "your little inside," not in your stomach and there were no words beyond "down there" to describe any itch or ailment in the lower parts of your body' (9). When Nicandra presents her scientific discovery, a 'double butterfly,' the sexuality of insects leaves everyone 'too stunned to utter a word' except for Mama who disinterestedly says, 'A freak, I suppose,' before Dada '[flings] out the double butterfly as viciously as if it had been a slug in the salad' (21).

Such situations, as well as the narrator's comments on them, expose the ideological structure of the symbolic universe into which Nicandra is being oriented. The workings of the symbolic network stand out as Nicandra negotiates the rules and learns new ones; she stumbles against this mechanism, revealing its limits, as she has not completely internalised its presumptions. Thus, she makes vague and uneasy connections between the 'secret' or the 'nasty' and the limits of the unspeakable. After seeing Anderson preparing to slaughter a sheep ('His green eyes gleamed with pleasure'), Nicandra thinks: 'what she had seen was indecent and terrifying, and she could tell her fear to nobody. It was a secret as dark as that couplet (written in pencil on the back page of "First Lessons in English Grammar") read over and over and never to be spoken aloud: "Pee-Po-Bum-Shit-Piddle-Bugger-Damn ..."' (26). As she leaves the scene of the cat giving birth, 'She [knows Twomey is] hiding something from her about the cat, something nasty, that should not be spoken of' (13). Here, she does not make distinctions between categories of the forbidden. She is aware of symbolic law, which determines what is 'secret' and 'nasty' and 'never to be spoken aloud', and she knows the expected code of conduct, but she makes no distinctions between a list of obscenities and the slaughter of a sheep. She has not yet grasped the hierarchical logic of these symbolic decrees. Indeed, we might more accurately say that she perceives correctly or that she has not yet learned to gloss over ideological contradictions, for there is no real difference in their status as abject/Real. Because of the instability of symbolic repression, which Keane fully reveals and explores with Nicandra, such incidents become for Nicandra traumatic memories that trigger related incidents of secrecy or prohibition.

As the novel progresses, we see Nicandra's internalisation of the codes presented to her on that day in her youth, just as Aroon's decision to become Mummie signals the completion of and the necessity of maintaining one's own symbolic identity. When Aunt Tossie's breast pops out of her dress at a dinner party, Nicandra reacts with a horror that never relents; it becomes 'the event that Nicandra was to remember, squeamishly and for always':

> Aunt Tossie's left breast bulged out, pale against the background of black velvet. Suddenly, all saw, and all talk stopped. The silence welled through the room.
>
> Only Aunt Tossie was unperturbed by the presence of the dreadful thing that, freed of its supports, hung bare and toppled over. (78)

The horror for Nicandra is exacerbated by the resemblance of Tossie's breast to the creamy dessert trifle being served – 'the great trifle rose in a stalwart bulge of whipped cream, topped by a single cherry', and as she eats her portion of the trifle, Nicandra feels cannibalistic, 'sick as if she were eating Aunt

Tossie' (78). Nicandra's exaggerated sense of bodily privacy, underscored here at the publicising of Aunt Tossie's breast, presents another example of her confusion and inability to distinguish between levels of abjection.

Nicandra's confrontations with the Real progress from signifying infringements on the taste of the gentry to signifying the traumatic entry of the Real into the flow of symbolic existence. Her marriage to Andrew Bland secures advancement into Anglo-Irish ideology as a recognition of 'the invaluable importance of belonging to the Anglo-Irish "Family"' (88). But her subsequent pregnancy leads to her most profound confrontation with abjection. Searching for a justification to borrow money from Aunt Tossie for an abortion, Andrew devises the excuse that the money is needed to 'drain the west bog,' an arresting, analogously abject metaphor. This metaphor, then, becomes a way to hide the existence of a child ('neutralized by the word'), and Nicandra, accepting it, convinces herself that six weeks of pregnancy could only yield a 'shadow of "it" – "baby", "embryo" were words she didn't speak, even to herself' (108). When the abortion is rendered unnecessary by a miscarriage, Nicandra must confront the material reality that would otherwise have been conveniently hidden through metaphors and medical procedures:

> She stopped, put the bottle between her knees, straining and tugging, her hands searing into blisters on the rough horn handle of the long corkscrew. It was when the cork yielded that pain struck, paused, struck again. She knew exactly what was going to happen now – she would lose her baby and he would commend her. (127)

As Nicandra confronts the physical reality of the event, she becomes a spectacle of abjection on display when Andrew arrives: 'She was propped in bed, soaking bath towels between her legs when Andrew came back' (127). The spectacle of Nicandra mopping up the remains of her foetus allows Keane to confront and disrupt the metaphoric dismissal of the pregnancy. She thereby highlights language's ability to gloss over the Real and 'disappear' regions of the body (just as the phrases 'down there' and 'my little insides' function earlier in the novel) while, at the same time, presenting the failure of such an endeavour. Yet Nicandra's habitual erasure of the material body through language and her characteristic lack of differentiation between levels of abjection leads to her relative lack of reaction to this failure in the return of the Real. Indeed, she seems more horrified by the appearance of Aunt Tossie's breast at the dinner table than by the graphic scene of her miscarriage.

Abjection challenges Nicandra again at the end of the novel when, upon returning to Deer Forest, she finds Gigi, Tossie's beloved parrot, now stuffed, covered with 'bald patches' and 'white mites squirming at the roots of feathers which remained' (226). Nicandra insists on the bird's destruction and

Tossie's removal from that 'filthy bug-house' (229). Her rage and authority are tied to the removal of abjection as she attempts to voice the symbolic law that she has never fully internalised. A flood of memories returns to her when the Irish Catholic Silly-Willy (now William) argues, 'Don't do that – that's dirty' (229):

> When had he said that before? ... They both remembered. It was in the morning when he had clung to his navy-blue shorts as, curiosity and cruelty the panaceas for the loss of love, in her loneliness, she held the tiny creature by the back of his jersey and whipped round his bare knees until he obeyed and stood, stripped to his school boots and stockings, so that she might see what it was that girls didn't have. She laughed at what she saw and switched round his legs again until he showed her how he made a trickle ... that was when his mother found them. (229)

The narrator notes:

> now the obscenity was alive again between them, freed from the impenetrable reserves of childhood, those silences that have no confidante. For who could understand such a strange caper? Or explain away the horror of kittens drowning in a bucket? Or the light in Anderson's green eyes? All were dark in places, staying powerful with their hoards intact. (230)

This scene and the recollections that it stirs synthesise the abject challenging the subject from its place of banishment, a regimented banishment that we have seen constructed and reinforced throughout Nicandra's life and throughout the novel. Nicandra's life is a series of attempts to 'explain away the horror', that is, to keep the Real at bay, while she sustains the proper life of an Anglo-Irish girl and woman. In the mind of Nicandra, Keane explores the insufficiencies of the symbolic network. Nicandra exemplifies the Kristevan maxim, 'to each ego its object, to each superego its abject', for her subjectivity relies upon this distinction which, to the horror of her and everyone else, she every so often erases.

Nicandra and Keane's cast of abject characters are parts for the whole of the Anglo-Irish gentry. Their abjection and their reactions to it reveal the limits of the manners and codes of Anglo-Irish society and create a subjectivity for the decaying Anglo-Irish class. Keane transposes the metaphor of the rotting Big House onto the bodies of its occupants and thus, defamiliarises the Anglo-Irish and the codes of the Big House genre. Though she offers plenty of rotting architecture, the materiality of the characters suggests a more powerful symbol of a class in turmoil. The rotting bodies of the once elite highlight the precariousness of the symbolic order upon which their subjective identity is based. Such an extensive use of abjection, however, amounts to more than a fascination with 'very nasty' stuff and more than a transposition of the rotting architecture onto the Anglo-Irish body. Her decision to abjectify Anglo-Irish bodies should also be read in the context of the abjectification of Irish Catholics throughout the history of Anglo-Irish writing, especially the history of the Big House novel. In this context we can appreciate the power of Silly-Willy's critique, a power which lies in his role as the Irish Catholic 'other' challenging the symbolic authority of the Anglo-Irish by pointing to their own abjection: 'that's dirty.'

The connection between Irish Catholics and abjection is reiterated explicitly by Keane in Aroon's assumptions about Rose's natural connection to the ill and the dead and her firm belief that '[Catholics] revel in death' and eagerly anticipate 'the nasty rituals' (7). Keane is clearly critical of these associations here; Aroon, repeatedly characterised as the epitome of Anglo-Irish prejudice ('I was, after all, Aroon St Charles, and I felt it too'), illustrates the security of a belief in the abject 'other.' Nicandra's fascination with the body of Silly-Willy functions similarly. Her power over him encourages her to enact the aforementioned scene of his cruel exposure which he challenges as 'dirty'. Upon their discovery, she retreats to 'her approved playthings: the pony, the bantams, the dogs, proper friends and companions for the little girl in the Big House' (229), but she cannot dismiss the existence of her own fascination with the grotesque: 'The nastier the faces she made, the dirtier the words she chose, the happier she grew' (31). In these situations Keane displays the workings of Anglo-Irish 'othering' of the Irish Catholic through interpretations of the body. Keane's decision to confront the abject bodies of the Anglo-Irish, thus, constitutes a metacommentary on the signifying systems of the Big House genre, which contain no shortage of abject representations of a Catholic peasantry.

The Big House novel, of course, is but one instance of a cultural semiotics which renders the Irish Catholic abject. Thus, before we consider specific instances from Big House texts, we might also note the context of other Irish writing or writing about Ireland in which the Big House novel developed. One context might be colonialism's reliance on the binary oppositions between metropolitan and native culture. The Anglo-Irish need to construct an identity that was not Irish (Catholic) but also not English was complicated by the long-standing fear of English degeneration into English-Irish savages expressed as early as 1571 in Edmund Campion's *A History of Ireland* (1571). The difficult material circumstances of the Catholic Irish created an Anglo-Irish and English fascination with them as material bodies wallowing in self-produced filth that also served, of course, to justify separate spheres and an imperialist ideology.

The body of the Irish Catholic appeared as an equally central figure in famine literature. Famine writing depended upon images of the starving, abject Irish, and Ireland itself was identified as an abjectified corpse. An article published in *The Times* in 1847 uses the language of abjection to reconstitute the symbolic structure of England: 'Before our merciful intervention, the Irish nation were a wretched, indolent, half-starved tribe of savages ... they have never approached the standard of the civilized world' (cited in Kinealy 133). But, it is important to note that even charitably-oriented accounts rely as heavily upon the bodies of the Irish masses: '[The sight] was enough to have broken the stoutest heart to have seen the poor little children in the union workhouse yesterday – their flesh hanging so loose from their little bones, that the physician took it in his hand and wrapped it round their legs' (cited in Kinealy 109). Similarly, William Bennett in 1847, expressing the need for 'Christian responsibility', observes a Catholic peasantry through an 'almost intolerable stench' to be so wretched that 'language utterly fails [him]' (cited in Hadfield and MacVeagh 263).

The extensive body of travel literature on Ireland, often written by leading European cultural authorities and marketing itself as tourist adventure, ethnographic study, or historical documentation, offers similar views of the Irish. As 'realistic' accounts laced with grotesque Irish bodies proliferate, abjection functions as a kind of prop to legitimise the account of any given text. Richard Twiss's *A Tour in Ireland* (1776) focuses on the cabin as a site of Irish abjection: 'The out-skirts of Dublin consist chiefly of huts, which are termed cabbins; ... and in these miserable dwellings, far the greater part of the inhabitants of Ireland linger out a wretched existence' (cited in Hadfield and MacVeagh 253). The workhouse offers another architectural site of abjection. In *Reminiscences of My Irish Journey* (1849) Thomas Carlyle records his visit to Westport Workhouse which inspires him to write: 'Human swinery has here reached its *acme*' (cited in Harrington 258). In 1835, Alexis de Tocqueville observed, 'the poor are seated pellmell like pigs in the mud of their sty' and 'that they do not appear to be thinking' (121–2). In William Steuart Trench's account of a workhouse, the Irish behave as animals, 'kicking and screaming and some of them actually biting at my legs' (153).

Throughout writing about Ireland, then, an understanding of Ireland and the Irish is presented through categories of abjection; this opposition between the abject and the subject has been a way of constituting and reproducing notions of class difference. Even contemporary historians, depicting the problems of Catholic poverty, rely on a pattern of material subjectivity for making their points. Giovanni Costigan's *A History of Modern Ireland*, for example, provides this look at the Catholic poor inhabiting the former townhouses of the Dublin rich:

> Elegant cornices, delicate mouldings, painted ceilings, marble mantle-pieces, looked down upon the squalid litter of the undifferentiated poor. Privacy was impossible. Opportunities for decency did not exist … In once-fashionable residential areas like Dominick Street … From open doorways came the stench of unwashed bodies … The stunted race that occupied such dwellings was clad in torn, ragged, or parched garments, filthy with age. Their children ran about half naked. Such people never knew clean linen until the day they were laid out in their coffins. (294)

These examples of Irish Catholic abjection continue to highlight the presence of an architectural context containing the abject bodies of the 'other.' The cabin and the poorhouse become mythic sites of filth with subjects so materially debased that writers like Tocqueville see no signs of thought. Indeed, Costigan's point relies, in part, on the unsettling contrast between the architectural grandeur of the Dublin tenements and the decaying bodies of its inhabitants.

Such literary and historical examples demonstrate a discursive habit in which the Big House participates. With its architectural premise, the Big House novel in particular depends upon this contrast between the classic body and the grotesque body and a corresponding distinction between the Anglo-Irish estate and the Catholic cabin. Thus, as the Big House represents classic, finished man, the cabin symbolises the unfinished, grotesque body of the peasant. It is not surprising, then, that Big House literature capitalises on this image to define distinctions between the classes. The cabin's dilapidated status is accompanied by the rotting body of its inhabitants, and the Big House's fortress-like status is accompanied by the closed body of its inhabitant. This metonymic function informs the entire genre:

> In Anglo-Irish literature, as in Irish life, the houses of the Anglo-Irish – sometimes called 'Ascendancy houses' or 'great houses' but, most commonly, 'Big Houses' – acquire a deeply symbolic value. In large measure, this is due to the discernible difference between the dwelling places of the Anglo-Irish and the majority of the population. Literature provides ample evidence of the respective points of view: those inside the houses regard their neighbors as the 'mere Irish'. Those who inhabit cabins and small farms see the people of the Big House as alien garrison and the houses themselves as the territory of strangers and interlopers – who live in their midst. (Madden-Simpson 44)

Thus, true to the semiotic necessity of difference for meaning, the Big House fails to signify without the correspondent notion of the cabin, and the refined Anglo-Irish body requires its abject opposite.

In *A Drama in Muslin* (1886), George Moore imagines the interior of the cabin as 'a dark fetid hole, smelling of potato skins and damp' (322) and depicts 'the peasants [rising] out of their wet hovels' (144). The necessity of their physical decay for highlighting the preservation of the Anglo-Irish appears when their 'vague faces' peer through the window panes to gaze at the 'warm bright room' of an Anglo-Irish ball. The peasants of Somerville's and Ross's *The Real Charlotte* (1894) function to offset the romance and intrigue of middle and upper-class characters and plots; they possess subjectivity as offshoots of their physicality – from the 'very dirty' (280) tailor's wife of Ferry Row to Billy Grainy with blood-shot eyes, a mouth that 'dribbled like a baby's' and the stench of whisky 'poisoning the air around him' (337). Figures of abjection are tied to the predominant concept in Anglo-Irish writing of the embattled gentry, subject to the decline of their economic power at the hands of an angry populace – the 'now-familiar literary image of the embattled Anglo-Irish, gallantly facing the inexorability of the new Ireland and the concurrent demise of their own' (Madden-Simpson 41). Such narratives are demonstrated in the house burning plots of Bowen's *The Last September* and Fitzgerald's *We Are Besieged* or Bence-Jones's historical text *Twilight of the Ascendancy*. Yet, Big House fiction, which witnesses the fall of the house, rarely offers a correspondent rotting Anglo-Irish body. Thus, Keane's decision to construct abject Anglo-Irish bodies and to present Anglo-Irish characters who continue to articulate a notion of Catholic abjection while succumbing to their own exaggerated abjection suggests a critique of both the Anglo-Irish and the Big House symbolic system.

Keane's apparent awareness of the complex signification of abjection could be offered in response to critics who charge Keane with an elitist avoidance of the 'native population.' Pondering the question of whether recent Anglo-Irish literature offers a voice different from that of nineteenth-century and early twentieth-century Anglo-Irish literature, Patricia Kelly argues that a one-sided representation of Ireland 'does seem … to be reflected in some of the recently-published Big House novels, especially those which deal largely with the early part of the century', and she adds that the 'native population is almost entirely non-existent in Molly Keane's marvellous extravaganzas' (232). Yet, representing the Anglo-Irish as positively grotesque (perhaps what Kelly refers to with the phrase 'marvellous extravaganzas'), as incorporating the abject Real, is undeniably a different voice, indeed a politically relevant one, challenging a traditional picture of the grotesque as only Irish Catholic. In Keane's novels, then, a binary system collapses. Given its presence in Irish literary meaning, abjection should also be considered when the question of where to situate her novels arises. On this subject, for example, Mary Breen writes:

> Although her novels have been described as Big House novels, in my view, they refuse to be so classified. The settings are those of the Big House, but her concerns ... are not those of the conventional Big House novel of Anglo-Irish literary tradition. Although there is a wealth of realistic detail, the fictional form she adopts is not exactly realist: there is no moral critique in Keane, no controlling irony. Neither are her novels romances, although a superficial reading might presume them to be so, and Keane herself certainly thought about her early novels in this way. Keane does not romanticise her world or treat it nostalgically, she ruthlessly satires it; her Big Houses are not the center of dignity that Yeats presents in *Ancestral Houses*. (206)

Critics such as Breen who places Keane outside the Big House tradition or Kelly who does not contextualise the contemporary 'voice' of Keane, tend to ignore the signifying system upon which the ruthless satires and the 'marvellous extravaganzas' are constructed and the potential within that system to radically alter it.

After almost two hundred years of Big House fiction, in an effort to understand the genre's history, its capacity for interpreting Anglo-Irish experience, and its current status, we might consider the difference between modernism and postmodernism. Critical work on Keane's contemporary vision repeats words like 'boldness', 'relentless', and 'merciless,' but such words are more descriptive than evaluative. What do such qualities mean exactly for this literary genre? Žižek offers one idea:

> Postmodernism thus accomplishes a kind of shift of perspective in relation to modernism: what in modernism appeared as the subversive margin – symptoms in which the repressed truth of the 'false' totality emerges – is now displaced into the very heart, as the hard core of the Real that different attempts of symbolization endeavor in vain to integrate and to 'gentrify.' (*Symptom!* 123)

Given Žižek's understanding of a postmodernist shift, Keane's Big House at the end of the twentieth century could be said to exemplify that shift; certainly, his metaphor of gentrification, directly applies to the novels under discussion here. In the traumatic kernel of the Real that confronts the idea of the Big House (in the material reality of the subject) lies the undoing of the Anglo-Irish gentry. The repressed status of abjection, formerly displaced onto the 'uncivilised', Catholic margins of an elite aristocracy, arrives at the centre ('of dignity'), 'displaced into the very heart' of Anglo-Irish life. This relocation of the Real establishes the 'merciless gaze' (Boylan 155) that Keane sets upon Anglo-Irish life. Far more disturbing than the outside intrusions of the

Land League or the arson of *The Last September*, are the confrontations in Keane's texts of the Anglo-Irish with the return of their very own Real.

This context allows us to consider why these last three novels inspire comments on its shocking, bold, and relentless vision or to explain why Sir William Collins refused the manuscript of *Good Behaviour* because it was 'too black a comedy' (cited in Lynch 77). Abjection itself does not cause such reactions, for abjection, in its Irish Catholic manifestation, has been a staple of Irish literature for centuries. What shocks us in Keane's vision, then, is not simply the presence of abjection, nor its excess, but the challenge that the abject poses to an Anglo-Irish ideology, the representational reversal of the Anglo-Irish and the Irish Catholic that it enacts, and the context of the Big House in which it functions. To suggest, as Ann Owens Weekes does, that Keane's work establishes a 'corrective' to Bowen's remains understatement; she most certainly offers a 'corrective' – one might say an emetic – but one that firmly forces the meaning systems of the Big House novel into the open, calling into question not only the Anglo-Irish themselves but the modes of discourse which represent them and with which they represent themselves. To purge a tradition which after two hundred years must dramatically rethink itself, Keane offers us the abject Anglo-Irish wallowing in self-produced filth in their 'very nasty' Big Houses while the formerly abject Catholic looks on and proclaims, 'that's dirty'.

Fattening out memories: Big House daughters and abjection in Molly Keane's *Good Behaviour* and *Loving and Giving*

KELLY J.S. McGOVERN

'You can't name it, and I won't name it. It's a nasty name for a nasty thing,' Nurse declares to Aroon after witnessing Rose give Papa a 'foot rub' in Molly Keane's novel, *Good Behaviour* (189). Nurse's shrewd use of the words 'can't' and 'won't' simultaneously forces the 'nasty' into conversation and exposes the peculiar squeamishness of her Anglo-Irish interlocutor. Nurse acknowledges what really happens during Papa's 'foot rubs' and chooses to condemn the sexual activity.[1] Aroon, the daughter of the Anglo-Irish Big House, has been thoroughly educated to recognise that the standards of 'good behaviour' forbid mention of such activities. Further, Aroon's construction of her clean and proper self and sexuality makes her particularly incapable of recognising Rose's action as sexually pleasing for Papa. Keane notoriously attends to 'nasty' – abject – details in her novels. Yet, both Nurse and Aroon refuse to admit this 'nasty' event into language. Nurse's euphemism and Aroon's deliberate incomprehension reveals the complexities inherent in Keane's use of 'nasty' details. When Keane's characters treat Papa's 'nasty' foot rub different from the way they treat other 'nasty' events, events like vomit and defecation, we see abjection splitting into two categories. I argue that the relationship of these two types of abjection undergirds the construction of Keane's female characters, specifically her classic character types denoted by Iris Aroon St Charles in *Good Behaviour* (1981), and Nicandra Forester Bland in *Loving and Giving* (1988). Keane's skillful deployment of abjection allows only voluptuously asexual Big House daughters to survive the downfall of their class, homes, and the end of their family lines.

The women of Keane's comeback novels and her descriptions of the decay in their lives have attracted attention since their publication. Ann Owens Weekes, Rachael Lynch and Mary Breen, among others, discuss Keane's illustrations of bodily impropriety and decay in terms of comedy.[2] Lynch in particular describes

---

1 Nurse's outrage makes it clear that Ascendancy landlords no longer possess their ancestors' power to compel sexual favours from women in their employ. See Vera Kreilkamp's discussion of the *droit du seigneur* in 'The persistence of illusion in Molly Keane's fiction' in *The Anglo-Irish novel and the Big House* (1998), 176–7.   2 Ann Owens Weekes, 'Molly Keane: Bildungsromane Quenelles', *Irish women writers: an uncharted tradition* (1990), 155–73; Rachael Jane Lynch, 'The crumbling fortress: Molly Keane's comedies of Anglo-Irish manners', in

Keane's technique as a form of 'women's humor' and asserts, 'Keane enables us to laugh even as we recoil, and perhaps for the author herself and her Anglo-Irish readers, to laugh *because* they recoil' (74). Readers love Keane's characters, especially her female ones. We love hating them, too. Vera Kreilkamp explains the maliciously good behaviour on the part of Anglo-Irish mothers as a response to their Ascendancy husbands' emasculating loss of power in postcolonial Ireland. She claims that in twentieth-century Anglo-Irish fiction like Keane's, 'mothers who turn against their young respond to the ascendancy's waning authority. Underlying the streak of sadism that motivates these matriarchal monsters lies rage at male social and political impotence' (186). Indeed, the women in *Good Behaviour* and *Loving and Giving* do turn against their daughters. Likewise, daughters turn against their mothers. Postcolonial Anglo-Irish descendancy may be in play in Keane's novels, but so too are the constructions of femininity and sexual difference that shape these mother/daughter power struggles. Abjection factors prominently in these constructions.

Like Ellen L. O'Brien, I advocate foregrounding Keane's use of bodily decay, which I believe illuminates Keane's attempt to rework the internal gender dynamics as well as the class politics of the Anglo-Irish. O'Brien claims that 'if we situate [Keane's] use of putrid excess within the category of abjection rather than comic irony, we can refocus our attention on the causes of the laughter that these representations elicit' and reads abjection as functioning in the class and cultural relations between Keane's Anglo-Irish characters and their Irish Catholic servants (O'Brien 35). In order to achieve her incisive reading of class and ethnicity, O'Brien approaches abjection as a whole, after noting and then setting aside the two categories of abjection, excremental and menstrual, that Julia Kristeva differentiates in *Powers of Horror*.[3] While O'Brien largely elides how abjection functions in relation to sexual difference, I read the abjection of certain sexual appetites as a mode of survival for Keane's large women.

Abjection breaks into two categories because it threatens the subject from the outside and the inside. Many of the body's own materials are abject, espe-

Theresa O'Connor (ed.), *The comic tradition in Irish women writers* (1996), 73–98; Mary Breen, 'Piggies and spoilers of girls: the representation of sexuality in the novels of Molly Keane', in Eibhear Walshe (ed.), *Sex, nation and dissent in Irish writing* (1997), 202–20. 3 Kristeva constructs the process of defining the social self, which involves determining the boundary between what is inside and what is outside the self, between self and other, subject and object, by pointing towards what the self is not: not filth, not waste, not dung, not dead matter. The abject locates the other side of a border of propriety. Recognising the existence of this boundary allows the self to simultaneously know the body as proper and institute symbolic order; the self pushes abjection away with its conception of a pure, rational and solid body. Abjection constantly threatens this boundary, however, by betraying its presence in the subject's internal struggle to construct the self. See *Powers of Horror*. For discussion of the Bakhtinian idea of the 'completed man' in Keane, see O'Brien, esp. 37–9.

cially materials related to bodily orifices, where the inside of the body comes into contact with what is outside. Kristeva discusses how excrement and decay 'stand for the danger to identity that comes from without: the ego threatened by the non-ego, society threatened by its outside, life by death' (37). This first category, excremental abjection, contains materials that originate outside of the self and materials that pass through the body, such as food. The body takes the outside in, uses it, and then disposes of it in abject form: excrement. The second category, menstrual abjection, is inherently more difficult to define than excremental abjection; sexuality and interiority resist any containment, including restrictive definitions. I read Kristeva as associating this more ambiguous category with menstrual blood, which 'stands for the danger issuing from within the identity (social or sexual); it threatens the relationship between the sexes within a social aggregate and, through internalization, the identity of each sex in the face of sexual difference' (71). Menstrual abjection originates within the body and passes out of the body into the world. This category is dangerous because menstrual abjection threatens to spill the self out of the body. It has the potential to 'use up' the finite self it spills out.

As it is for Kristeva – evidenced by her choice of the specifically female associations of her label for sexually abject materials and her claim that sperm does not 'have any polluting value' (71) – the threat offered by menstrual abjection is asymmetrically feminine in Keane's novels. Keane's Anglo-Irish daughters may find a way out of the Big House, but they cannot escape the larger Western tendency to pair femininity with pollution and malign women as the embodiment of sexual difference.[4] Anglo-Irish patriarchs like Aroon's Papa die off, disappear, and lose body parts during the course of these narratives. In contrast, Keane's Anglo-Irish women become more immediately corporeal. Their responses to excremental and menstrual abjection, however, provide a way to explore the identity structures of Keane's Big House mothers and daughters and to trace Keane's attempt to create a space for these Anglo-Irish women outside the boundaries of the Big House.

Good Behaviour and *Loving and Giving*, the first and last novels of Keane's literary rebirth in the 1980s, mirror one another in ways that make them particularly apt for a study of character responses to excremental and menstrual

---

4 For this point, I depend on Elizabeth Grosz's 'Sexed bodies' in *Volatile bodies: toward a corporeal feminism* (1994), 187–210. Grosz critiques the way that Kristeva 'seems to think there is a link between menstruation and dirt', as I would critique Keane because 'this coupling is itself significant insofar as menstrual blood ... becomes associated with the characteristics of excrement. The representation of female sexuality as an uncontainable flow, as seepage associated with what is unclean, coupled with the idea of female sexuality as a vessel, a container, a home empty or lacking in itself but fillable from the outside, has enabled men to associate women with infection, with disease, with the idea of festering putrefacation, no longer contained simply in female genitals but at any or all points of the female body' (Grosz 205, 206).

abjection. Both plot the lives of the last and only daughters of their respective Big Houses. The lists of characters, when placed side by side, reveal several correspondences within the family structures. Each traces the development of the protagonist from the nursery into womanhood. Emotional distance and romantic affairs on the part of at least one parent stymie both daughters. Nicandra's Maman elopes with a hired hand and abandons Nicandra at a young age, though it is Aroon's Papa who enjoys a series of extramarital affairs and whom Aroon progressively loses, via amputation, illness, and death. Both families find themselves slowly draining their inherited coffers, though the influx of Aunt Tossie's money maintains Nicandra's beloved Deer Forest for a time. The mothers in both novels are beautiful, thin, and prone to ruling over their daughter's relationship with food; in *Loving and Giving*, Maman ties Nicandra to a chair until she eats a plate of spinach, even after a nauseous Nicandra makes 'a horrid defilement' out of her first serving (*LG* 35), while in *Good Behaviour*, Mummie seeks to deny food to overweight Aroon in an effort to reduce her weight and save money. She cruelly chides Aroon, '[p]erhaps if you were willing to eat just a little less, we wouldn't have this appalling bill' (178). Nicandra is an only child. Aroon becomes one when her homosexual brother, Hubert, dies in a car accident. Both houses have Catholic servants able to actively resist the daughters: Silly Willy at Deer Forest, and Rose at Temple Alice, Aroon's home. The chronological endings of both novels leave one woman inhabiting a smaller home on the periphery of the Big House property and another woman dead. The dead and the survivors have distinct modes of response to abjection.

The materials of excremental abjection make their presence known in great detail in both *Good Behaviour* and *Loving and Giving*. Each major encounter with these materials occurs when a character recognises that he or she has misjudged the symbolic order, thereby exposing its fragility and allowing the abject a temporary escape from its banished position. As O'Brien has noted, Mrs Brock's diarrhoea and Aroon's vomit serve as 'protective excrement ... Like Mrs Brock, Aroon is restored by the expelling of her own abjection' (41–2). In both of these instances, abjection appears as a defence mechanism. It evidences Mrs Brock's uncomfortable incorporation of the symbolic order. After her diarrhoeic episode, Mrs Brock quickly seeks to distance herself from her contact with abjection and reaffirm the fragile symbolic order through cleansing and ritual behaviour. Making reparations for abjection's interruption provides Mrs Brock with an opportunity to reinstate the symbolic order by transferring her attention to a social breach she has the power to address and contain. In this sense, the physical abject material provides a welcome outlet for social anxiety because it reminds her that she can reassert control over her own physical boundaries, if not her social environment. Aroon's encounter with abjection serves a similar function. Not only does her

need to vomit temporarily divert her attention away from the crushing revelation of Richard's engagement to another woman, it provides her with an
exit strategy. It gets Aroon out of the room and away from the other party-
goers, disallowing their witness of her social humiliation.

For Aroon, this encounter serves an additional function. It defines the
moment where Aroon embraces her position as the spinster daughter of the
Big House, the culminating moment of becoming when, in Kristeva's words,
'I give birth to myself amid the violence of sobs, of vomit.'⁵ Only in Mr
Kiely's car, covered in and smelling of this excremental material, and after a
burst of 'loud crying', does Aroon declare 'I was, after all, Aroon St. Charles,
and I felt it too' (210–11). This declaration dismisses the Anglo-Irish ideal
Aroon briefly envisioned for Richard and herself and delivers her as 'the truly
unwanted person' capable of surviving in the twentieth-century Big House
(211). In order to do so, Aroon must erase all desire for sex by transferring
her attention to the consumption of food.

This is not to say that excremental abjection is always protective or formative in Keane's novels. While Aroon can use excremental abjection as a tool
or a weapon for her own preservation, Mummie can only see it as a threat.
Mummie spends her life denying the power of the outside world to affect her
Anglo-Irish self. She dies protecting the symbolic boundaries she has constructed for herself. Mummie rejects rabbit, a meat she has determined fit
only for Aroon and the dogs (178). When Aroon serves it to her disguised as
a chicken mousse, its mere presence at the boundary of her nasal cavities elicits her final, violent assertion of control over her bodily boundaries: '"the
smell – I'm –" She gave a trembling, tearing cry, vomited dreadfully, and fell
back into the nest of pretty pillows' (6). Her fixation on the maintenance of
her personal boundaries ultimately leads Mummie to expel herself rather than
incorporate excrementally abject materials from outside the boundaries of the
Big House. Aroon might be able to reconcile herself to a life without sex, but
no body can survive without food.

Mummie represents a certain type of Big House woman – the thin, elegant, dependent, self-deluded variety that dies at the end of a Keane novel.
In *Loving and Giving*, Keane produces a similar character: Nicandra. Each
devotes herself to her love affair with her Anglo-Irish landholding husband to
the neglect of her self, her home, and her other relationships. Mummie's
malevolent neglect of her daughter is already apparent. She clearly falls into
Kreilkamp's category of the monstrous mother. Nicandra, on the other hand,
never has a child to wield power over. She devotes herself so fully to caring
for her philandering, opportunistic husband, Andrew Bland, that she deprives

---

5 Kristeva 3. Tossie experiences a similar moment in the redecorated bathroom when '[a]s she
sat, relief flowing through her, a resolve was absolute in her mind' (*Loving and Giving* 214).

herself of motherhood in order to suit him; though she regards her single pregnancy as a 'kind of subdued glory, a triumphant secret warmth', in the face
of his apathy, her 'glory dwindle[s] into a nuisance, a practical difficulty, since
that was how he saw a child' and she acquiesces to an abortion (106). Later,
when Andrew asks for a divorce, Nicandra sacrifices her role as wife because
she defines love as 'giving all you had' (165). Nothing satisfies Nicandra like
giving herself away. Keane suggests that Nicandra will continue to devote herself to 'loving and giving'. She will transfer her attention to another love object
and devote herself to (s)mothering Aunt Tossie, the woman who substituted
as a maternal figure for Nicandra after Maman ran away. Nicandra's powers
of loving and giving make Aunt Tossie into the child Nicandra never had; the
'more Aunt Tossie showed herself obstinate and baby-like, the stronger
Nicandra felt her protective love to grow' (205). If allowed to continue
unchecked, Nicandra would grow more and more like Mummie.

Loving and Giving traces the development of a woman who learns early
to construct her boundaries against the outside world. Nicandra's incident
with Maman and the spinach parallels Mummie's incident with Aroon and
the rabbit. Nicandra refuses to ingest that 'brown-green mountain on her
plate' served to her out of 'Twomey's injurious spite', thereby rejecting the
intimation that she would condescend to allow the servant to control her
behaviour (34). She models this assertion of her power as a woman of the Big
House on the behaviour of her mother, who, after instructing Nicandra to eat
her spinach, declines her own glass of wine. '"I don't want it," she said. It
could have been spinach she was refusing. The glass rocked and wavered for
an instant before it fell and a dark pool of wine spread over the tablecloth'
(36). Maman's behaviour schools Nicandra about the power that comes alongside the refusal to allow external control over her self. Through her relationship with Maman, Nicandra learns that obeying others threatens to eat away
at the self she has constituted. At the same time, Maman models Nicandra's
romantic ideal. She realises that her 'love for Maman, with its consuming
passion to please, belonged to the times before Maman had, as she now
realised, so gallantly followed her love' (108). Nicandra inherits the understanding that the power of Anglo-Irish womanhood derives from internal control over the self and selective expenditure of the self for the cause of romance.

Nicandra operates according to the rules of menstrual abjection. Keane
structures *Loving and Giving* such that Nicandra, rather than allowing the
external world to cross her symbolic boundaries, keeps the outside out by
flushing the inside out as well. Her self-immolation symbolically enacts the
'good curetting' – the scraping out of body cavities with a surgical instrument
– her friend Lal suggests to her the night she meets Andrew (68). The full
extent of her aptitude for menstrual abjection becomes clear when Keane indicates that Nicandra miscarries by her own volition. Nicandra acts upon the

'midwife's warning' that she hears in Lal's voice when she tells her, 'Don't pull corks, Nico' (125). The exaggerated force required to open the bottle of wine betrays her dual effort:

> She drove the corkscrew in, twisting it like a knife in an enemy, stretching her shoulders back and pulling, with no result. Her will to pull the cork redeemed for the moment her grief. She stooped, put the bottle between her knees, straining and tugging, her hands searing to blisters on the rough horn handle of the long corkscrew. It was when the cork yielded that pain struck, paused, and struck again. She knew exactly what was going to happen now – she would lose her baby and he would commend her. (126–7)

The soaking bath towels attesting Nicandra's willed abortion signal her downfall: she proves willing to curette her self for an obsolete ideal. Nicandra dies ready to abandon her own needs and the borders she has set up in order to protect herself during her estrangement from her husband. She empties herself out with her selfless devotion to her ideal of the Anglo-Irish wife. By the novel's end, the old Big House devours her self-sacrifice literally and figuratively, leaving '[h]er body, heaped together on the stones ... coffined and certain in her happiness' after she falls through what remains of Deer Forest's dining room floor (232). The Big House becomes a container for Nicandra and her sexuality.

As she depicts Nicandra's progressive and characteristic relationship with menstrual abjection, Keane establishes the trajectory of the thin Anglo-Irish woman. This category of Big House women is helpless in the face of excremental abjection: witness Mummie's death and Nicandra's reaction to the condition of Aunt Tossie's caravan and the maggots inhabiting her stuffed parrot, Gigi. While Nicandra sees the infestation as a 'cogent reason to overrule Aunt Tossie's absurd determination to defend (with Silly-Willie's entire co-operation) that horrid fortress' and thereby generate her maternal hold over her aunt, Tossie responds to the instance of excremental abjection with the vague suggestion that William should 'just try the Mothproof' (226). Tossie accepts her friend Gigi, maggots and all. She (like Aroon) can handle herself around excremental abjection. Mummie and Nicandra cannot.

For Aroon, however, encounters with menstrual abjection are another matter. Aroon treats materials relating to sexual difference with a mode of communication unlike the frankness she awards excremental materials. This form of communication becomes explicit as Aroon searches for an excuse to enter Hubert and Richard's room. She decides to use menstrual cramps as her ticket to admission to their fellowship:

I was in a haze of melancholy which was to find its climax in one of those pains I had been taught to disregard as slight monthly discomforts, not to be over-rated; to take them seriously was to be guilty of a social nuisance. This time I had the remedy near. At last I knew what gin could do for me. (94–5)

Aroon can only refer to menstruation, even when speaking to herself, through euphemism, a borderland form of communication that at once conceals and reveals its referent. O'Brien states that Aroon 'calls attention to the abjectification of the menses when she notes its banishment from language and the social implications of complaint' (60–1, n2). This slide into euphemism flags the way that Aroon, unreliable narrator that she is, is searching for a suitable way to express the situation. The actual statement she voices, 'I'm feeling rather awful,' registers on the scale of sexual difference only in the most oblique sense (95). Aroon can only present her menstrual complaint in general rather than specific terms. She is more comfortable narrating vomiting and bowel upsets than menstruation, which she treats with far less precision and detail.

As we have already begun to see, Aroon and Aunt Tossie constitute a second type of Big House daughter: the fat, awkward, independent, self-deluded variety who survives the close of Keane's novels. Though liable to find themselves in the clutches of Mummie and Nicandra, these women resist. Indeed, both Aroon and Tossie fight for survival. Their voracious appetites and careful attention to their own physical and financial needs help them find a way out of the Big House and into smaller satellite abodes. Tossie's caravan satisfies all of her physical needs and offers her access to her animal comforts (even if they have maggots in their feathers and stuffing). She comes to prefer it to a redecorated Deer Forest, and resolves that '[n]o loving coercion would succeed in keeping her caged and closeted for her own good. Her own good, or her own bad, were her own concern, her own sacred cows and causes. Even though Nicandra, this child she so loved, was to be her warden, she could never yield up her independence' (214). Aunt Tossie's defiant move back into her caravan demonstrates that Nicandra would never fully dominate her mother-figure as Aroon manages to do, even if she were to survive the narrative. Tossie 'was in no way a dependent old member of the family. Generous and unthinking as she had always been, she could not quite forget whose money, as long as it lasted, had maintained Deer Forest' (197). Nicandra could not overcome the fact that Aunt Tossie's dissipated financial inheritance has left her residual power.

As she does with Nicandra, Keane illustrates how Aroon's relationship with abjection develops. She throws off her mother's model of sexuality at a young age and finds pleasure in food.[6] A key event occurs at the dinner table,

6 For discussion of Aroon's first memory, alienation from her mother, see Weekes 162.

as Aroon struggles to define herself as a sexual being in the presence of her brother Hubert's friend, Richard. When Hubert tells her 'Just be your natural self,' Aroon interprets that 'natural' self as insatiable:

> Right, I thought, I can't talk. But I can eat. I can be the fat woman in the fairground ... So ... I wolfed down sensational quantities of food. Almost a side of smoked salmon, and I ate a whole lemon and its peel as well; most of a duck; four meringues and four pêches melbas, mushrooms and marrow on toast; even cheese ... I was a joke again. I was a person. I was something for them to talk about. (85–6).

Aroon identifies herself as a large woman with a voracious appetite. This identity sticks; it is how Richard remembers his 'Pig. Pig-wig. Piglet' (110). She equates personhood with the incorporation of food and womanhood with being loved by Richard, whose staged and asexual bedroom visit allows her to proclaim, 'I can never look on myself as a deprived, inexperienced girl. I've had a man in my bed. I suppose I could say I've had a lover. I like to call it that. I do call it that' (108). For Aroon, the language of euphemism serves its purpose; she remains a virgin, but can play language games and pose as an experienced woman.

Aroon's power of narration becomes entangled with her construction of a viable maturity for herself. She validates un-initiation into adult sexuality: 'I was loved although still untouched by that thing men do. Untouched because no doubt he had held me too dear' (120). Aroon's twisted logic and her abjection of sexuality creates a space in which she can regard herself as a desired being while simultaneously banishing sexual experience from her version of Anglo-Irish womanhood. Aroon protects herself with these memories and these euphemisms; there are no other romantic possibilities in her future, thanks to the combination of Mummie's economic decision to not present Aroon in London as a debutante and the class snobbery that rules out local businessman Mr Kiely's marriage proposal. She intentionally transfers even the pseudo-sexual moment of Richard's staged visit to her bed from a menstrual (sexual) to an excremental (food-related) register; 'I fattened out my least memories, slyly building up a future,' she tells herself after Richard departs Temple Alice (110). Aroon will not have a sexual future. She will have fat memories. In order to survive, she must redirect what can only be futile sexual appetites toward other modes of sustenance and accommodate herself to life as the last daughter of her Big House in a decaying Anglo-Irish world.

It is no wonder that Aroon refuses to acknowledge sexuality. As she sees it – or refuses to see it – sexuality has separated her from every form of masculine love she imagines she has had access to. She blames it for her father's increasing emotional distance, as well as for his death. Aroon circumvents rather than communicates references to sexuality and materials marked by sexual difference. She can euphemise sex as masculine behaviour; in Aroon's world, sex is the 'nasty things [Hubert's horse does] to the donkey' (167). It is 'that thing men do' (120). Keane's novel (despite the unreliable narrator) manages to intimate that sexual materials circulate abundantly: Papa impregnates both Mrs Brock and Blink.[7] Further, Hubert and Richard have a series of homosexual liaisons.[8] Keane's masterful display of abjection's power becomes clear even as Aroon attempts to elide sexuality. Aroon's efforts to eject menstrually abject materials only spotlight their presence.

This identity of desexualised yet corporeal womanhood is reinforced when Aroon comes home from the party and Mr Kiely's proposal covered with vomit. Her narrative skills allow her to elide the sort of sexual experiences she will never have. When she comes across Rose and Papa together on his bed, she immediately desexualises their activity through euphemism. She finds her narrative banishment so convincing that she is surprised that Rose finds it necessary to give an explanation, 'as though I might not see or understand that she was warming his feet' (212). Aroon knows her father can no longer withstand exertion and blames Rose for his death. Her accusation transfers Papa's last sexual experience (leading up to an ejaculation of sexually abject matter) into an encounter with forbidden drink (the stuff of excremental abjection). It was 'Rose who had killed him with her spoiling and her whisky. I would have given him anything except whisky. Surely he might have needed me most' (223). Because Aroon refuses to register any source of desire that comes from within – sexuality – she can only register any desire on the part of her father for something that comes from without – thirst.

Both Aroon and Aunt Tossie become active agents of change upon their environments and therefore achieve for themselves the power to dispose of modes they find distasteful, stultifying and emotionally starved. Like Aunt Tossie's move to her caravan, Aroon's move from Temple Alice to Gull's Cry supplies her with a space in which to order her world, complete with a drawing room that functions as a shrine to Papa and a kitchen well-stocked with appliances capable of creating deliciously murderous meals. While Kreilkamp is quick to point out that if 'Aunt Tossie's insistence on remaining in her caravan suggests her defiant choice of independence over gentility, it also underscores the downward social trajectory of the Anglo-Irish' (90), I would emphasise that this trajectory is tenable in a way that Nicandra's and Mummie's is not. Keane decrees that Nicandra and Mummie must die, signifying that the pair have come to represent a defunct ideal of Anglo-Irish

---

7 Indeed, it is no wonder that Papa worries that Aroon may be pregnant by Richard; he is used to watching his women head toward the ocean, whether to cross over to England for an abortion or to drown themselves and he thinks Aroon may follow their example. 8 See Breen for further analysis of Keane's use of hetero- and homosexuality.

womanhood. Even Papa, the symbolic Anglo-Irish patriarch, has made his choice: Mummie will not re-inherit the Big House she signed over to her husband. Aroon will.

If Mummie were to retain power over Temple Alice, she would spend her time exerting it over her adult child. Aroon predicts that if 'we lived on at Temple Alice a ceiling cornice would fall or a dog would die; those would be the interests and tragedies to mark passing time. And as time passed there would be new devices invented and contrived for my restriction and humiliation' (237). Nicandra would also devote herself to shaping her environment and the people in it to her vision of suitable Big House living. Upon her return to Deer Forest, she tells herself 'occupation was to be her discipline and her religion now … irritation only became part of her new code of discipline… She found the rank discomfort very nearly agreeable' (209). Nicandra intends to 'be a good steward and put the house back as it ought to be' (210), but a single telephone call from her estranged husband undoes these plans (230–2). Mummie and Nicandra may as well be the ghosts of Ascendancies past: they will allow themselves to waste away within the Big House, unconcerned for their own survival. If left to Mummie and Nicandra, Big Houses would remain frozen (at times literally) relics from a former age and their occupants would sacrifice themselves to maintaining an outmoded code while their houses gradually moulder around them.

Like Aunt Tossie, Aroon inherits power alongside a financial bequeath, at Mummie's expense. Keane makes it clear that though Temple Alice originally belonged to Mummie, Papa's choice will stand and the household will live according to Aroon's code: '[e]mpowered by Papa's love I would be kind to them. Now I had the mild, wonderful power to be kind, or to reserve kindness. I looked at them with level, considerate eyes' she says (244). Her first exercise of that power, of course, is to order Rose to fetch the Tío Pepe – the good sherry – and her second order is the dinner menu, including the woodcock that 'Mummie couldn't bear' (236). Aroon evinces her power through food, that much contested terrain. She also shows signs of continuing to play the old game in her new location.

The move away from the Big House is an epochal shift nonetheless. Aroon and Tossie fight for their lives while they can and in ways that more rigid female characters cannot conceal. Lynch cautions that Aroon and Tossie's inherited power has its limits; '[i]f Ascendancy women wish to control their own lives, perhaps they need to direct these lives themselves rather than living out a reaction to those of their forebears'(84). Yet, Keane depicts these excrementally-oriented Big House daughters as controlling the lives of the servants who formerly served in their Big Houses. While he condemns Nicandra for her sexual misbehaviour, Silly Willy pledges complete devotion to Tossie; 'if even there was a mouse in the place I'd catch it in my teeth before I'd upset her,' he claims, knowing full well how likely this service will be, given Tossie's permissive attitude toward excremental abjection and threats that come from the outside world (229). Keane hints that Aroon will come to have the same type of relationship with Rose when she depicts Aroon transferring her attention towards Rose and away from Mummie's corpse. 'I can afford to be kind to Rose. She will learn to lean on me. There is nobody in the world who needs me now and I must be kind to somebody', Aroon tells herself (9). Aroon will shape Rose until she responds to Aroon the way Silly Willy does to Tossie. Aroon and Tossie are doomed to be the last of their family lines, yet they each forge new relationships that appear devoid of sexuality.

O'Brien may claim that Keane has overturned Anglo-Irish and Irish Catholic power relations as she 'offers us the abject Anglo-Irish wallowing in self-produced filth in their 'very nasty' Big Houses while the formerly abject Catholic looks on and proclaims, 'that's dirty,'' but I argue that there is a finer distinction to be made here (60). It is significant that Silly Willy, when reminding Nicandra of her sexual mistreatment of him, chooses not to involve Tossie. Willy will remain loyal to this woman for whom Nicandra's sexual life was 'a subject not forbidden so much as not existing' (12). Tossie and Aroon may have large appetites for food, drink, and the devotion of servants, but they do not have sexual appetites. These Big House daughters only survive because they displace their sexual desires. In Keane's novels, the Anglo-Irish Ascendancy finds a way to live on, but only in the fattened out memories of the fattened out daughters who exist palatably outside the traditional boundaries of the Big House.

Queering the Big House

Piggies and spoilers of girls: the representation of sexuality in the novels of Molly Keane

MARY BREEN*

When the Irish novel *Good Behaviour* was short-listed for the Booker Prize in 1981, few people had ever heard of its seventy-seven-year-old author, Molly Keane. Such a polished and sophisticated novel excited interest among a wide range of readers. Research found Molly Keane, a widow with two daughters, living quietly in the small, secluded village of Ardmore, in Co. Waterford. Keane had had a previous literary career, between 1926 and 1961, when her work had been published under the pseudonym of M.J. Farrell. During this period she had written eleven novels and six plays, of which, according to an interview with Polly Devlin, two 'were big successes, three ... weren't and one ... was a staggering failure'. (Introduction to *Conversation Piece* unpaginated). The sophisticated and black literary imagination displayed in *Good Behaviour* is clearly evident in all of the eleven early novels. This essay examines some of the main preoccupations of all of these novels, concentrating on two of the early ones, *Taking Chances* (1929) and *Devoted Ladies* (1934), and on her later masterpiece *Good Behaviour* (1981). Primarily I am interested in Keane's representation of sexuality.

Molly Keane was born Molly Skrine in Co. Kildare in 1904 and died in April 1996 (during the completion of this essay). Her family belonged to the privileged Anglo-Irish Ascendancy. She described them to Polly Devlin as 'a rather serious hunting and fishing, church-going family'(*CP* unpaginated). Her mother, Moira O'Neill, was a poet known as 'the poetess of the Glens', and she also did literary reviews for *Blackwoods* magazine; her best-known work *Songs of the Glens of Antrim* was published in 1900.[1] According to her daughter, she took very little interest in her children's lives, devoting her energies to writing; Keane remembered her childhood as one of neglect and isolation. She explained to Polly Devlin how she 'was always disliked as a child. My mother didn't really like me and the aunts were ghastly to me and my father had absolutely nothing to do with me'(*CP* unpaginated). Until she was fourteen years old she received no formal education, but suffered at the hands of a succession of governesses. At fourteen she was sent to 'a prim,

---

* An earlier version of this essay was first published in Eibhear Walshe (ed.), *Sex, Nation and Dissent* (1997). This reprint is courtesy of Cork University Press.
1 See John Quinn, *A portrait of the artist as a young girl* (1986). This collection of interviews with Irish women writers contains an interesting piece by Keane, pp 65–78.

suburban boarding school' in Bray, Co. Wicklow. She was desperately unhappy here and told Polly Devlin that:

> I might never have become a writer had it not been for the isolation in which I suffered as an unpopular schoolgirl. My unpopularity, that went to the edge of dislike, drove me into myself. I was walking among stars that had a different birth and I certainly learned the meaning of the black word 'Alone'. (*CP* unpaginated)

Keane tended to present herself as a philistine, describing her interests as a young woman as 'hunting and horses and having a good time' (*CP* unpaginated). She wrote her early novels under the pseudonym M.J. Farrell in order 'to hide my literary side from my sporting friends'(*CP* unpaginated). We may note that the neutral initials M.J. also hid the gender of the author. Although her family lived the elegant life of the Ascendancy, there was very little ready money, and Keane says that she began writing as a way of supplementing her dress allowance. It seems likely, however, that she used this rather frivolous reason as a blind to protect herself and her early writing from serious critical attention. A young woman who completes her first novel at seventeen and who goes on to write prolifically over the following years, and who was still writing novels in her eighties, is a serious novelist. In her interviews Keane presents a kind of depreciating self-parody, which reveals very little about her serious attitudes to her writing. Because of her unhappy childhood, she left home at the earliest opportunity and went to live with family friends, the Perry family of Woodruff House, Co. Tipperary. Here she met Bobby Keane, whom she later married, having first lived with him for six years, and John Perry, who worked with her on several of her successful stage plays in London. These details of Molly Keane's social and family background are important because the decaying Anglo-Irish Big House and its daily routine form the setting for all of her novels. Her experiences as a child and a young woman, in particular her relationship with her mother, and her isolated life as an unpopular schoolgirl clearly inform the imagination of the novelist. The settings of the novels are confined and detailed; her intimate knowledge of the way of life of the Anglo-Irish in their Big Houses in the early part of this century is deployed in minute detail. Selfish and emotionally manipulative mothers occur frequently in Keane's novels, as do isolated and unhappy daughter-figures. There is a concentrated focus on unattractive women who stand 'alone'. The settings of all of Keane's novels are very similar, and so too are the families who lounge elegantly in these exclusive settings. The decadence that Elaine Showalter associates with cultural decline is everywhere in Keane's representation of this social world (Showalter 3). Voracious, cruel and power-hungry mother-figures dominate many of these households unchecked by indolent, foxhunting, uninterested fathers. Like Charlotte Brontë's Mr Rochester, these men 'are hack-neyed in all the poor petty dissipations with which of the rich and worthless try to put on life' (Brontë 119). But, unlike Rochester, these characters are without critical self-awareness: They are presented as complacent and self-sat-isfied. Children struggle to maturity in this debilitating environment where the primary concern is 'good behaviour', in the drawing-room and in the hunt-ing-field. Unattractive, very often overweight, unmarried daughters flounder about in search of husbands, and when that fails, they fill their days with end-less small tasks, like washing dogs and arranging flowers, and in futilely giv-ing their love to those who don't want it.

Very little critical work has been done to date on Keane. In Ann Owens Weekes's 'Seeking a Tradition: Irish Women's Fiction' she discusses *Good Behaviour*, a novel she sees as 'a needed corrective, a widening, of Bowen's pic-ture' and 'a satirical glance down fifty years to the last September of Anglo-Ireland' (*Irish Women Writers: An Uncharted Tradition*, 22). In *The Irish Novel* James Cahalan is much more dismissive of her work: 'At worst, her fiction seems a lighter rehash of the fading Ascendancy world explored by Bowen' (207). My argument will be that Cahalan's criticism fails to observe the critical difference between Bowen's Irish novels and Keane's: although both deal with the Ascendancy world, Bowen's novels are realist, while Keane's are satire or black farce. Rather than seeking to produce a 'rehash' of Bowen, Keane approaches her subject from a totally different imaginative perspective, and her writing can more successfully be compared to certain elements in the work of Maria Edgeworth, particularly to *Castle Rackrent,* than to Bowen's *The Last September*, which Cahalan seems to have in mind. Cahalan does concede, however, that 'at her best Keane explores the sexual conflicts of Ascendancy women with a bold-ness not found in Bowen'(208). It is this 'boldness', which Cahalan does not further define, that marks Molly Keane's work and may, as I shall suggest, draw readers nurtured on the absurd of the 'Theatre of Cruelty'. There are also some interesting essays on Keane in collected works on women novelists.[2]

Tamsin Hargreaves, in 'Women's Consciousness and Identity in Four Irish Women Novelists', observes that 'no one in Keane's fictional world is

2 Tamsin Hargreaves, 'Women's consciousness and identity in four Irish women novelists' in Michael Kenneally (ed.), *Cultural contexts and literary idioms in contemporary Irish literature* (1988), 279. See also Katherine Lilly Gibbs, 'An introduction to the fiction of Molly Keane'; Clare Boylan, 'Sex, snobbery and the strategies of Molly Keane' in Robert E. Hosmer (ed.), *Contemporary British women writers: narrative strategies*; Rudiger Imhof, 'Molly Keane, *Good Behaviour, Time after Time* and *Loving and Giving*: a collection of interpretations' in Otto Rauchbauer (ed.), *Ancestral voices: the Big House in Anglo-Irish literature* (1992); Bridget O'Toole 'Three writers of the Big House: Elizabeth Bowen, Molly Keane and Jennifer Johnston: essays in honour of John Hewitt', in Gerald Dawe and Enda Longley (eds), *Across a roaring hill: the Protestant imagination in modern Ireland* (1985).

capable of love' (279). For Hargreaves, 'Keane offers a deeply ironic, witty and painful critique of alienated being' (279). The Virago editions of the M.J. Farrell novels all have substantial introductions, which supply some information about Keane's background but not much discussion of the novels themselves. Keane herself wrote the introduction to her first novel, *The Knight of Cheerful Countenance*, in 1993, almost seventy years after its first publication. In this she sketched in the lifestyle of the Ascendancy, in a situation where 'the world of my youth has vanished' (5). *Conversation Piece*, which was reissued in 1991, has an interview with the author by Polly Devlin, who also wrote introductions to five of the other novels. *Taking Chances*, one of the novels focused on in this essay, has an introduction by Clare Boylan. *Treasure Hunt*, which is dedicated to John Perry, is introduced by Dirk Bogarde, who remembers seeing the successful play of the same name which preceded the novel and which ran successfully for a year in 1949. Bogarde recalls that the tired post-war British audience 'welcomed it with roars of delight' (unpaginated). The cast included Sybil Thorndike, Irene Brown, Alan Webb and Milo O'Shea. In 1987 Russell Harty wrote a brief and self-deprecating introduction to *Loving without Tears*, which contains one of Keane's most bitter satires on motherhood. Harty's introduction is not concerned with the novel itself, but with his friendship with Keane and this forms the major subject of the preface. He does, however, give warning, however inadequately, of a certain bitterness, indeed, a certain cynicism in the novel. Caroline Blackwood, in her perceptive 1986 afterword to *Full House*, points out the profoundly philistine nature of Keane's Anglo-Irish society, where books and reading are looked on with contempt. She notes too Keane's representation of a stagnant world where love affairs are like games that are played to break the monotony, cruel games where nobody wins, and the 'unkind' mothers who create emotional devastation (320).

The most difficult task when discussing Keane is to find a genre into which she can fit comfortably; in fact it is easier to decide the genres to which she does not belong. Although her novels have been described as Big House novels, in my view, they refuse to be so classified. The settings are those of the Big House, but her concerns, as I shall show, are not those of the conventional Big House novel of Anglo-Irish literary tradition. Although there is a wealth of realistic detail, the fictional form she adopts is not exactly realist: there is no moral critique in Keane, no controlling irony. Neither are her novels romances, although a superficial reading might presume them to be so, and Keane herself certainly thought about her early novels in this way. Keane does not romanticise her world or treat it nostalgically, she ruthlessly satirises it; her Big Houses are not the centres of dignity that Yeats presents in *Ancestral Houses*. Her novels belong, I believe, to the Irish comic tradition, the tradition of Swift and the Maria Edgeworth of *Castle Rackrent*. In Vivian

Mercier's definition, Keane would appear to belong among these satirists. Mercier defines satire in the context of Irish tradition as employing 'wit, humour, parody, and even word-play besides the irony which is often regarded as its most characteristic device' (184). Mercier also discusses the motives for satire, of which in his view the most spurious are those whose 'ultimate aim is to inflate their authors rather than to deflate the foolish and the evil' (184). The more laudable motives are those which, 'though mixed, include selfless indignation and a desire for abstract justice' (184). Keane's childhood experiences of Anglo-Irish life – the lack of emotional and imaginative nourishment, the total philistinism of her world – gave her every reason to feel 'indignation' and every right to seek 'abstract justice'. Keane chose her subject and her form well; as Mercier points out, 'Satire demands a spice of danger; it cannot be achieved by denouncing the weak and impoverished' (184) Keane satirises the world of the privileged Anglo-Irish, her own world. The idle, pleasure-seeking lifestyles of the decadent Anglo-Irish were a worthy subject. Like Swift and Edgeworth in their time, Keane belonged to this world herself and, except for her childhood, seemed in real life to have been a contented member of it. Nevertheless, satire does not condone or accept; it condemns what it represents. Presumably in order to protect herself and her life in her milieu, Keane wisely used a pseudonym, not simply because her 'set' frowned on literary pretensions, including even reading, but also because all her characters and settings, as she admits, are drawn from life.

In all of her novels, with the exception of *Good Behaviour* which has a first-person narrator, Keane uses omniscient narrators. The action is frequently focalised through a central character, whose view seems to closely mirror that of the narrator. Her narrators appear more as voyeurs than as the judging, ironic narrators of classic realism. Classic examples of unreliable narration, they are intensely interested and usually deeply implicated in the ugly but compelling sexual power-struggles that are enacted between the characters. There are no good or sympathetic characters in Keane, no idealised figures for the reader to identify with. Neither is there a central ground of moral rightness; indeed, there are no generalising or explicit judgements, and the narrators do not direct or guide us. Keane might even be seen as parodying realist fictional form, for although she often ends her novels with marriage, these are never happy endings. These challenges to realism and moralising satire make Keane an intensely interesting and disconcerting novelist, and they also complicate and qualify any interpretation of her representation of sexuality.

The rest of this discussion explores her satiric depiction of heterosexual, gay and lesbian relationships and her recurrent unsympathetic representation of sexually undesirable women. Her novels are concerned with two groups of people: those who are involved in sexual relationships and those who remain outside. The central relationship in *Devoted Ladies* is a lesbian one; in *Good Behaviour* the narrative focus is on the homosexual relationship between two young men; and in *Taking Chances*, the novel is dominated by the heterosexual attraction between a young man and woman. In all three novels there are unwanted women who are marginalised by the central sexual relationship, which excludes them. Keane is unusual in presenting gay and lesbian desire as an integral part of a complex range of sexual possibilities. This might be seen as an advance on Victorian and Edwardian repression of the very existence of such desire. But although Keane makes alternative sexualities visible, she also circumscribes them very decisively. In her influential essay 'Compulsory Heterosexuality and Lesbian Existence' Adrienne Rich argues: 'Any theory of cultural/political creation that treats lesbian existence as a marginal or less "natural" phenomena, as mere "sexual preference", or as the mirror image of heterosexual of male homosexual relations is profoundly weakened thereby, whatever its other contributions'. (63)

Keane does not marginalise lesbian existence; in fact in *Devoted Ladies* she centralises it. But she does present it as a 'mirror image' of heterosexual relationships. Rich goes on to argue in the same essay that it is not enough merely to tolerate lesbianism, 'Feminist theory can no longer afford merely to voice a toleration of "lesbianism" as an "alternative life-style", or make token allusion to lesbians. A feminist critique of compulsory heterosexual orientation for women is long overdue' (63).

Keane does not, of course, construct the kind of critique that Rich has in mind here, but she does, however negatively, treat lesbian existence as a legitimate subject. In this study I have grouped heterosexual, gay and lesbian relationships together because Keane does not present gay and lesbian relationships as marginal or apart. They are, in fact, an interwoven part of a complex series of interpersonal relationships depicted against a background of decaying Ascendancy life. This is not to suggest that gay and lesbian relationships are presented as enabling in Keane's novels; they are seen as imprisoning and debilitating, but no more so than the heterosexual relationships her characters are involved in. I shall argue that these heterosexual, gay and lesbian relationships are strikingly similar because the same heterosexual trope of desire is used throughout. In accordance with this, masculine desire is presented as strong and active, and feminine desire as passive and submissive; in all her same-sex relationships, traditional masculine and feminine roles are adopted. E.A. Kaplan argues that:

> As long as the structures of sexual attraction are locked into defining
> the masculine as dominance – cold, driving, ambitious and manipu-
> lating – and the female as the submissive – kindness, humaneness, moth-
> erliness – the fact that some women are allowed to step into the mas-

culine role leaves the structure intact: the gaze is not male but masculine and phallocentrism remains. (43)

Paradoxically, in Keane's representation of heterosexual desire in *Taking Chances* she constructs her female subject, ironically called Mary, as sexually active and desiring, thus questioning her traditional active / passive dichotomy between the male and the female. Yet, her homosexual and lesbian protagonists seem to remain imprisoned in a predetermined heterosexual trope of desire.

Keane's novels concentrate intensely on sexual desire, which is presented as the cornerstone of identity, and on its consequences. Desire is represented as a destructive force in the lives of her characters, dividing those characters into two distinct groups: 'they who have power to hurt', and those who, lacking this power, are hurt. If identity is dominated by sexuality, then those who are not considered sexually attractive, to either sex, have no recognisable value. In Keane's novels it is significant that only women are sexually unattractive; her male characters never fall into this category. Sexually unattractive women must search elsewhere for status and power in a society whose value system is so narrowly constructed. Unattached women abound in Keane's fiction; they are the marginal others in a society obsessed with sexuality and sexual gratification. This focus on the ability to marry (or mate) is not, of course, new or peculiar to Keane. The characters in Jane Austen's novels display a kind of spinster-baiting, similar to that in Keane, and Austen's marriage-obsessed society views unmarried women as an aberration and a horror to be avoided; a typical example is Miss Bates in *Emma*. In Austen's novel, however, Emma is criticised by Mr Knightley, the perfect gentleman and the voice of correct behaviour, for her treatment of Miss Bates, while in Keane the novels themselves cruelly lampoon these women and no corrective or consolatory moment is ever staged.

It is worth noting that while, as I have said, same-sex desire is presented in Keane's novels as frequently, or almost as frequently, as heterosexual desire, the undesirable single woman is perceived as the true aberration, the freak of nature. In Keane it is sexual desirability which is essential for the successful formation of identity. The society that Austen critiques in her novels sees marital status as the chief source of female identity, whereas Austen presents marriage as a prize awarded for moral self-knowledge, rationality and self-control. This draws a clear distinction between Austen and the world whose values she critiques. This distinction, as I have suggested, is not so clear in Keane. Without the moral guidance of the narrator, it is the implied reader who judges.

Good Behaviour traces the decline of an Anglo-Irish family, the St Charles of Temple Alice. The novel has a first-person narrator, the only daughter of

the house, Aroon St Charles. Aroon is obese, unattractive and desperately willing to please; she is naïve and sexually ignorant, and constantly presents facts
in order to show herself in a favourable light. By constructing Aroon as an
unreliable narrator, Keane ruthlessly exposes her lies and pretensions and the
ridiculous façade behind which she hides her manipulative and jealous nature.
Aroon's fake exterior is a paradigm of her world, where every economic and
political reality is ignored or manipulated to buttress a decadent and diseased
way of life. One of the great ironies of this novel is that this sexually naïve narrator presents a story which is dominated by the sexual exploits of its other
central characters. Aroon's father, a major in the British army, conducts affairs
with almost all the female characters in the novel, and several others whom we
never meet, while remaining securely married to Aroon's mother. Major St
Charles's sexual desire is presented as active and demanding, although it is hidden by a deceptively helpless charm, while the women he seduces are passive
and accepting, some to the point of self-annihilation. Mrs Brock, the children's
governess, commits suicide when she discovers that she is pregnant and the
Major has ended their affair. Nod and Blink Crowherst have to leave their
home and go to England when Blink too becomes pregnant by the Major. She
desperately, but unsuccessfully, attempts abortion by means of hot baths and
bottles of gin. But the Major's sexual exploits merely form the backdrop for
the central sexual relationship in the novel: the homosexual relationship between
Aroon's brother Hubert and his sophisticated friend from Oxford, Richard
Massingham. *Good Behaviour* is a retrospective novel in which Aroon, in an
attempt to understand her life, looks back from her bleak middle-aged spin-
sterhood to her childhood and adolescence. Her story is one of loneliness and
isolation, except for the middle section of the novel which deals with the glorious few weeks that Hubert and Richard spend in Temple Alice. Aroon
describes lovingly and with minute attention to detail, but little understanding,
the relationship that develops between her brother Hubert, his friend Richard
and herself. The young men are physically beautiful and seemingly totally at
ease with their sexuality, although unwilling to disclose it in public, being well
aware of the punishment meted out to those who step outside accepted male
homosocial behaviour:

> There was a quick, hard grace about their movements, in the way they
> put links quickly into the cuffs of evening shirts, such a different tempo
> from a girl's considered gesture. They wore narrow red braces and
> their black trousers were taut round waist and bottoms. (90)

The gaze here is female; although Aroon presents herself as naïve, passages like this reveal her consciousness of active sexual desire or longing. The
boys bring an extra glamour to Temple Alice; their days are idle, they drink

gin and lemon in their room before dinner, and dance languidly with Aroon in the drawing-room in the evening. Their relationship is exciting, even dangerous; there is a constant power struggle between them, and a threat of infidelity. Despite the homoerotic nature of their relationship, however, their roles are allotted in a conventional way. Richard is aggressive and predatory in his desire – 'masculine' – while Hubert is passive and malleable – 'feminine'. As a representation of gay desire, this limits the relationship, trapping it in a set of predetermined oppositions which are the traditional hallmarks of heterosexual relationships. An air of exclusiveness surrounds Hubert and Richard even when they are doing something as prosaic as taking fleas from a dog:

> Hubert was sitting, a dog on his knees, below the Negro's shaded lamp. The light on his bent head shone his hair to blue-black, and the forward turn of his neck, between hair and white shirt collar, was as dark a brown as his hands on the white dog. Richard standing behind the tall wing chair, stooped his extraordinary height over Hubert and the little dog. His eyes, when he raised his head towards us, held a look of anger and loss as if he suffered some unkind deprivation – something quite serious, like getting left in a hunt. (97)

But even this subtly lit cameo of the two young men groups them in a standard Edwardian pose of the happily married couple. The 'wife' sits passively on a chair, head bent, while the 'husband' leans devotedly and possessively over her. The mystery and glamour that surrounds them even affects the old house. Temple Alice, although large and imposing, is a cold comfortless house, full of ugly furniture; it has a leaking roof, hard beds and soft, cold bath water. But when Richard and Hubert come to stay, the old house is transformed by their presence and the excitement that surrounds them:

> But in this eternal August the place took on a sumptuous quality. Every day the lean deprived face of the house blazed out in the sunlight. Sun poured onto the damp-stained wallpaper, through the long windows. It shone on us from when we woke until we changed for dinner. (89)

Despite their careless and arrogant attitude to life, the boys are vulnerable to the social threat of homophobia. As Eve Kosofsky Sedgwick says, 'For a man to be a man's man is separated only by an invisible, carefully blurred always already-crossed line from being interested in men' (89). In order to protect themselves from being thought 'interested' in each other, Hubert and Richard involve Aroon in their cruel games of deception. Aroon is a willing accomplice, but this does not excuse the arrogance of the boy's behaviour.

In those last days the boys kept me with them continually. Each day
of early September was more perfect than the last. Grapes were ripe
in the battered vinery – those muscatels Mummie knew how to thin
and prune. Butterflies – fritillaries, peacocks – spread their wings on
scabious, sedum, and buddelia, waiting heavily, happily for death to
come. We sat among them, eating grapes, the sun on our backs. (99)

In this passage Aroon captures imaginatively the fleeting nature of the boys'
relationship: for a short but glorious time, like the butterflies, they are happy,
but the inevitable conclusion of this intensity must be death. Driving back
through England on the way to Cambridge, Hubert is killed in a car crash.
Keane here makes the direct connection between same-sex desire and death
– the standard ideological response to 'perversion'.[3] In Keane this fate awaits
not only the 'pervert', but many of her female heterosexual characters who
love too much. Mrs Brock is an example of this, as is the central female character, Maeve, in *Loving and Giving*.

Because of her marginality as one of Keane's unwanted women, Aroon
finds in her relationship with Richard and Hubert an opportunity to develop
a sense of herself as a sexually desirable being. From this she forges a sense
of identity which is as false as Richard's pretended desire for her, upon which
it is based, and which lasts throughout her life despite the fact that Richard
never returns to Temple Alice. As Aroon tells us, she 'knows how to build
the truth' (142). But this meagre proof of herself is not enough to sustain her,
for despite her ability to transform in fantasy the smallest display of interest
shown in her by Richard into a consuming desire, Aroon still has to find an
expression for her own sexuality. In the event, she displaces her own sexual
desire into an obsession with food and its consumption. Food becomes a source
of power and control. As we learn in the opening chapter, she eventually uses
it to kill her mother and then asks for the same dish to be kept warm for her
own luncheon. Keane suggests that those who never find a way to express
their sexual desire end up as cruel and destructive self-deceivers. As a large
and sexually unattractive girl, totally lacking in self-confidence, Aroon strives
to attract attention to herself by other means. When she first meets Hubert's
friend Richard, the only way she can think of to make the boys take notice of
her is to eat enormous quantities of food at dinner. The boys do notice, and
are amused by her. These gastronomic feats earn her the nickname Pig.
Aroon's relationship to food is a complex one; it at once empowers and enslaves
her. It provides solace in an otherwise lonely life, but it is also fraught with
anxiety. When Aroon's father dies and she thinks that her mother will inherit

---

3 For a discussion of this topic see Jonathan Dollimore, *Sexual dissidence: Augustine to Wilde,
Freud to Foucault* (1991).

everything, she is agonised by the fear that her mother will ration her food. By the end of the novel Aroon is a lonely and isolated figure possessed by a strong desire to justify herself, but she is also free and independent. That desire to speak about her life which motivates the narrative is a product of this newly found independence. Aroon is not liberated by weight loss, or by suddenly becoming sexually attractive, or by an offer of marriage or of love, but by the fact that her father has left the estate to her. From being the undesirable daughter, she becomes the head of the family. She directs their affairs and takes charge of her now elderly mother and at last attains what she always wanted: the power to exercise complete control over other people's lives. She gets what Sara Sceats calls 'revenge-by-looking-after' (121). All of Keane's unwanted women seek continually to be included, to be part of a relationship; but all experience moments of dreadful clarity when their isolated and unwanted state is brought home to them with appalling finality. Aroon, who has thought of Hubert, Richard and herself as a 'trinity' (101), is brought to the full realisation of the exclusiveness of the boys' relationship and her own marginality when she overhears them laughing at her:

> I stood outside the door with the dreadful glass in my hand. Inside the room I heard them begin to laugh, relieved giggling laughter, and when they supposed I had gone, shouts of laughter followed me – laughter that expressed their relief from some tension and left me an outsider. Puzzled and anxious I sat in my bedroom, sipping at the disgustingly powerful gin without gaining from it any lift or exuberance. I waited for the minutes to pass, minutes that I had so carelessly expected to spend in their company. Soon the gin overcame the pain, but not my mistrust, or certainty in happiness. (96)

The moment of clarity when Aroon, the unwanted single women, vividly sees her exclusion is a recurrent motif in Keane. In *Devoted Ladies* and *Taking Chances* the unwanted women, Piggy and Maeve, have similar epiphanies.

Devoted Ladies was published in 1934. In the opening chapters the action takes place in London, in a world of chic parties, beautiful flats, Bohemian lifestyles and talk of literature and art. But the action very soon returns to the familiar setting of an elegant but decaying Big House in rural Ireland, where life centres on horses and hounds, fishing and shooting. The central relationship in this novel is a lesbian one. In the introduction to the Virago reprint of the novel, Keane has explained to Polly Devlin why she chose this as a subject:

> I suppose I was rather curious and shocked by coming upon all that. Before then no one thought anything of two elderly ladies setting up

house together. I'd certainly never heard a murmur. I was excited by
finding out about lesbians and homosexuals. It was new. It made a
subject. My interest went in spasms, there would be a sudden arousal
of interest that took over, something new – like this – that would be
the start of a new book. (iv)

From this rather innocent statement it would seem that Keane did not
have a particular agenda when she began to write *Devoted Ladies;* lesbianism
was simply a new subject. Belying this casualness, however, the narrative itself
displays an intense, almost voyeuristic, interest in the relationship between
the two women. Although the novel has an omniscient narrator, its action is
frequently focalised through Sylvester, an Anglo-Irishman who has a successful career as a writer. He lives mainly in London, but retreats to Ireland
to write. There he stays with his two unmarried cousins Piggy and Hester.
The action of the novel traces the complicated relationships that develop
between a group of ill-assorted people who come to stay with them. We see
much of the action through Sylvester's eyes; he is observant, distant, and at
times intensely cruel and manipulative. His main interest is in Jessica and
Jane, the lesbian couple. He is fascinated by the cruelty of their relationship;
when Jane falls in love with a friend of his, George Playfair, he abandons his
status as an observer and strives to help Jane escape from Jessica.

In this discussion I will draw on Adrienne Rich's analysis of the use of
the word 'lesbian':

> I have chosen to use the term lesbian existence and lesbian contin-
> uum because the word lesbian has a clinical and limiting ring. Lesbian
> existence suggests both the fact of the historical existence of lesbians
> and our continuing creation of the meaning of that existence. I mean
> the term lesbian continuum to include a range – through each
> woman's life and throughout history – of woman-identified experi-
> ence: not simply the fact that a woman has had a consciously desired
> genital sexual experience with another woman. (80)

Considering Keane's representation of woman-identified experience and
using Rich's concept of a 'lesbian continuum', we find in this novel two relationships between women which could occupy positions almost at either end
of such a range: one between Jessica and Jane, which is genital/sexual, and
the other between Piggy and Joan, which is apparently non-sexual. I shall
argue that these two, seemingly very different, relationships have startlingly
similar elements. Jessica and Jane's lesbian existence and Joan and Piggy's
female friendship parallel each other throughout the second half of the novel.
Keane satirises the butch/femme roles that Jessica and Jane adopt by exag-

gerating them into grotesque figures of fun. Jessica is strong and assertive, and she has a violent temper which she relieves by chewing on the side of the bath until her teeth bleed or by deliberately cutting herself. Her physical appearance is a ridiculous contradiction between her feminine body shape and her desire to appear 'masculine':

> Jessica's dark hair was cut with charming severity. If her dark face had been less heavy and turbulent in expression Jessica would almost have succeeded in looking as hard and boyish as she hoped she looked. But this plan of hers had been spoilt by God in the beginning, for he had given her a positive bosom and massive thighs. She was a heavy-minded woman too, without much gaiety of spirit. It was typical of her to break chains and bite baths in moments of stress, so did she grind her teeth into life and with as little satisfaction to herself. (42)

Jane, by contrast, is slight, fair and pretty, except for the scar of her hare-lip, and exaggeratedly feminine and helpless. From the beginning of the novel their relationship is described in sado-masochistic terms. Jane, alcoholic and helpless, is in constant fear that Jessica will kill her. This is not simply a pose, although Jane adopts many poses. When at a party at Sylvester's Jessica sees Jane lying on a sofa talking to George Playfair, she is consumed with rage:

> 'I can't bear to see her like that', Jessica went on, 'half asleep – half drunk. It disgusts me. Why, I'd rather see her dead, I think'. And with this she picked up a bottle of tonic water and made menancing gestures with it across the room at Jane.
> Jane had just time to scream: 'Now, Jessica, don't throw that bottle at me' – when Sylvester saw the crash of broken glass and heard Jane scream: 'Oh – you're horrible to me,' as she bowed her bleeding head upon his divan. (16–7)

This is followed by a reconciliation between the women that makes Sylvester feel:

> slightly sick, partly from the sight of Jane's nasty blood and partly from his understanding of that fierce instinct to cherish that Jessica – drunken, pallid and tender – displayed now as she sponged Jane's head with his favourite sponge; dreadfully protective where five minutes ago she had been to all intents and purposes a murderess. Jane … her crooked mouth a little open and her whole attitude as drained of emotion as that of any woman at the conclusion of a blood quarrel with her mate. It was unbearable. (18)

Frank O'Connor, lamenting the lack of a good modern Irish satirist, complained: 'None of us could ever fashion a story or play into a stiletto to run
into the vitals of some pompous ass' (quoted in Mercer 182). Keane seems to
have mastered the technique; in this passage she manages to satirise not only
the two women but her narcissistic camp observer Sylvester as well. But she
does not reserve her ironic presentation for her lesbian and camp characters;
her straight characters receive similar treatment. Although Jane protests, with
good reason, that she is afraid of Jessica, she is also intensely aware that
Jessica's strength gives her a sense of vitality: 'Now Jessica – although she is
horrible to me – she's a real live woman' (19).

The appropriately named George Playfair, a charming but boring man,
is to be Jane's rescuer. The relationship between Jane, Jessica and George
develops into a bitter contest. Jane sees George as a means of escape from the
exciting but deadly grip of Jessica. The narrator constantly reminds us that
it is Jane's weakness that ties her to Jessica: 'Jane was easily defeated in any
emotional contest. All her opponent's points of view became instantly and
agonisingly her own' (200). This relationship, which is held together by
Jesscia's strength and Jane's weakness, is mirrored in the other important
woman-centred relationship in the novel: the friendship between Joan and
Piggy. Piggy is totally subservient to Joan; she allows herself to be abused and
used and still remains devoted and loyal. Piggy, as her name suggests, is fat
and unlovable, while Joan is beautiful and happily married. Throughout most
of the novel we see Piggy through Sylvester's eyes. He despises her and
searches constantly for ways to humiliate her, as do most of the characters in
the novel. Jessica describes her as a 'fidgety, over-sexed woman' (201).

As her relationship with George develops, Jane becomes obsessed with
escape. She learns very quickly that the life she and Jessica and their gay valet
Albert live in London will not be acceptable in Ireland. When Albert begins
to behave secretively, Jane is appalled:

> He can't have an affair here. His affairs belong to another life where they
> were faintly amusing and anyhow did not matter … Here she would not
> have such rudeness. No, she would deny it all, all. This life and that
> were a world apart; one could escape, surely one could escape. (257)

In Keane it would seem that Ireland is represented as narrower and more
prescriptive than England. Yet, ironically, Jane wants to escape from England
to Ireland. The ambiguity in Keane's writing is evident here, as it is extremely
difficult to decide which place the novel approves of; again, the lack of a moral
judgement leaves the reader puzzled.

The two woman-centred relationships in *Devoted Ladies* are destroyed in
order for the heterosexual relationship between George and Jane to survive.

But this 'happy' ending is weakened by the way in which Keane represents the love between George and Jane:

> The stupidity and tenderness of such love as George's encompassed Jane entirely ... She was enthralled and held away from herself. She was the Jane he thought her to be. She would forever protect him from the Jane she was. (264)

This extremely cynical statement, which for once is unfocalised through character and seems to be the voice of the narrator, is another good example of the radical denial of moral statement in Keane.

Devoted Ladies ends with a resounding climax, suitably at the end of a bloody and successful day's foxhunting. Piggy and Jessica, the two unwanted women, are excluded from the hunt: when they arrive, the others want nothing to do with them:

> Jane, George and Joan and Sylvester, all so quiet and aloof after their morning's endeavour, belong to the moment and to each other, not to any outsiders. Certainly not to Piggy and Jessica. With Piggy and Jessica they were in no accord. (279)

Jessica, the outsider, comes 'Obviously screaming for her lovely' (280). She is consumed with a desire to punish: 'She would require no more of Jane after she had destroyed her. She only required her destruction' (281). The scene that takes place between the two women shows Jessica's power and cruelty and Jane's helplessness. Jane knows that George will not want her if Jessica tells him about her past. In order to love George and be loved by him Jane cannot be herself. As Jessica remarks:

> I just can't stand aside and see you make such an absurd sentimental mess of your life. Of course, if this man should have enough vision to want you when he has some idea of the real you, then I have nothing to say. (291)

This disturbs the seemingly happy resolution of the novel. If Jane can only truly be herself with Jessica, then that, no matter how difficult, must be preferable to playing a part. (This is an implied reader's comment, because the narrator makes no judgements about the matter.) Yet this is complicated by the fact that Keane constantly shows Jane as playing at life; she is presented as a woman without ideas, as a hollow shell that must be defined by a stronger character. In her relationship with Jessica she found a way to think; Jessica's ideas 'fitted well into the hollow place in her mind where her opinion might, had she owned such a thing, have belonged' (200–1). The motif of exclusion used in *Good Behaviour* is even more frequently used in *Devoted Ladies*. Piggy is constantly aware of her own marginality:

> And Piggy stood beside them. Alone, burningly alone, terribly apart and unwanted. This was typical of so many moments in Piggy's life, sickening, frightening moments in which she was impotent and alone. (193)

– and again:

> Piggy endured one of those terrible poisoning moments when she knew herself to be outside love forever. Blindly aware that this thing was never for her. (170)

In Keane, exclusion from love is the only marginality to be feared. To be in a relationship, no matter how cruel, is to be whole; to be outside is to be 'impotent' and 'terribly apart and unwanted'. When Joan insults Piggy, beyond even her capacity to forgive, she turns to George and finds in his kindness a new location for her loving and giving: 'Every desire that Piggy had was sublimated into a single wish to serve.' It is this desire to serve George that drives Piggy to kill Jessica:

> Piggy did not think. She only felt and knew. Her blind gift of serving where she loved cast out all fear. She put her foot down on the accelerator and the car leapt forward and dropped. (303)

In one violent impulse Piggy kills Jessica and herself. This emphasises the capacity for destruction that characterises Keane's unwanted women, Piggy and Aroon.

In *Taking Chances* (1929) Keane's focus is on heterosexual love and its all-consuming power. She uses a familiar plot structure and setting. Sir Ralph, Maeve and Jer live in their elegant Big House, Sorristown. Maeve is engaged to Rowley, the handsomest man in the county. Jer's beautiful friend Mary arrives from London to be Maeve's bridesmaid, and the quiet contented lives of these young Irish people are shattered. Popular understanding of sexual relationships between men and women has been largely informed by Freud and Lacan, who have not essentially dispelled the time-honoured notion that women are 'naturally' passive and men 'naturally' active in sex. Women are seen as having no sexual autonomy. In almost all her novels Keane too fails to challenge this essentialist view of women's sexual desire as passive. We have seen in *Devoted Ladies* how Jane the 'feminine' partner in the lesbian relationship is without sexual autonomy. Even in her new relationship with George she remains passive; her escape from Jessica is orchestrated by others. In *Good Behaviour*, where the homosexual lovers replicate the conventional heterosexual pattern, Hubert, in his relationship with Richard, is weak and submissive. In *Taking Chances*, however, Keane constructs a woman, ironically called Mary, with an active sexual will. She is charming and selfish, cruel and destructive, and almost all the men in the novel are in love with her. Instantly attracted to Rowley, she actively pursues him, and very shortly after Rowley's marriage to Maeve they run away together. Maeve is virtuous and honest but sexually naïve. Keane, as Boylan points out in her introduction to the novel, 'manages to make virginity seem a kind of short-sightedness which turns marriage into Blind Man's Buff' (xiii).

> Soon – in a few hours – they would be together for always, and each day would be a day to love each other more. And the nights. But Maeve's nice thoughts stopped short there in a mysterious, hallowed glow. (122–3)

Keane has no patience with sexual naïveté or passivity. She pillories Aroon and Maeve for their blindness to sex and power. The relationship between Rowley and Maeve is presented using the conventional binary opposition of masculine and feminine. Rowley, thinking of Maeve, 'was not too disturbed by the most negative acquiescence which was all he knew of her love for him' (16). Maeve loses Rowley because of her passivity, and Mary wins because of her clearly displayed active sexual will. The virtuous Maeve, who should be the heroine, but whose suffering is dismissed in the novel – she has only 'the vitriolic, futile importance of a slighted woman'(271) – voices her opinion and condemnation of Mary:

> Girls who have no respect for their slack, lustful bodies, who love and demand and take other women's dear mates; who never stop for fear or for favour; for whom ostracism is not punishment, but an amusement which they faintly deride. (235)

This may be Maeve's opinion of Mary, but how does the narrator view her? As always in Keane, any judgement of her characters is omitted or, as in this case, judgement is pronounced by the other, equally unreliable, characters. Above we have Maeve's judgement of Mary, but counterbalancing this is Jer's opinion. At many of the important moments in the novel the narrative is focalised through Jer; in love with Mary himself, he judges her with kindness and tolerance. But Jer, while morally more creditable, has proved himself unreliable as a reader of character many times in the novel. We are left, therefore, oscillating between many different moral perspectives, several of which seem to be irreconcilable.

Keane's novels are concerned with sex and power and with how the intimate connection between them influences the lives of her characters. For the purposes of her novels, she is evidently not interested in creating regulatory sexual categories, central or marginal. She is interested in how sexual attraction between people of opposite or the same sex works. Nevertheless, her representation of same-sex desire, although glamorous and exciting, is problematic. Both the lesbian relationship in *Devoted Ladies* and the gay relationship in *Good Behaviour* end in death. The only relationship which is based on mutual subjectivities is the illicit heterosexual one between Rowley and Mary in *Taking Chances*. As I have stressed throughout this essay, there are no clear moral judgements in her novels, which makes it difficult to come to any clear conclusions about her representation of sexuality. She is, however, an important figure in any consideration of the homoerotic in Irish writing, because in her fictional world lesbian and gay characters learn to suffer equally with their straight counterparts under the tyranny of love.

'Now the day is over': bourgeois education, effeminacy and the fall of Temple Alice

EIBHEAR WALSHE*

> Molly Keane's great achievement as a novelist was to reject the nostalgia that is a major cultural production of a declining imperial state ... Molly Keane's last three novels, however, insistently reject the formulations of a lost organic cultural tradition and ruthlessly expose the fictitiousness of personal memory.
>
> Vera Kreilkamp (1998, 174)

> 'Now the Day is Over' ... the hymn I had chosen for Hubert's funeral. Mrs Brock's hymn ...
>
> (*Good Behaviour* 131)

Cool ruthlessness, an antipathy towards nostalgia, and a clear-eyed exposition of the 'fictitiousness of personal memory' are Molly Keane's strongest characteristics as a Big House novelist, and these characteristics are most evident in her 1981 novel, *Good Behaviour*. In this essay I want to suggest that Keane's fictive writings, both as M.J. Farrell and latterly under her own name, overturn the dominant literary and cultural tropes of previous Ascendancy novels, particularly in her depiction of bourgeois education and a consequent destabilising 'effeminacy' for the heirs to the Irish Big House. *Good Behaviour* is her swan song for the Ascendancy novel, a novel of termination where the narrative begins with the end of the Big House, Temple Alice, voluntarily abandoned by the childless Aroon St Charles, the last of her family. Writing in her late seventies, Keane is marking out a kind of imaginative closure for her class and for the literary genre produced by them but this is a closure without any sense of lyricism or elegiac regret. Now that the day of the Irish Big House is over, Keane suggests that collapse and final annihilation was self-fulfilling, that the Anglo-Irish Raj fell because it was a cruel, emotionally redundant world and that its day is properly over.

*An earlier version of this essay appears in the proceedings of the Spanish Association of Irish Studies, edited by Patricia Traynor and published by the University of Malaga, 2005.

Keane's starkness as authorial presence and as practitioner of the genre of the Ascendancy novel cannot simply be accounted for by the fact that she was writing towards the end of the twentieth century. Other contemporary Irish novelists like William Trevor and Jennifer Johnson still locate a kind of distinguished pathos in the fall of the Big House and a graceful (if limited) future in Ireland. Keane's writing is the nail in the coffin for the Anglo-Irish Big House, and by, implication, for the literary form of the Big House novel. What sets Keane apart from other late twentieth-century Irish writers within this literary genre is that she ends the Big House tradition from within, imploding the fictive world of the novel by undermining the notions of family, of heterosexual identity, of all the modes of education, of Ascendancy 'Good Behaviour'. Critics of Keane like Mary Breen argue that 'Keane does not romanticise her world or treat it nostalgically. She ruthlessly satirises it. Her Big Houses are not the centres of dignity that Yeats presents in Ancestral Houses' (206). In addition, Rachael Jane Lynch comments that 'Keane herself is bringing down her house, killing and burying a decaying microcosm with an overwhelming sense of relief' (74). In all of this, Molly Keane is determined to bring down the house and end the family and somehow she manages to lay the blame right within the power structures of the Anglo-Irish family.

As M.J. Farrell, Keane published a series of popular comic novels of the Irish Ascendancy in the late 1920s and 1930s, including *Mad Puppetstown* (1931), *Devoted Ladies* (1934) and *Full House* (1935). In 1961, Keane retired to Ardmore, Waterford in Ireland and stopped writing for nearly twenty years. Then in 1981, at the age of seventy-seven, she published *Good Behaviour* and found a new voice as a writer with two further novels, *Time after Time* (1983) and *Loving and Giving* (1988). Writing as Molly Keane, she proceeded to overturn the codes of Ascendancy behaviour and identity already interrogated by M.J. Farrell. Perhaps she felt free to do so because so many of her own contemporaries from her own class were now dead.

It is striking that the social and cultural backdrop in Keane's later work is ahistorical – in particular all reference to the key events that went into the making of the new Irish state. As V.S. Pritchett notes:

> After the Treaty in the Twenties, the Anglo-Irish gentry – the Ascendancy as they were called – rapidly became a remnant. Some stormed out shouting insults at the receding Wicklow Hills. Those who stayed resorted to irony … As one who knew something of the period of Molly Keane's *Good Behavior*, I was astonished to find there was no hint of the Irish Troubles, the Rising of 1916, the later Civil War or the toll of burned down houses. (89)

Many of her predecessors within this genre incorporated discourses of Irish Republicanism, rebellion and land agitation into their Big House narratives – even in Keane's own earlier novel *Two Days in Aragon* she integrates the precise social and political conditions of the Irish War of Independence into the narrative. However, in *Good Behaviour* she focuses her narrative away from the historical and concentrates on the fall of the Anglo-Irish house in utter imaginative isolation. This stripping away of the political context renders the Ascendancy class and their beleaguered houses socially isolated and places her protagonists into even more liminal positions. By banishing history to the periphery, Keane licenses a greater predominance of comic grotesquery in her later fictions, creating an imaginative world stranded on the outer margins of twentieth-century Ireland and at the edge of its own history.

Irish history disappears from Keane's later fictions but the dark comedy of her last novels, particularly *Good Behaviour*, does have an implicit political context in the juxtaposition of class with categories of sexual identity. In this relentlessly unsentimental novel all of the social norms of the Big House novel are under attack. As Keane presents it, the codes of politeness and noblesse oblige that go to make up Anglo-Irish 'good' behaviour are all predicated on a denial of emotion and a consequent impotence in the face of destruction. In Keane's remorselessly cruel fictive world, heterosexuality (and more subtly, homosexuality) is either duplicitous or bankrupt, Ascendancy families die out, and houses crumble or slip away. The ethos of hunting and of the outdoor life, hitherto valourised by Ascendancy writers like Somerville and Ross, is, in *Good Behaviour*, represented as a symptom of the destructive denial of the emotional. The courage of Bowen's Anglo-Irish is now transformed into a willful blindness in the face of obliteration. Within Keane's imaginative world, it is this denial that cannot be sustained and so the Big House is at risk. But I would contend that it is bourgeois education and effeminacy, and not the more usual Irish Republican violence, that brings down the Big House.

In all of her fictions, early and late, duplicitous sexual intrigue is one of the key impulses driving her protagonists. Keane entangles her representations of the erotic with other discourses around authority and money. There is nothing radical at all about the deployment of non-heterosexual eroticism within the tradition of the Irish Big House novel. Most of the Ascendancy novels before Keane also deal with sexual ambiguities, interrogating normative gender roles. In George Moore's 1886 novel, *A Drama in Muslin*, one of the central female protagonists, Cecilia, is clearly figured as both lesbian and man-hating, finding a refuge and an escape from heterosexuality by turning Catholic and entering a convent. Charlotte Mullin, the main protagonist in *The Real Charlotte* (1894) by Somerville and Ross is, I would argue, figured as cross-gendered and occupies a representational space somewhere between

male and female, between Irish and Anglo-Irish. Also, in Elizabeth Bowen's
1929 novel *The Last September*, the relationship between the young Anglo-
Irish protagonist, Lois and the older, sophisticated Marda suggests an unspoken homoerotic attraction between the two women, undermining the dominant heterosexual romance between Lois and the young British officer, Gerard.
Keane's fictions clearly draw inspiration from these novels. Most importantly,
Keane's own 1934 *Devoted Ladies* brings to the fore same sex desire and
homoerotic entanglements.

What makes *Good Behaviour* distinctive is the fact that she uses these
tropes only to subvert them. She suggests that the destruction of her particular Big House, Temple Alice, is a kind of implosion, a corruption of the code
of good behaviour from within by the middle-class governess, Mrs Brock.
Usually the middle class characters in the Big House novels operate as the
secretive mechanism for deceitful usurpation of land, house and heirs. For
example, the Irish land agent or lawyer is often the scheming usurper, using
his new found wealth and his innate Catholic cunning to buy out the impoverished ascendancy family and thereby take unlawful possession of the house.
Jason Quirke in *Castle Rackrent* is one example (1800) and the Whelans in *The
Big House at Inver* (1925) are another, with eventual possession of Ascendancy
land as their avowed aim. Likewise, middle-class English visitors like Captain
Hibbert in *A Drama in Muslin* or the unfortunate Gerard Lesworth in *The
Last September* are seen as unwelcome suitors for the daughters of the Big
Houses and must be rebuffed to keep the caste of the Anglo-Irish pure. The
encroachments of the middle class, both English and Irish, are resisted by the
Anglo-Irish, even if the houses are sold, lost or burned down.

In Keane, the corruption of the heirs of the Anglo-Irish Big House comes
about accidentally from the 'corrupting' domesticity of the bourgeois, the middle-class English governess character Mrs Brock. When these bourgeois values come into contact with the sterile Big House code of good behaviour,
calamity is brought down on the house. Although the middle class protagonist is a figure of threat within this genre, the interloper neither servant nor
master, unusually Keane makes Mrs Brock uncanny as she brings unwitting
destruction by nurturing and mothering. The house falls because Mrs Brock
is an influence towards humanising and self-actualising for her pupils. Mrs
Brock's middle-class decency, her quasi-maternal nurturing abilities, brings
disaster into a house where the Anglo-Irish women have somehow been alienated from these qualities and these emotional capabilities.

Earlier Keane governesses had been powerless figures for comic satire or
pathos, but this is not the case here. I take my title for this essay from the nursery song taught by the governess Mrs Brock to the children of the Ascendancy,
'Now the Day is Over', a children's devotional hymn written by Sabine Baring
Gould (1834–1924), a standard in late Victorian and Edwardian schoolrooms.

The words of the hymn are elegiac and mournful, denoting ending and the drawing to the close of a twilight world 'Now the Day is Over/ Night is drawing nigh; Shadows of the evening/ Steal across the sky'. As ever with the Irish Big House novel, the middle class character brings closure to the house and to the family and Mrs Brock fulfils this role in *Good Behaviour* with her (inadvertently) effeminising system of education. To make my argument specific, I want to look at Keane's structuring of the novel and, in particular, at her figuring of the English governess, Mrs Brock and her system of education.

Joseph Bristow's cultural history of male education of Britain in the late nineteenth century is useful in this context, particularly his 1991 *Empire Boys*, and his 1995 study *Effeminate England*. In *Empire Boys*, Bristow describes the ideal of a manly education for the empire building young gentleman of the upper classes:

> There is no doubt that the sexual style that caused the greatest confusion and anxiety about homosexual identity in the late nineteenth-century was its perceived attachment to feminity – and thus by extension, to effeminacy. (10)

Bristow considers the kinds of adventure stories aimed at young boys and men of all classes in late Victorian and Edwardian Britain, by writers such as Kipling, Conrad Haggard and even Baden Powell (with his Boy Scouts manual, the wonderfully titled 1908 *Scouting for Boys*). He argues that writers like Baden Powell promulgated a version of imperialist manliness to 'uphold a highly reactionary form of patriotism in an effort to defend a demoralized empire at a time of crisis after the pyrrhic victories of the second Anglo-Boer war of 1899–1902' (61). The hunting, manly outdoor ethos of the Anglo-Irish was perfectly attuned to this mainstream imperialising education and Keane registers her quiet rebellion against this dominant ethos in her subtle countering of an idea of art: effeminising, indoor, poetic art. Thus, the discourse of imperial manhood is threatened by the counter education and degenerating influence of effeminate art.

I would suggest that Keane exploits this crisis, the clash between these two opposing traditions of Edwardian education, to introduce the undermining influence of bourgeois effeminacy. Thus, in *Good Behaviour*, the middle class governess provokes a crisis in masculinity and precipitates the fall of the house. It is Mrs Brock's system of education which subverts the Big House, rather than the greed of the emergent Irish Catholic middle class or the anger of Irish republican militants.

Mrs Brock's encoding within the narrative is carefully prepared by Keane right from the start. She is English, middle-class and adrift emotionally and economically:

> She was the widow of an organist who had saved very little money before he died at a medium sort of age, leaving her, (fortunately childless, though she longed for kiddies of her own) to drag a living from a world out of which she had been cozily embedded in a nice little house with a nice little man who had a nice and not so little job in a large London parish. (18)

Into the relentlessly undomesticated world of the Anglo-Irish, Mrs Brock brings personal affection, domestic order, poetry and music. Yet she is destroyed by her emotional encounters with the world of the Big House. Firstly, she is the governess in England to the Massingham family at Stoke Charity, and there she 'corrupts' the eldest son, simply by her sincere love and her maternal nurturing:

> Richard was Mrs Brock's favourite and years afterwards she was to be my first intimate link with him ... Richard was a beautiful child and, despite a proper interest in and all the aptitudes for all the importances of outdoor life, there were times when he would lean in silence against Mrs Brock as she played the piano or even join her in singing ... He liked dressing up, too, but Mrs Brock felt that such games were not quite the thing for little boys. Sometimes she allowed herself to read him her favourite pieces from the *Children's Golden Treasury of Verse*, when they would charge with the light brigade or even lean from the golden bar of heaven with the Blessed Demozel. (19)

Keane deploys a series of discourses around education to link the loss of economic and political power in Ascendancy Ireland with a re-ordering of the notion of masculinity and heterosexual fixities. As Vera Kreilkamp observes, 'Anglo-Irish novelists writing about the Big House have registered the unmanning of the colonizer ... Keane's fictions suggest that as Anglo-Irish power erodes, gender identities shift' (184). In *Good Behaviour*, Keane is knowing and slyly comic in her representation of Richard's education, her signalling of his homosexuality. Mrs Brock's efficiency as a teacher, and her enabling qualities of affection and empathy with the young child of the English Big House, allow the boy Richard to become the adult outsider – her good education simply allows his 'singularity' to flower. As Keane presents it, the notion of a developing sexuality is something innate, essentialist even, and so Richard is already interested in the non-masculinist discourses that will connect with his adult sexuality. Mrs Brock's system of education, and indeed Richard's own qualities and sensibilities, are all qualities that jar with the dominant ethos of hunting, the outdoor life of the gentry. Mrs Brock is dismissed, partly because she falls in love with the lady of the house and more because she dared to educate her charges in poetry, in music, in feeling. By implication, she has sown the seeds of nurturing and of 'decadent' literary tastes by which the eldest son and heir, her favourite Richard, will be empowered to reject the pretense of heterosexuality. Witness the description of the measures taken by Nannie, the longstanding servant and upholder of proper feudal relations, in the English house against Mrs Brock's literary nurturing of Richard:

> Nannie took the book of poetry straight to Lady Grizel, who talked it over unhappily with the Captain. His response was a genuinely worried: 'Yes, we'll have to put a stop to this book worming. No future in that. And he was having a music lesson yesterday when old Sholto was schooling his pony.'
> 'That's hardly the point, is it? The awful thing is, he told me quite a big fib.'
> 'That's more natural – it's this poetry that bothers me. What's the book called?'
> 'The Children's Golden Treasury of Verse.'
> 'Unhealthy-sounding stuff.' (30–1)

Keane is unrelenting in her ironising of the philistinism of the Edwardian upper classes, where the strict control of male education was seen as a crucial safeguard against the dangers of art and effeminacy. These dangers were most keenly felt by this class in the wake of the Oscar Wilde trials of 1895, where effeminacy, literature and homosexuality were dangerously co-joined in the public eye. As a result of her transgressive system of education in England, Mrs Brock is sent off to Ireland, a dumping ground for rejected servants. There she is employed at Temple Alice, where she takes care of the St Charles children, Aroon and Hubert. 'Mummie', Mrs St Charles, the Anglo-Irish chatelaine, is represented as cold, unfeeling and unmaternal. At one point Mummie is disgusted when her young son's near fatal bout of appendicitis interrupts her private dinner with her husband. Earlier, Elizabeth Bowen, in her Irish War of Independence novel, *The Last September*, presents a heroic chatelaine of the Big House, Lady Naylor of Danielstown, heroic in her insistence of living her everyday life in the face of death and violence, with her policy of not noticing the Irish rebels lurking out in the fields seen as a positive virtue. Now, for Keane, not noticing is no longer a virtue but a cruelty, and the children love the governess Mrs Brock because she provides the maternal attention lacking from Mummie: 'With her in the schoolroom, there came to us a daily security in happiness and with it the delightful prospect of such a state continuing into an untimed future' (17). During her time in Temple Alice, Mrs Brock uses her bourgeois skills as a teacher in swimming lessons, horse riding and even her mending of clothes and linen to win the children's love, 'Sorting and piecing and darning, her hands never ran out of skill or tired of work'(48). In her countering system of education, she embodies the virtues of care and concern, all of the bourgeois qualities despised by the spendthrift, Ascendancy family.

Mrs Brock's downfall comes with her seduction by Aroon's father. Pregnant and abandoned, she gives the young Aroon a terrible lesson into the dangers and the cruelties of heterosexual relationships for women. She tells Aroon about the nursery mice and their mating:

> 'You're always asking me how they do It,' Mrs Brock went on. 'Well, I'll tell you. It's that horrible Moses; he sticks that thing of his, you must have seen it – Hubert has one, too – into the hole she pees out of, and he sows the seed like that.' 'Oh.' I felt myself become heated; horrified and excited. 'That's how it happens', Mrs Brock went on, 'that's how it happens with people, too. It's a thing men do, it's all they want to do, and you won't like it.' (61)

Perhaps the most chilling element within this cruel and unpleasant final scene between governess and child is that Mrs Brock has been 'converted' to Big House values of maternal cruelty. Desperate and at the point of suicide, the nurturing bourgeois governess becomes vindictive and relentlessly truthful. In fact, Mrs Brock has come to behave like Mummie.

Aroon's adult sexuality is stunted by this last cruel scene between herself and Mrs Brock, the only negative lesson taught by an otherwise enlightened and caring governess. Thus Aroon's subsequent cherishing of Richard as a pretend lover and suitor comes as a saving illusion in the face of Mrs Brock's final harsh words. Mrs Brock's memory and the resultant legacy of her system of education haunt the rest of the novel. Keane makes it clear that the consequence of Mrs Brock's instinctual nurturing is linked to the downfall of Big Houses, English and Irish, and she invokes her ghost at moments of danger and crisis in the rest of the novel. When the adult Anglo-Irish Aroon and Hubert finally meet with the adult Richard, the memory of Mrs Brock is the bond between them all, a bond they are unwilling to acknowledge. Keane invests the ghost of Mrs Brock with the only lyricism, the only sense of grief and loss in the whole novel.

We can see this lyricism, this haunting when Keane re-unites the adult Aroon with the grown up Richard. In the interval, apparently 'cured' into heterosexuality, Richard has become the empire boy, to all appearances. As Aroon recalls:

> I was appalled when I met the present Richard ... Long legs I saw (I had expected that), eyes discriminating and critical as a bird's small

ears, crisp hair; rolled umbrella, swinging stylishly as a sword, he
came straight from the middle pages of the Tatler and Bystander.
The right family, the right school, the right regiment had all been
his. I was stunned between fear and admiration. He was brown (from
Cowes week), lean and hard (polo at Hurlingham); he had ridden the
winner of a Grand military (Sandown should have been written on
his forehead). (85)

Yet this is all appearance, as Aroon is unwittingly aware, the outward
codifying of imperialist masculinity, the brand names of Cowes, Sandown and
others all providing the outward semblance. In addition, a reference to a key
incident in the history of late Victorian homosexuality, the trials of Oscar
Wilde, is made by Keane when she names Richard's younger brother Sholto.
This was a family name for the infamous Black Douglases, the Scottish aris-
tocrats that included the marquis of Queensbury, the man sued for libel by
Oscar Wilde and his son, Lord Alfred Douglas, Wilde's lover. Keane was a
close friend to several gay men during her career as a West End London
dramatist and drops this reference into her text as a deliberate encoding, a
knowing 'insider' reference for those familiar with gay history and urban subculture. Keane thus deploys the discourse of homosexuality both as a code
for deconstruction, but also as a code for disclosure and for eventual sexual
honesty. It is implied that the two families are brought to an end by the sexual relations between the two heirs and Mrs Brock is the link between the
two male lovers. The memory of Mrs Brock, Richard's most beloved childhood memory, is now used as part of this adult game of sexual deceit between
the two men:

> We had all forgotten Mrs Brock; we never gave her a thought in
> those days – just a dead governess ... We had forgotten Mrs Brock,
> but it was by her methods that we deceived and defeated fear ...
> That was the start of the Mrs Brock cult. It grew into a game that
> Richard loved playing. He drew Hubert and me into it. First
> remembering things about her; then inventions, sad, funny, intimate
> details. It was a charade ... They took to dressing and undressing
> her like a doll, like an effigy. Hubert screamed at some of the dis-
> gusting things he thought up. I laughed, not always hearing, not
> always or quite getting the point but determined not to be left out,
> frightened yet longing to be party to this violation ... Everything I
> remembered was a betrayal and a denial of the other things she was.
> But between us we almost called her into being. It was such fun
> sharing in her persecution. (90)

This childish, nasty cult of Mrs Brock, the adult mockery of a beloved childhood figure by Richard and Hubert, is linked to their emotional dishonesty towards Aroon. As the novel progresses, all of the Ascendancy men betray the women around them. Aroon is the victim of duplicity both from her father, her brother and her pretend lover Richard, and throughout the novel it is the women who must bear the consequence of male sexual dishonesty. Aroon becomes the dupe of her brother, Hubert, who masks his sexual relationship with Richard by pretending that his overweight sister is the object of sexual desire for Richard. The two male lovers are a kind of mirage for Aroon, a vision of physical beauty and confident erotic selfhood beyond her own sense of self, and their beauty betrays her:

> I liked to watch the boys as they finished dressing. There was a quick, hard grace about their movements, in the way they put links quickly into the cuffs of their evening shirts, and such a different tempo from a girl's considered gesture. They wore narrow red braces and their black trousers were taut around waists and bottoms … How dear they were. Spoilers of girls. (90)

Men are the objects of desire or agency in this novel, women either victims or passive observers but, as the narrative unfolds, the men die or are exiled. As part of this process, Mrs Brock's name becomes a talisman for destruction, and, as the novel progresses, Temple Alice never burns, unlike Danielstown in *The Last September*, or Aragon in *Two Days in Aragon* or indeed like Keane's own family home, Ballyrankin. Instead, Hubert, the heir to Temple Alice, is killed in a car crash, leaving the future of the Big House bleak and the family line at an end. Here, at this moment of grief at the loss of the brother, the spectre of the drowned Mrs Brock is invoked in Aroon's description of Hubert's funeral, 'Praise elated me, grief was a spasm. "Now the Day is Over" … the hymn I had chosen for Hubert's funeral. Mrs Brock's hymn …' (131). The day is indeed over for both the Anglo-Irish family and the house and Mrs Brock is the touchstone for this demise, the lost chord of emotional connection and nurturing.

Mrs Brock has also 'queered' the other heir to the English house. Richard is sent off to Africa on safari after Hubert's death, to quell any potential scandal. This contains the threat of homosexual exposure by placing Richard beyond the pale of the Imperial mainland. This strategy of denial and containment rebounds when Richard places himself outside the pale of heterosexuality. Richard's homosexuality is overtly revealed in his final decision to 'out' himself by running away with an old school friend, now his new lover and living openly with him in Kenya. Here Keane suggests that the Colonies offer possibilities for self expression, unavailable in Britain or even in Ireland.

Keane uses the male tropes of English public school and the Colonies as shifting fault lines to unsettle the heterosexual consensus of imperial manhood. As Richard's father tells Aroon at the end of the novel, again invoking Mrs Brock:

> 'Wrong from the start ... Reading books in trees. Nannie was right, unhealthy stuff. Then there was that governess – we sacked her. She was in it, too. Queer person [...] Trouble at school. Who hasn't, after all? Forget it, I always think [...]'. He looked like an angry blue-eyed baby with a pain it can't explain. 'Broken off his engagement, broken up the entail, upset his mother and taken himself off to farm in Kenya with Baby Kintoull' (226–7).

Ironically, in running away and breaking the entail, Richard behaves with an honesty and directness around sexuality that is unique in the novel, and it is Mrs Brock who, it is implied, has facilitated this honesty. Ironically, or maybe not, Keane's only honest man is an openly gay one. It is possible Keane was drawing on her own knowledge of gay theatre life in London to suggest out-ness, openness and sexual identification, but only away from family, the Big House and the Imperial mainland.

For Anglo-Ireland, the early death of the heir to Temple Alice renders the father old before his time and when he too falls gravely ill, Mrs Brock again is invoked, unconsciously:

> In the dog shaped shadow cast by the stolid little church on grasses and graves I found him. Rose was sitting on the grass, her knees spread, holding him in her arms ... Her flowered hat was lying on the grass. There was mushroom dew on it and on the graves. I remembered Mrs Brock's hat, dripping from the wet grass, one silly hat recalled the other, clear and meaningless, conjuring together that night with this evening. (145)

The conjuring together of these two evenings is deliberate. The dew on the grass where Mrs Brock made love with Papa, a lovemaking that left her pregnant, abandoned and then suicidal, is now his own death knell, the moment where he is paralysed. The Captain wills the house to his daughter, Aroon, but Temple Alice is then abandoned by Aroon, who, most tellingly, had been rendered middle-class and bourgeois by Mrs Brock's education.

In conclusion, in *The Last September* Gerard is killed and Danielstown burns, and in Somerville and Ross the Big House at Inver is sold. Uniquely, Keane allows for the voluntary surrender of the Big House to the invading middle class when Aroon gives up her home and creates another home in the

ideal mold of bourgeois domesticity. Thus the novel ends with the success-
ful infiltration of Ascendancy codes of behaviour by Mrs Brock, with the St
Charles family at an end in Gull's Cry, and with a voluntary surrender of the
Ascendancy to middle class comfort and respectability.

Molly Keane's *Devoted Ladies*:
the apparitional Irish lesbian

MOIRA E. CASEY

It is difficult to locate the figure of the lesbian in Ireland in the first half of the twentieth century. Few examples exist to give us an idea of how lesbians might have lived and what kind of sexual and emotional relationships they might have engaged in. And yet, it seems safe to assume that women who sexually desired other women did in fact exist in Ireland despite the culture's hostility toward sexual deviation. The fictional Irish lesbian – pre 1960, at least – might be linked to Terry Castle's 'apparitional lesbian,' a figure that seems be 'hidden from history':

> The lesbian is never with us, it seems, but always somewhere else: in the shadows, in the margins, hidden from history, out of sight, out of mind [...]. What we never expect is precisely this: to find her in the midst of things [...]. (3)

The lack of information about lesbians in Ireland at this time could lead us to the conclusion that though lesbians existed, they were tragic figures, 'hidden from history' and somehow distanced from the heterosexual centre of Irish life and Irish fiction. And yet, when we do look at the fiction, there she is, quite nearly 'in the midst of things', demonstrating Castle's theory that the figure of the lesbian has been present in this literature, but in a ghosted form.

The application of Castle's theory to certain Irish women writers might help critics to understand better the significance of the lesbian characters in these writers' works. For when lesbian characters and examples of lesbian desire surface in the works of two of Ireland's celebrated and critically acclaimed women writers of the first half of the twentieth century – Kate O'Brien and Molly Keane – it would seem that the Irish lesbian is in fact 'in the midst of things.' The fact that these well-known and popular authors addressed the issue of lesbianism raises questions about the invisibility of the Irish lesbian: to what extent did Ireland's cultural environment really render lesbian expressions of desire invisible if these works were published and read? In *Mary Lavelle* (1936), O'Brien features a lesbian character as one of the heroine's closest friends, and her later, more famous novel, *The Land of Spices* (1941), depicts male homosexuality as well as intense female relationships developed in the convent school setting; Molly Keane, in *Devoted Ladies* (1934), centres the entire plot on two clearly lesbian characters and works in a third, equally central, but less overtly lesbian character. Much later, in 1958, O'Brien produced her last novel, *As Music and Splendour*, in which one of her two heroines openly engages in a lesbian relationship.

Both *Mary Lavelle* and *Devoted Ladies* appeared within ten years of an event that, in England, marked the emergence of a new public discourse about lesbianism that added to the sexological studies from the early part of the century: the obscenity trial of Radclyffe Hall's lesbian tragedy, *The Well of Loneliness*. As Laura Doan has shown in her book *Fashioning Sapphism*, the 1928 publication of *The Well of Loneliness* and the ensuing trial served to provide the public with a tangible sense of what lesbianism is and what types of clothing styles, preferences, and behaviours might mark the woman who erotically prefers other women: 'The highly publicized obscenity trial of Hall's novel, which is generally recognized as *the* crystallizing moment in the construction of a visible modern English lesbian subculture, marks a great divide between innocence and deviance, private and public, New Woman and Modern Lesbian' (xiii). As Doan and others have suggested, the fact that lesbianism was never successfully criminalised helped to keep it invisible and vaguely defined. But the combination of the sexological discourse of the 1920s and the publicity surrounding *The Well of Loneliness* and its author brought lesbianism to the public consciousness in a particular way – the mannish lesbian, or female sexual invert, embodied in Hall's own image, became the dominant image of the lesbian.

Published just six years following the publication of *The Well of Loneliness* and the ensuing trial, Keane's *Devoted Ladies* (1934) seems to draw on some of the new public knowledge about lesbianism and lesbian identities. Emma Donoghue has suggested that the fervour over Hall's novel provided some Irish writers with a new theme with which to experiment: 'For those Anglo-Irish writers who looked to London as their barometer, lesbianism had a certain cachet as a theme, if carefully handled' ('Noises' 161). 'Carefully handled' seems to have meant that these writers used language delicately and did not explicitly describe sexual acts *and* that they dealt with their gay or lesbian characters harshly; few of these characters find sexual or personal fulfillment and novels like *The Well of Loneliness* do not offer much hope. If we take novelists such as Keane and Elizabeth Bowen as in any way representing the real cultural attitudes in Ireland toward sexual alternatives, then such alternatives were problematic during this period. The lesbians of Molly Keane's *Devoted Ladies* (1934) do not survive as lesbians when the setting moves from London to Ireland; two die in a murder-suicide while the third ends up in a heterosexual marriage. The intriguing attraction between Marda and Lois in Elizabeth Bowen's *The Last September* remains unexplored at the end of the novel, when Marda leaves for England.[1] The earliest Kate O'Brien

---

1 For a discussion of lesbian links between Bowen's characters, see Patricia Coughlan's 'Women

novel to openly involve a lesbian character, *Mary Lavelle* (1936), is set not in
Ireland, but in Spain, but its frankness about sexuality (lesbian and hetero)
caused the Censorship Board to ban it.[2]

Polly Devlin's 1983 introduction to the *Devoted Ladies* quotes Keane discussing her own discovery of lesbianism as a novelistic subject:

> I suppose I was rather curious and shocked by coming upon all that
> ... Before then no-one thought anything of two elderly ladies setting
> up house together. I'd certainly never heard a murmur, though now
> everyone murmurs about everything. I was excited by finding out
> about lesbians and homosexuals. It was new. It made a subject. (iv)

Although it is unclear what year 'then' refers to in the passage, given the publication date of the novel 'then' could certainly refer to the years following
the Hall trial in which, as Doan has outlined, a public discourse arose in
England about homosexuality in general and lesbians in particular. This passage also illustrates some of the changes in attitudes toward sexual deviance.
Keane implies that until the terms 'lesbian' or 'homosexual' were in circula-
tion in Ireland or England, women could have been participating in lesbian
relationships fairly freely; two women setting up house together was not considered suspicious because of the public's general innocence. Interestingly,
Keane also accounts for the way in which public knowledge about homosexuality functions in the 1980s – 'now everyone murmurs about everything.'
But in England and Ireland in the 1930s, the general invisibility of lesbians,
the same invisibility that protected lesbians from labels or prejudice, and
allowed two women to set up house together without suspicion, was just
beginning to be eroded, in part because the terms for non-normative sexual
behaviours were increasingly coming into more common usage.

Similarly to Hall's *The Well of Loneliness*, *Devoted Ladies* employs what Castle
might call a 'dysphoric' plot structure, in which the lesbian characters' search for
social, sexual and emotional fulfillment ends tragically, and heterosexuality is
thereby implicitly affirmed. Keane's lesbian characters are not spared the romantic masochism experienced by the great majority of her female characters; as Mary
Breen notes, Keane's fictional world is populated by 'unattractive ... unmarried

and desire in the Work of Elizabeth Bowen' in *Sex, nation and dissent in Irish writing*, 103–34.
2 However, I must admit that it is not entirely clear why the Censorship Board banned *Mary
Lavelle*. Emma Donoghue, for example, writes that 'it has been presumed that the offending
passage occurred at the point where the Irish governess, Mary, demands that the married son
of her Spanish employer should deflower her, but O'Brien's explicit validation of Agatha
Conlon's love for Mary must have scandalized the Board too' ('Noises' 163). In *Mary Lavelle*,
Mary's sexual experience with Juanito is described fairly explicitly, whereas in *Devoted Ladies*,
no one's sexual activities are detailed.

daughters … [who] fill their days in endless small tasks … and in futilely giving their love to those who don't want it' (204). For the most part, *Devoted Ladies* is no different, except that in this novel the unattractive, unmarried women are futilely giving their love to other *women* who don't want it. In the end, Keane allows no place for devoted ladies to be devoted to other ladies, and she reasserts the heterosexual and patriarchal order that the lesbians of this novel threaten. London, and its social and sexual freedoms, is implicitly contrasted with the Irish countryside, in which sexual alternatives are literally killed off. This conclusion to a homosexuality associated with British decadence and the lack of explicit sexual passages such as those in *Mary Lavelle* may have allowed *Devoted Ladies* to escape the disapproving eye of the Censorship Board.

Devoted Ladies is, therefore, an important fiction in terms of its representation of the sexual attitudes of the time, but it also has importance as a version of the novel form, in which the marriage plot is radically re-envisioned. Significantly, by placing a lesbian relationship at the novel's centre, Keane disturbs the triangle of desire employed by conventional domestic novels. However, in what may be seen as a conservative plot trajectory, Keane also reaffirms the heterosexual social order at the novel's end. Yet, the novel is radical in that it primarily deals with female-female desire, bases the plot on such desire, and promotes an obviously flawed heterosexual relationship with the novel's end. Simultaneously, throughout the course of the novel, Keane interrogates both the power of language and its limitations for the representation of ostensibly unspeakable sexual desires.

Within the growing body of criticism on Keane's work, very few writers fully explore the import of her homosexual characters, and little has been written about *Devoted Ladies*. In Anne Owen Weekes's article, 'A Trackless Road: Irish Nationalisms and Lesbian Writing,' which attempts to trace a history of Irish lesbian writing, she mentions *Devoted Ladies* but dismisses the use of homosexuality as negative and stereotypical, thus denying the work's import as a precursor for later Irish lesbian narratives. But Keane's interest in homosexuality did not end with *Devoted Ladies*. In two of her more recent novels – two that received greater critical examination – gay male characters figure prominently. In *Good Behaviour*, the main character's deluded self-perception is based on her memory of a one-night stand with her brother's male lover. The brother's homosexuality is shielded from the family, but notably it is not dealt with harshly in the text. In *Time after Time*, Jasper's homosexuality is handled matter-of-factly.

According to Breen, one of the few literary critics who does take a close look at Keane's treatment of sexuality in *Devoted Ladies*, Keane does not take a condemnatory stance on lesbianism: '[Keane] is evidently not interested in creating regulatory sexual categories, central or marginal. She is interested in how sexual attraction between people of opposite or the same sex works' (219). And yet, Breen notes that 'nevertheless, her representation of same-sex desire, although glamorous and exciting, is problematic' (219). 'Problematic' for Breen means that the homosexual relationships in *Devoted Ladies* and *Good Behaviour* end in death; presumably, a less problematic depiction would be one in which lesbian and gay characters actually live through the novel's conclusion. The ghosting techniques utilised in the narration of *Devoted Ladies* would seem to support Breen's argument. Without passing judgment, without creating a clear 'central ground of moral rightness' (Breen 207), Keane draws attention to the way in which lesbian desire is simultaneously central to and marginalised from the Anglo-Irish social order. Although I agree with Breen that Keane's omniscient narrator avoids clear moral judgments, the fact that the Anglo-Irish marriage of Jane and George Playfair is based on lies of omission, George's ignorance of the lesbian desire operating around him, and Jane's cipher-like personality, must amount to a critique of the Anglo-Irish social order.

The novel begins in London, where Jane and Jessica enjoy a decadent life supported by Jane's wealth; at the outset, the relationship between Jane and Jessica has been going on for some time. Jane's love of sporting novels set in the Anglo-Irish Big Houses, and her mild attraction to George Playfair, the paradigm of Anglo-Irish masculinity, inspire her to persuade Jessica to travel with her to Ireland. Once there, Jessica and Jane are involved in a car crash, which results in Jessica being injured. They are taken to Kilque, the country house of their London friend, Sylvester, where Jessica can convalesce. There they meet Sylvester's cousin, Piggy (coincidentally the driver of the other car involved in the crash). Jessica's immobility allows Jane the time and freedom to develop the relationship with George Playfair, whose sister Joan lives not far from Kilque. Jane's growing relationship with George not only upsets Jessica, but also wreaks havoc with Piggy's life. Jane usurps the role that Piggy imagines is her own – best friend to Joan and romantic partner to George. The end of the novel sees Piggy driving herself and Jessica off a cliff in order to preserve George's and Jane's future happiness together, a happiness threatened by Jessica's readiness to reveal Jane's past to George.

To achieve her critique of the Anglo-Irish in this novel, Keane employs a version of Castle's apparitional lesbian, a figure who is marginalised, but who also exercises a certain degree of power from her ghostly margin:

> [...] in nearly all the art of the eighteenth and nineteenth centuries, lesbianism or its possibility, can only be represented to the degree that it is simultaneously 'derealized,' through a blanching authorial infusion of spectral metaphors. [...] One woman or the other must be a ghost, or on the way to becoming one. (34)

The ghosted form of Castle's 'apparitional lesbian' appears in this text in the character of Jane. Her feeble personality and lack of physical substance contrast sharply with the physically and psychologically threatening presence of

Jessica, who embodies the powerful aspect of the apparition. Jane's slight physique, small bones, and her 'blanched' coloring (Sylvester also later refers to her as 'blanched') conspire to render her ghostlike, and she is also frequently referred to as 'unreal.' As Jessica admires Jane's appearance in Sylvester's apartment, the narrator admits that Jessica is correct in her admiration:

> Jane did look well, for her lines were faintly geometric, as though flesh had been put on her body only to be ruled off again with extreme exactitude. Her bones were no more than small enough to justify the theory that she was ghostlike, not gaunt. As it was she escaped that unattractive state of body by very little. Her coarse fair hair was a lovely blanched colour and she arranged it with much care like a little girl's. [...] (7–8)

Indeed, she lacks a certain emotional substance as well, partly due to her excessive drinking and her passivity in the face of Jessica's violent physicality. As the narrator tells us, 'Jane was terrified of pain and sickness and her fear was not without cause for she had very little strength of mind and body with which to combat either' (56). Additionally, she and Jessica evolve in opposing ways. Jane becomes increasingly healthy (after her sickness at the novel's start) as she is separated from Jessica and gradually absorbed into the Irish heterosexual social order. Simultaneously, Jessica, the more threatening and stereotypically 'butch' of the pair, becomes injured and immobilised and dies violently at the novel's end, thus enabling Jane's escape.

The growing relationship between George and Jane seems, in fact, to be based on her spectral qualities, and is thus a key element in Keane's satire of both the Anglo-Irish and heterosexual romance. For George, the idealised embodiment of Anglo-Irish masculinity, Jane remains a kind of cipher, as the narrator here explains:

> Although she might say no more than 'Fascinating!' 'Frightening!' 'Are you being horrible to me?' she enclosed within herself a sense of the undiscoverable – a completely false sense, but that did not matter, for it was always round a corner. There was in Jane for those who loved her the illusion of an unknown place, obscured from them – forever obscured from them because indeed it was not in her. She was not reticent by nature, but she could not communicate, and for her this was a most fortunate disability. The mirage of lovely secrecy was in her, never discovered for it was never there. (184–5)

This aspect of Jane – the idea that she is only the illusion of a complex personality- contributes to her physical unreality and creates the effect of Castle's derealisation through the use of spectral metaphors. Later in the novel, when George is looking at Jane, he is clearly attracted by her 'unreality': 'She was a masked creature sitting there beside him in this small wood – faint and unreal and hidden from him entirely, as apart from him as she was from this glade of brith trees, as distant from all this life. George was encompassed and excited by this sense of her absurd unreality to him' (185). George's attraction to the promise of psychological depth in Jane, rather than any actual knowledge about her sense of identity, renders their entire relationship suspect; their relationship, like Jane, is without substance – a mirage.

If Jane functions as an apparitional lesbian in this novel, then Jessica functions as the other side of the metaphorical coin – she represents the threatening, challenging aspect of the apparitional lesbian. Castle writes that,

> the case could be made that the metaphor meant to derealize lesbian desire in fact did just the opposite. Indeed, strictly for repressive purposes, one could hardly think of a *worse* metaphor. For embedded in the ghostly figure, as even its first proponents seemed at times to realize, was inevitably a notion of reembodiment: of uncanny return to the flesh. (63)

With her heavy physicality, and her vicious and powerful personality, Jessica appears to function as the embodied lesbian – the 'uncanny return to the flesh' that Castle argues remains a part of the apparition's threat. In contrast to Jane's pale complexion and diaphanous personality, Jessica is dark, severe, and 'heavy-minded':

> Jessica's dark hair was cut with a charming severity. If her dark face had been less heavy and turbulent in expression Jessica would almost have succeeded in looking as hard and boyish as she hoped she looked. But this plan of hers had been spoilt by God in the beginning, for He had given her a positive bosom and massive thighs. She was a heavy-minded woman too, without much gaiety of spirit. It was typical of her to break china and bite baths in moments of stress, so did she grind her teeth into life and with as little satisfaction to herself. (42)

In Keane's fictional world, the apparitional lesbian is, as Castle has indicated, less threatening to the heterosexual order than the lesbian with substance and strength. The two women's contrasting appearances and personalities symbolise their respective functions in the novel: Jane's distinctively feminine weaknesses allow her to be folded back into the patriarchal order, with her match-up with George Playfair. Jessica's aggressive sexuality, on the other hand, cannot be contained, and her physical appearance (the combination of her 'heavy and turbulent expression' and her 'positive bosom') does not allow her to fit easily into conventional gender categories.

Although the nature of Jane and Jessica's relationship is never explicitly articulated as a sexual one, the oblique references to it in the text engage questions of how to express lesbian desire in language. Jessica's repeated expressions of jealousy and Sylvester's musings about the pair imply that Jane and Jessica's 'passionate friendship' has a strongly physical element to it. Significantly, Sylvester's musings about George and Jane also reveals the inadequacy of language to describe Jane and her past relationships. After a conversation with wealthy, Anglo-Irish George Playfair, in which Sylvester encourages George's romantic interest in Jane, Sylvester considers the possibility of George learning about Jane's sexual past and present:

> How explain to him that Jane's husband and lovers and passionate friends were as unreal as she? For first George would have had to learn a whole new language of life and having learnt it he would still have found Sylvester's explanation of Jane unsatisfying. Antichrist, that was how Jane typified all that she was to George could George have understood about her. A thing of the Groves. Unclean. Incredible. (27)

This passage is fundamentally about the language of sexuality, and the narrator's choice of terms here reflects the linguistic dilemma Sylvester faces. Sylvester feels he lacks the language with which to explain Jane's past to George, and he also recognises George's lack of vocabulary with which to understand Jane fully. Jane's lesbianism and her sexual liberties would be 'unreal' and 'incredible' to someone so intertwined with patriarchy as George is. I read Sylvester's description of Jane's husband as 'unreal' in the sense that the marriage was probably motivated by money and not love or sexual attraction. This application differs from the use of 'unreal' to describe Jane's 'passionate friends,' which I take to mean lesbian lovers. The use of the term 'passionate friends' points to the coded language for lesbian desire that Emma Donoghue has explored in *Passions between Women*, her work on eighteenth- and nineteenth-century women's writing. Donoghue examines so-called passionate friendships between women and posits the use of this term as prior to or as a substitute for the more explicit term 'lesbian'. *Devoted Ladies* reveals that such coding lingered on into the twentieth century, in settings in which more specific and explicit language may not have been available, appropriate, or functional.

Language and the potential communication of Jane's past create the major conflict within the text and lead to the novel's climax. Jane is keenly aware of how Jessica could ruin her future with George. Jane envisions her relationship with George as based on her protection of him from the person she really is and the world that she has previously inhabited:

> She was the Jane he thought her to be. She would forever protect him from the Jane she was. This she knew with a surprising shock

of strength, and knew too a gentleness towards him that she might never dismiss. [...] There was power in her to hurt him and she would never hurt him. (265)

Jessica, of course, is the force that could defeat Jane in her protection of George: 'Jessica could break and ruin and reveal all that Jane had done and all that Jane was. Jane's lovers and sins made a sad story, and to George it would be more than sad, it would be desolating and unholy. [...] And Jessica would tell and tell and tell' (265). Jessica seems more confident than Sylvester about her ability to narrate Jane's past for George: while Sylvester wonders how he could possibly tell George the truth about Jane, Jessica actually seems to possess the power to do so.

Although Jane's lesbianism is never named, Jessica presents it as doubly damning; it becomes both the reason for a prediction of her marriage's future failure as well as Jessica's trump card that she could use to wreck the marriage before it begins. When Jessica confronts Jane about the future of her relationship with George, she questions Jane about how much George knows and how much he could possibly know and yet still desire to marry Jane: ' "And how much does he know about you? The you," said Jessica, gently, "that *I* know. [...] It's important, you know," Jessica went on, "that the poor young man should know *something* about you. Have you told him anything?"' (289–90). Jessica is, of course, tormenting and manipulating Jane in this scene, but Jane admits that George knows little about her past. Jessica, with some degree of accuracy and a great degree of malice, points out that George's love could not mean much and their success in marriage seems futile if he should love Jane and yet know so little about her:

'You don't believe anything could survive for you when I've told him, do you?'

'Oh, *no.*' That sweet, empty note was grievous and final. 'He won't want me any more then.'

'And *still* you imagine you could make a success of living with any one so entirely apart from you.' (291–2)

Jessica asserts that George's love for Jane is meaningless if he is 'apart' from her, in terms of his knowledge about her and the differences between them. Without ever actually articulating what the 'something' is that Jessica would tell George, Jessica wields the power that comes with the threat of telling, and simultaneously exposes the absurdity of the central heterosexual relationship of the novel.

Jane's past thereby functions to subvert the traditional marriage plot; even if her past is never narrated, Jessica has exposed to the reader how the Jane-

George marriage is far from an ideal companionate marriage. By contrast, George's past presents the reader with an example of the canonical structure of male homosocial bonding, an example that Keane presents through Sylvester's eyes. George's first love, Blanche, was the object of desire in a triangle involving George and his best friend Stephen, who is now engaged to Blanche. Sylvester thinks of George's relationship to Stephen and Blanche in idealistic terms, as if the canonical triangle is the ideal state in which to exist:

> George who was Blanche's friend and Stephen's friend – who for the last week had sat by Blanche's side while she [...] had watched Stephen play his glorious part in swift games of polo [...]. George had come to [Sylvester's] party to-night with Blanche and Stephen. He was Stephen's best friend [...].
>
> But luckily for George [...] he had not discovered for himself the nature of his need until she was irrevocably another's. That she should be Stephen's, Stephen's – his best friend's – was so fittingly in keeping with the situation that Sylvester almost envied George. (23–4)

The George–Stephen–Blanche triangle represents the type of plot that would conventionally drive a novel. Sylvester regards this triangle as perfect in a tragic way – 'faintly unhappy love' is what he calls it. Sylvester, who is himself a writer, recognises that this arrangement of desire fits the traditional mode of romance in novels, and conspires to extricate Jane from the unsatisfactory (and entirely uncanonical) relationship that she is involved in with Jessica:

> For why should Jane – poor silly – not be as happy as Blanche? As serene as Blanche, thanking Heaven (on a full stomach) for a Good Man's Love? Why contrarily should she be loved and bullied and perhaps even murdered by that frightful Jessica? Surely the thread of her fate might be snipped, as with nail scissors, so that she could swim away in time, back to the warm mud-flat of domesticity. (23)

Through the character of Sylvester, Keane thus manipulates the fictional world of Jane and Jessica, and juxtaposes the plot of lesbian desire (represented by Jane and Jessica's relationship) with the canonical plot structure based on homosocial bonding and heterosexual love.

Keane's revision of the canonical plot structure corresponds with her exploration of various contexts for lesbian desire. When the novel opens, we are already in the world of the post-marital lesbian plot – Jane's husband has died some time ago, and her relationship with Jessica appears well established. For Castle, the 'world of schooling and adolescence' is one of the contexts in which lesbian desire flourishes, in contrast to the other clearly identifiable context, the post-marital world of 'divorce, widowhood, and separation' (85).

The reason that lesbian desire flourishes in these contexts, according to Castle, is because the canonical arrangement of desire shaped by male bonding cannot take hold – there are no men in these contexts to bond with each other: 'In each of these mimetic contexts, male erotic triangulation is either conspicuously absent or under assault' (85). In *Devoted Ladies*, Keane leaves out male homosocial bonding almost entirely (the only fully drawn male characters are Sylvester and George), and the operations of female bonding (however perverse and masochistic they may be) take central stage.

In the case of *Devoted Ladies*, Keane employs both contexts for lesbian desire: Jane and Jessica's post-marital lesbian bond and Piggy's prolonged adolescent attraction to the self-centered and heartless Joan, which closely resembles Castle's pre-marital lesbian model. However, Keane modifies the pre-marital lesbian model slightly; unlike Castle's figure, both Joan and Piggy are adults, Joan is married, and while Piggy is certainly in love with Joan, no actual sexual relationship exists between the two women. When asked about the real-life model for Joan and her Piggy-like 'acolytes' (Intro. xiii), Keane asserted that 'there was nothing lesbian about it at all. Perhaps part of it was because there was a great scarcity of young men [in the Anglo-Irish community]' (Intro. xiii). Despite Keane's denial of the lesbianism in Piggy's devotion to Joan, her assertion about the scarcity of Anglo-Irish young men indicates that the Anglo-Irish community, lacking homosocial bonding, would have been a fertile setting for the emergence of lesbian desire.

Although the models for Joan and Piggy might have been innocent of sexual desire, I think we can usefully apply the term 'lesbian' to Piggy's desire for Joan. For one, Piggy's initial love for Joan is based on a moment of physical attraction, when as girls Joan demonstrates how a 'calf' can be not just a young cow, but a part of the anatomy: 'She put her leg on the schoolroom table and showed Piggy what a calf was. Piggy's heart thumped' (148). The narrator also describes the relationship between Piggy and Joan in heterosexual terms:

> In all her romantics for Joan she was least sincere in that on this she most believed her life was founded, and so deceived herself with the most energy, persuading herself of Joan's necessity towards her and bolstering up her own belief in this in a hundred ways – in the giving of little gifts and in the giving of rich, expensive gifts; in this like nothing so much as an amorous and impotent old man, buying a rich jewel for a teasing young Miss to see her lovely gratitude for a moment. (147)

Piggy is likened to an 'amorous and impotent old man', a simile that acknowledges the fact that any sexual desire on Piggy's part is unrealised, but not that this desire is entirely absent. The narrator also describes Joan as

Piggy's 'girlfriend' (89) and tells the reader that Piggy 'loved her with a flaming devotion that was her one true excitement in life' (89). Although Emma Donoghue has asserted that Jessica is the novel's 'only clearly lesbian character' ('Noises' 161), Piggy's lesbian desire for Joan is significant in that it presents readers with a version of female-female desire that differs from the examples of Jane and Jessica and also creates the circumstances for the novel's dysphoric ending in which the three versions of lesbianism are eliminated – Jessica and Piggy through death and Jane through marriage.

The use of apparitional metaphors and the predominantly female-female arrangement of desire in *Devoted Ladies* create what Castle might call an archetypal lesbian fiction. According to Castle:

> by plotting against what Eve Sedgwick has called the 'plot of male homosociality,' the archetypal lesbian fiction decanonizes, so to speak, the canonical structure of desire itself. Insofar as it documents a world in which men are 'between women' rather than vice versa, it is an insult to the conventional geometries of fictional eros. It dismantles the real, as it were, in search for the not-yet-real, something unpredicted and unpredictable. It is an assault on the banal: a retriangulating of triangles. (90–1)

Although *Devoted Ladies* concludes with the implied canonical ending – Jane will marry George – the pathway to that ending has been structured around lesbian triangles, and not the Sedgwickian male homosocial triangle. Instead of men competing for Jane, women – Jessica and Piggy, primarily – are linked in competition for control of Jane's future. When, in the novel's conclusion, Piggy kills herself and Jessica by driving off a cliff, their deaths represent a simultaneous sacrifice of both the threatening embodiment of mature lesbian sexuality and the pre-marital lesbian figure; neither, according to Keane, are viable expressions of sexuality in 1930s Ireland.

In conclusion, Keane's attitude towards lesbianism seems to be one of authorial curiosity and, frankly, exploitation; as the above-quoted interview with Polly Devlin indicates, lesbianism represented a new and intriguing subject for her. In *Devoted Ladies,* Keane exploits the possibilities for how lesbian desire might fit into her dark satire of the Anglo-Irish. The lesbian depictions might be problematic (as Breen, Weekes and Donoghue have noted), but the range of lesbian expressions – Piggy's perennially adolescent crush, Jane's apparent bisexuality, Jessica's resemblance to Hall's mannish lesbian – reveal an impressive sophistication about the varieties of sexual desire. Keane's exploration of lesbian desire, its function in narrative structures, and its linguistic representation mark *Devoted Ladies* as a useful literary landmark in the development of Irish lesbian narratives and in twentieth-century definitions of 'lesbian.'

Bringing down the House

Big House home improvements?
Troubled owners and modern renovations in
Mad Puppetstown

SARAH McLEMORE

What's so scary about renovating an Anglo-Irish Big House? In the few novels by Molly Keane that involve the renovation of a home and its demesne, redecorating and rebuilding are depicted as horrific and haunted tasks comparable only to the experience of surviving the Anglo-Irish War physically, emotionally, and architecturally intact. It's not just the Troubles that wreak havoc on the psyches of Keane's Big House residents. The psychological consequences involved in renovating after the Troubles, and Keane's Gothic, personified images of Big Houses-in-transition, point to new ways of thinking about Anglo-Irish fear and architectural metaphoricity within the Big House genre. I will suggest in this essay that Keane's novel *Mad Puppetstown* (1931) illustrates the end of a particular type of life and style within the walls of the Big House. Like other contemporaneous works, such as Elizabeth Bowen's 1929 novel *The Last September* and Keane's 1941 novel *Two Days in Aragon*, *Mad Puppetstown* implies the end of Anglo-Irish authoritative rule in Ireland. However, Keane is careful to pen a series of possibilities for the future of Puppetstown. In *Mad Puppetstown* the house is not ruined by fire or abandoned but neither is it preserved as a monument to life before the war. The text complicates the matrix of writerly tropes usually associated with the Big House and 'the Troubles' in two interrelated ways. First, Keane elides the burning of the Big House of Puppetstown. Accordingly, the text lacks the series of architectural images – or what critic Vera Kreilkamp terms the 'fatedness or 'design' of a political 'execution' of the Big House' – that we have grown to expect from an Anglo-Irish Big House novel set during the Troubles (1998, 151). Second, Keane makes the prospect of renovating Puppetstown after the war a source of incredible anxiety. This is most clear in the final chapters of *Mad Puppetstown*, which discuss in detail the emotionally and physically painful process of its renovation and redecoration. Although both Easter and Basil – the two youthful architects of the renovation process – wish to make Puppetstown as it was before the Anglo-Irish war, they are also intent on endowing it with modern conveniences and other touches that reflect their own modern aesthetic sensibilities. Wanting to both make it new and put it back the way it was leads, after many Gothic twists and turns, to a new aesthetics of hominess within the Big House of Puppetstown. While the primary focus of this essay is on Keane's deploy-

183

ment of Gothic renovation in *Mad Puppetstown*, I also read it against *Two Days in Aragon*,[1] her only other novel which is explicitly concerned with the Anglo-Irish war. As in *Mad Puppetstown*, *Two Days in Aragon* depicts renovation as a contentious issue which illustrates the loci of family power and Anglo-Irish fear both during and after the Troubles.

One might ask whether Molly Keane's anxiousness about renovation isolate her as a home improvement-phobic, or whether the textual renovation fears in *Mad Puppetstown* are indicative of a broader literary or cultural trend. Although somewhat unique among Big House novelists, Molly Keane's turn to Gothic renovations and debates over life and style within the Big House might be said to situate her squarely within the discourse of modernist debates regarding tradition, innovation, and the aesthetics of homeness. For example, Adolf Loos's 1908 treatise 'Ornament and Crime' is both a schema of ornament, or interior and exterior decorations, and an exhortation to decorate in a way that reflects the historical, economic, and geographical realities of where one lives. Loos argues that those 'who measure everything by the past impede the cultural development of nations and of humanity itself' (32). Furthermore, ornamental styles which overly invoke the past are, in Loos's manifesto, criminal and capable of damaging a nation's economy and cultural development (32). While Molly Keane makes the process of home improvements and redecoration Gothic, Loos asserts that to *not* renovate would be criminal and degenerate. Literally 'living' in the past stymies the growth and sophistication of the nation in ways that are both scandalous and terrifying. Keane's texts are not analogous with Loos's decoration manifesto. Loos proclaims the criminality of certain types of decoration and style while Keane insinuates the allegorical and physical potentials produced by large-scale Big House home improvements. Yet it is undoubtedly the case that Keane's chief renovator/zeitgeists do, like Loos, emblematise the desire to move beyond particular epochs of Anglo-Irish household style and history and to avoid the uncanny consequences of living in the past.

In each of Keane's Big House novels, the architectural space of the Big House works symbolically. At nominal and material levels, space is a source of power and intrigue as well as a means of illustrating belonging or anomalousness within and beyond the confines of Anglo-Irish society. In *Good Behaviour*, Aroon St Charles's inheritance of Temple Alice precipitates her smug and strategic movement of the family to Gull's Cry, thus supremely signifying her status as the new matriarch of the St Charles family. In many cases Keane's houses are blithely or ominously haunted by spiritual apparitions of deceased family members or servants.[2] The appearance of these ghosts force questions

---

1 For an in-depth discussion of this issue see Vera Kreilkamp's analysis of Molly Keane's literary engagement with the Troubles in Chapter 7 of *The Anglo-Irish novel and the Big House* (1998). 2 See for example *Young Entry* (1928) in which a cook's suicide is provoked by

of ownership and stability for residents within the Big House gates, while the ghostliness and contingency of Big House ownership and occupancy points to the precariousness of Anglo-Irish authority in Ireland. Thus, the Anglo-Irish residents' shaky hold over their demesnes is made manifest through the hints of ghostly presences and retributions, as well as through a seemingly endless series of textual battles regarding home ownership and home occupation.

Viewing Keane's literary production in this light propels us towards thinking of her work as focussed on a society verging on extinction. The precarious nature of the Big House – its physical decay, its financial indebtedness, its ability to harbour ghosts – comes to symbolise the decline and fall of Anglo-Irish power in Ireland. In Polly Devlin's introduction to *Mad Puppetstown*, she writes that to find a literal image of the fictitious house Puppetstown 'Open any book on the ruined houses of Ireland, or on existing great houses, and you will find its match' (page x). Here Devlin suggests that the textual house stands for both that which has been ruined and that which has survived. Yet thinking of homes such as Puppetstown in this way implies that houses are only capable of signifying ruin or an image of Ascendancy life before impending ruin. Devlin suggests a limited system of Big House signification which elides the complex evolution which Puppetstown undergoes in Keane's text. Puppetstown experiences two crucial transformations in Keane's novel. First, Aunt Dicksie and Patsy, a servant, turn it into a hermitage when they are left alone during the most volatile days of the Anglo-Irish war. The house is then subsequently transformed when Easter and Basil return to remodel it in a way that both evokes the past and incorporates modern conveniences, making Puppetstown a new symbol of Ascendancy life in a Free State countryside.

Commenting on the structural plan of *Mad Puppetstown*, Devlin notes, 'The book moves in episodic fits and starts' (xiii). The setting of the novel moves from Puppetstown to England and then, finally, back to Puppetstown. Likewise, Keane's style of narration shifts depending on the geographical and temporal locations of the text. The first sustained section of *Mad Puppetstown*, which focuses on a day in the life of the house in 1904, is vivid and exact. Like many of Keane's novels written as M.J. Farrell, this first section of *Mad Puppetstown* contains a lucid picture of Ascendancy life, complete with a cast of quirky but loveable servants, aloof adults, charming children, and the necessary menagerie of animals, including horses and hounds as well as peacocks, ferrets, and a dead badger. Vera Kreilkamp's 1986 review of *Mad Puppetstown* praises Keane's 'passionate and savagely ecstatic' description of an Anglo-Irish childhood, but this rapturous view of life changes in the next section of the text as it moves towards the traumas of World War I and the Anglo-Irish war (16).[3]

accusations that she has stolen a ham. The presence of the ghost-cook is later felt by Prudence, the novel's young heroine.   **3** Critics such as Marjorie Halligan have noted that Keane based

As the book progresses, its episodes darken in tone. In the second section of the novel, the hoyden days of tennis parties, racing, and hunting are
interrupted with the grim news of Easter's father's death in France during
World War I and new worries about the presence of the IRA in the Irish
countryside. By the close of the third section of *Mad Puppetstown* – the
episode most associated with the Anglo-Irish war – Keane's house, which had
before been described as being as comfortable 'as a wide-lapped woman, sitting blue-aproned in the sunlight', becomes a 'lonely, wicked old woman of
a house' (45, 165). Keane's use of personification recalls Elizabeth Bowen's
early descriptions of Danielstown in *The Last September* and it also foreshadows her portrayal of the Big House of Aragon which was to come in 1941.
Commenting on Danielstown, Gearoid Cronin describes Bowen's tone as
'apocalyptic' (153). The personification of the house signals the beginning of
the narrative's acceleration towards a nightmarish end: the burning of
Danielstown (153). As Bowen's novel progresses, Danielstown is continually
animated or described as a living character which seems to sense its impending doom as a means of metaphorically illustrating the grimly anomalous status of the Anglo-Irish in Ireland. The writerly architecture of Danielstown
and its surrounding landscape foreshadow their future as 'brittle staring ruins'
and, more broadly, the ominous future awaiting the Anglo-Irish in Ireland
(Bowen 152). Significantly, none of Keane's novels include the comprehen-
sive burning of a Big House in which the novel's protagonists make their
home, although Aragon's near total ruin in *Two Days in Aragon* comes quite
close. Instead, her novels seek their resolution in different forms which force
us as critics to consider how they work against the conventions of the burning Big House novel.

One of the most exhaustive analysis of these conventions is contained in
Margot Gayle Backus's important critical intervention *The Gothic Family
Romance: Heterosexuality, Child Sacrifice, and the Anglo-Irish Colonial Order*.
In her chapter 'Somebody Else's Troubles: Post-Treaty Retrenchment and
the (Burning) Big House Novel', Backus develops a grammar of post-Treaty
Big House novelistic conventions focused on issues of gender, colonialism,
and the recurrence of Gothic family secrets concerning sexual abuse and sexuality (175). Backus aligns the textual burning of the Big House with authorial foci on family conflict and deep-seated political issues. She explains that
if read collectively 'these "burning Big House" texts … reveal an Anglo-Irish
Gothic family romance punctured by the force of external events, which must
now be integrated rather than maintained as a dissociated cultural fantasy'

Puppetstown on her childhood home, Ballyrankin, which was burned down in 1920 (45). In
both *Mad Puppetstown* and *Two Days in Aragon* Keane utilises real rather than fictitious names
of houses in a departure from her earlier works in which fictitious names tended to be used.

(178). Accordingly, Molly Keane's *Two Days in Aragon*, which depicts the gruesome near-destruction of the Big House of Aragon, is one of Backus's prime examples of a burning Big House novel. As Backus notes, at the 'generative center of the novel's topoi of hidden and twisted relations is the architecture of the house itself, which is fully revealed to the reader only late in the novel' (199–200). Our knowledge of Aragon's architecture coincides with our understanding of the long history of sexual abuse and sadistic treatment of employees by Aragon's owners and employers. Soon after, the climax of *Two Days in Aragon* occurs during which the house is nearly annihilated, a retributive IRA attack that asserts the end of Anglo-Irish authoritative rule in Ireland.

In Keane's fast-paced novel set during a frenetic two days in which a series of sexual secrets, violent histories, and long standing grudges are elucidated, Aragon's near total burning is cathartic for Sylvia and Grania, the legitimate daughters of Aragon's Big House. The baroque description of the violent fire clears a path for a new future with a rebuilt Aragon expunged of its past ghosts and Gothic colonial secrets. Moreover, Keane allows Grania, the promiscuous, emotional, and less traditional of the two heirs to Aragon, to be depicted as the chief architect of Aragon's impending restructuring. Her sister Sylvia, a scrupulous and vicious upholder of the family's traditions and a firm believer in the greatness of the British Empire, will not live on in Aragon. Sylvia's ultimate reaction to the burning of Aragon is one of hysterical grief and loss; there is no future for her in Ireland and she will escape to England as soon as possible (250). If Sylvia's grief-stricken rejection of Aragon implies her wish for the house to live on only as a memory of the golden days of 'tennis parties and white hunting ties and blue habits,' then the violent death of Nan, Aragon's sadistic housekeeper, gorily symbolises the end of the Fox family's legacy of sexual abuse (250). As a product of the Fox's violent use of *droit de seigneur* and the mother of a child fathered by Sylvia and Grania's grandfather, Nan is a supreme signifier of what Margot Gayle Backus terms 'Big House miscegenation' (195). Moments before her death, Nan foresees the future of Aragon and opines:

> the house would rise again. A house would be built here for happy Grania's children. Grania looking back to the lusty foolish child she had been, and a little proud of the brave child she had been, would live here with her children, and the garden of Aragon [would] flower after its desolation. (255)

This fertile image of a flowering garden and a new generation of Aragon's denizens represents the paradigm shift implied at the end of Keane's text. The rebuilt house of Aragon will be a space for a happy family without the Gothic threats of miscegenation and sexual and domestic power struggles which haunted its earlier residents. Indeed Nan's death simultaneously suggests the end of a long line of sexual abuse of servants and the conclusion of her sadistic and cruel attempts to control the house and its residents. Likewise, the IRA assault on Aragon seems destined not to be repeated as its architects attacked the house both for its symbolic value and as a means of deploying an act of retributive violence against Nan. Nan's mistreatment of Killer Denny – one of the IRA members – when he was a young servant in Aragon was one of the primary reasons why Aragon was burned. Her death then makes the home an unlikely target for a second act of violence. The impending renovations suggest that a sense of closure has been achieved through Aragon's burning. Thus the end of the text, which includes Nan's death and the house's partial burning, does not insinuate a continuing cycle of violence either within or against the house. Instead, *Two Days in Aragon* depicts a brutal, exact, and brief moment in Aragon's history, which brings to the surface its Gothic histories and vivifies the architectural and human consequences of the Anglo-Irish war.

In contrast, Keane's literary analysis of the Troubles, which she caustically describes as 'the little bitter, forgotten war in Ireland,' is neatly contained in one of the shorter sections of *Mad Puppetstown* (123). The section is a stylistic miasma which never fully achieves the acceleration of architectural metaphoricity endemic in *The Last September* or in *Two Days in Aragon*. During the Troubles Danielstown and Aragon are rich sites of allegorical animism and Anglo-Irish guilt which culminate in their respective near demises. However, in *Mad Puppetstown* Keane paints the events leading up to the Anglo-Irish war with broad strokes and clichés in a montage of images that lacks temporal and spatial specificity. This lack of exactitude is remarkable when we consider her earlier minute catalogue of life in the Puppetstown of 1904 and, more broadly, her reputation as a writer who persistently attempts to render life in Ireland realistically. As Diana Petre notes in her introduction to *Young Entry*, 'You can *touch* a Farrell/Keane countryside and you can *smell* it' (x). Instead of more concrete realist visions of agrarian outrage during the Anglo-Irish war, readers are given the following description of the Troubles in which hackneyed images form a frantic, terrifying list:

> Meetings by night: oaths to their forgotten land sworn, signed and forgotten: drillings and revolver practice and always the romantic cup of dizzy words ... these things ran in a golden exciting vein through the years before the grim actual happenings took shape of horror in the land. (124)

The calculated wry exactitude of Keane's earlier writing is gone. In its place, and presented from the perspective of Irish men participating in assaults against the Ascendancy, Keane explores the discursive foundations of the Troubles. It is the 'romantic cup of dizzying words' spoken, presumably, by members of the Land League or the IRA that is privileged by Keane. She does not include any elaborate descriptions of physical or geographical conflict. This description of the catalytic and fearsome language of shadowy organisations is juxtaposed with a short description of Anglo-Irish fear during the Troubles:

> They were strange days for the gentry of Ireland these, strange silent, dangerous days. The morning's paper (and if the post was late it was because a bridge had been blown up the night before or the mail raided on its way from Dublin) might tell of the murder of a friend; or the burning of a house that had lately been like Puppetstown. (125)

Here, the narrative voice seems to suggest that the 'strange days' of the Anglo-Irish war are beyond the linguistic epistemology of the Anglo-Irish gentry. While it is possible to read of agrarian outrage in the newspaper, Keane asserts that, for the Anglo-Irish, silence rather than speaking or describing is the dominant method of response and commentary on the Troubles.

It is only in subsequent pages of *Mad Puppetstown* that Keane gives concrete, if fleeting, examples of the ways that the Anglo-Irish war affects Puppetstown's residents. Officer Reginald Grey is shot by an IRA man while in his car with one of Puppetstown's denizens, the lovely Aunt Brenda. His death, and Brenda's fears for the lives of her sons Basil and Evelyn and her niece Easter, drive her away from Puppetstown to England. Keane doesn't describe Reginald's death and there are no sustained personal descriptions of reactions to his violent passing. Grief, fear, and outrage are quickly felt and then moved beyond, owing to Brenda's overwhelming desire to remove herself from Puppetstown as soon as possible. Hours after Reginald's death, Brenda and the children are gone, leaving Aunt Dicksie alone in the house.

Reginald's death and the abandonment of Puppetstown en masse provoke a complicated portrayal of the house which is far less abstract than Keane's earlier attempts to describe the atmosphere of the Anglo-Irish war. The image is focalised or seen through the point of view of Aunt Dicksie who is to become the dictatorial caretaker of the house. Aunt Dicksie imagines that the house has 'lost her honour and now stood betrayed and forsaken and most desolately in sin and in shame before the world' (165). This description of the house is given to explain Puppetstown's status after the loss of Aunt Brenda and the children, an important juncture that signals the beginning of Aunt Dicksie's reign and the consequent erosion of Puppetstown. Keane's imagery of the house as a shamed woman is grim and ominous. However, its shameful appearance foreshadows life under the rule of Aunt Dicksie and

Patsy rather than a sense of impending doom related to the recent violence in the countryside.

The evening that Aunt Brenda departs, Aunt Dicksie keeps a lonely watch over Puppetstown's demesne. While Reginald's death seems to be the vivification of Keane's earlier mention of the newspaper story detailing 'the murder of a friend', Aunt Dicksie's presence precludes the realisation of the story of 'the burning of a house'. Keane informs us that IRA men watched Puppetstown the night of Reginald's murder but their sense that the house was occupied kept them from burning it. At this most precarious point in Puppetstown's history Keane forgoes the opportunity to describe the house as a Gothic, barren space. In contrast to the disgrace and desolation produced by Brenda's flight, Keane notes that Puppetstown on the eve of its possible destruction was 'Not so empty as it was vacant; not so desolate as it was sulky' (171). Here Keane shows that the descriptive terms we as readers might expect from an account of a nearly abandoned and almost burned Big House are not appropriate. Instead, Puppetstown's sulky vacancy points to its somewhat unique status as a survivor with an uncertain future.

Puppetstown's survival suggests that Keane's novel both contains and counters the conventions of the Big House novel set during the Troubles. Its permutations, first into a hermitage and then into a newly modern version of the past, take it beyond the archetypal signifiers of Ascendancy decline: the burned Big House and the Big House as ruin. The last sections of *Mad Puppetstown*, in which the narrative returns to Keane's earlier descriptive exactitude, are fundamentally concerned with exploring the architectural and stylistic future of Puppetstown. As Easter and Basil fight Aunt Dicksie and Patsy for stylistic authority over the house, the text becomes comically Gothic. Easter and Basil's initial bravado descends into fear and uncertainty as Aunt Dicksie, Patsy and Puppetstown brood and rebel against their plans for improvement. Given Keane's earlier more abstract descriptions of the Troubles and, indeed, her subsequent scrupulous description of a nearly burned Big House in *Two Days in Aragon*, it is important to consider what is at stake in her turn to the realistically portrayed horrors of renovation in *Mad Puppetstown*. While anyone who has embarked on a home improvement project might well understand the emotions, fears, secrets, and power struggles involved in seeing the project through to completion, the 'home improvement Gothic' is a less common subject of literary investigation for Big House authors. In making renovation rather than ruin the final focus of *Mad Puppetstown*, Keane's novel is somewhat unique among Anglo-Irish Big House novels written during the first half of the twentieth century. One exception is Bowen's 1955 novel *A World of Love*, but the home restoration that occurs in this text is executed by its *nouveau riche* owner Lady Latterly and does not precipitate the same anxieties as represented in *Mad Puppetstown*. Rather than portraying the renovation in Gothic terms, Latterly's ability to restore her house signifies her deviant status as newly-rich in a world of genteel poverty.

The infrequent textual emphasis on renovation corresponds with information available on the restoration history of Anglo-Irish country houses and, more particularly, the restoration of homes after the architectural violence of the Troubles. According to Terrence Dooley, author of *The Decline of the Big House in Ireland*, few of the approximately seventy-six houses burned during the War of Independence or the 199 houses burned in the subsequent Civil War were rebuilt (182, 189). Dooley's history of the Big House suggests that while some recompense was provided by the Free State government under the Damage to Property (Compensation) Act of 1923, few former Big House owners made claims (201).[4] Moreover, as the duke of Devonshire explained in a letter to the governor-general of the Free State, there 'are owners of property who feel that they cannot with safety return to Ireland or in view of the destruction of homes to which they were attached, do not wish to return' (cited in Dooley 202). Instead, many former Big House owners became deracinated, moving abroad or building new, smaller homes closer to the relative safety of Ireland's metropolitan centre, Dublin, thus abandoning their homes or the ruins of their homes.[5]

Given the frequency of Big House decline and Anglo-Irish deracination, it would seem logical that anyone attempting to improve a Big House in a text would be a happy exception to a grim rule. Yet in *Mad Puppetstown* no one is satisfied by the prospect and process of its renovation. Aunt Dicksie feels that Easter and Basil's return home means that she will lose her power over Puppetstown, while Easter and Basil, escaping from the competitive and claustrophobic world of English house parties and Oxford social life, are horrified to return to Ireland and find their former home simultaneously 'forgotten,' 'familiar,' and 'unfriendly' (251). Thus, in the last section of the text

---

4 One of the most common reasons that burned-out house owners were reluctant to make claims was due to the fact that the Damage to Property (Compensation) Act limited compensation for home furnishings and jewellery which would have represented a sizeable amount of the fiscal (and emotional) losses accrued during the burning of a Big-House. Furthermore, compensation would only be provided if owners could prove definitively that steps 'taken or which might reasonably have been taken by the owner of the property, his servants or agents to protect the property from anticipated injury, or to resist, prevent or defeat the committal of the injury' (cited in Dooley 202). Proving that these steps had been taken was next to impossible and, moreover, there were relatively few documented cases in which house owners or house staffs spiritedly defended their home or spaces of employment.   5 For more information on this matter see one or more of the several elegiac coffee table books which point to this sense of decline. The titles of this proliferation of housing indexes and social histories of the Anglo-Irish in the twentieth century such as *Ascendancy to oblivion, The decline of the Big House in Ireland*, and *In Ruins: the Once Great Houses of Ireland* suggest the downward spiral of the Big House and the diaspora of its owners.

there are two foci of anxieties regarding Puppetstown's present status and future possibilities. First, the renovation of the house calls into question issues of ownership and possession. While Aunt Dicksie knows that Easter is the rightful inheritor of the house, she is reluctant to give up the space that she has guarded over and scrimped for. During the renovation process, Aunt Dicksie's fears and anger seem to bewitch the house, causing it to rebel against the improvements proffered by Easter and Basil. The various projects that Easter and Basil begin result in an avalanche of more complicated repairs. For example, Puppetstown's leaky roof is discovered to be supporting rotten beams; a drain dug by plumbers displaces bushes of *Daphne Mezereon* whose mutilated floral corpses rest at Easter's feet seeming to flow with 'white scented blood' (272). Furthermore, the contractors and servants that Easter and Basil hire to help complete the home renovation project are angered and alienated by the squalor and decay of the house and by Aunt Dicksie's obliquely inhospitable disposition. Puppetstown's cook becomes 'violent and unruly', the plumber 'pliably unbiddable', and the house's other servants are bullied by Aunt Dicksie into helping her in the garden thus keeping them from their redecoration work in the house (271).

The second major foci of anxiety which Puppetstown's renovation provokes concerns issues of legitimacy and identity. I have already suggested in this essay that one of the dominant ways of textually being Anglo-Irish during or immediately after the Anglo-Irish war involves the ruination or burning of a Big House. To rebuild and revise their house as Easter and Basil do means thinking of Anglo-Irishness as a mutable identity which is not solely constituted by a sense of demise or impending doom. Moreover, renovation forces Puppetstown's residents to question the legitimacy of their status in Ireland after the Anglo-Irish war. As Easter and Basil begin to redecorate they question whether or not they have a right to reoccupy and reorder Puppetstown and, if they do choose to do so, how the house should reflect both its past history and its future hopes. Accordingly, renovation may be seen as a new means by which Anglo-Irish literary Gothicism, or what Terry Eagleton in *Heathcliff and the Great Hunger* has termed the 'political unconscious of Anglo-Irish society,' emerges (187). Nineteenth century Anglo-Irish Gothic writers from Maturin to Stoker and Le Fanu engage in writing the stories of Big Houses. According to Eagleton, these sorts of Gothic writings may be said to represent the political unconscious of the Anglo-Irish as they mirror back 'the recognizable characters, events and locales of daily life ... shot through with all the guilt, loathing and unnameable desires which had to be jettisoned from that existence if [they] were to operate as coherent citizens at all' (180). In *Mad Puppetstown* it is not merely the house's dramatic decay and sense of unhomeliness which are the sources of the text's literary Gothicism. Instead, renovation becomes a new precipitant of fear, anxiety and

Anglo-Irish guilt. Thus, Keane's Big House novel implies a new dimension of the Anglo-Irish political unconscious which attempts to negotiate the new troubles endemic in remaking an Anglo-Irish home in the Irish Free State.

Although they had been in exile from Ireland for several years, both Easter and Basil had formed romantic memories of their earlier life at Puppetstown. Their spontaneous decision to abscond from England was precipitated by a mixture of nostalgia, homesickness, and a sense of anomalousness in England. Yet Easter and Basil's arrival at Puppetstown is uncanny and the house itself is uncomfortable. Without the modern conveniences she has come to expect in England and without a sense of being at home, Easter is immediately ready to return to Oxford. Implicitly, Easter and Basil comprehend the nominal and material effects of the Anglo-Irish war. While not burned, Puppetstown's decrepit state and its anomalous location in the Free State countryside allegorises their uncanny senses of unbelonging. It is only by stressing the adventurous aspects of the home improvement project that Basil convinces Easter to stay, suggesting 'don't you see, we might have rather more sport putting it all right, putting it back to what it was, than we'd have had if it had been all complete and ready for us?' (263). Easter agrees but proposes that while they should restore the house to its former cosy glory, they should also endow it with aesthetic flairs that represent their cosmopolitan, youthful styles. The promise of electric lights, a vibrant green or yellow bathroom and other stylistic and technological changes will allow the house to finely balance the legacy of the past with prospects for the future. It is the series of alterations that Easter and Basil propose that illustrates the uniqueness of their project and makes both characters sympathetic to the reader as Big House innovators.

Yet Easter and Basil's jaunty optimism quickly dissipates. Like so many home improvement projects, the renovation of Puppetstown becomes a jarring and cacophonous headache:

> There rang through Puppetstown now the tingling beat of hammers, the volcanic jutting of blow-lams, the click of trowel on stone, and occasionally the slyly modest shrieks of the cook that Easter and Basil had imported from Dublin, as she dallied hopefully with the plumber. (265)

As *Mad Puppetstown* unfolds, the home improvements go increasingly wrong. Keane describes these darkest days of construction in terms that recall her earlier use of personification. Puppetstown becomes a spirit bent on sabotaging Easter and Basil's enthusiastic changes. As Easter and Basil contemplate the nightmarish qualities of their renovation or, as we hear from Easter's point of view, 'The world ... spinning on an axis of crowded, trivial miseries – raging cooks, weeping aunts ... plumbers, painters, and masons – all, abominable'

(273), it becomes increasingly clear that the only way that the project will ever be finished is with Aunt Dicksie's blessing. From its start, the project of renovating Puppetstown lacks the blessing of Aunt Dicksie, who fears that her position of authority will be usurped and that the house will become a decadent money pit of little-needed changes. Together with Easter and Basil's anxiety over how to renovate and what to change, Aunt Dicksie's fears of replacement as owner form the most sustained narratives of fear in the novel. Her fears, which seem to precipitate the house's Gothic animation, suggest the complicated ways in which the home allegorises Ascendancy life both before the Anglo-Irish war and Aunt Dicksie and Patsy's life within Puppetstown during the war under virtual 'house arrest'. For Aunt Dicksie to relinquish even partial control over Puppetstown's demesne means she must first accept the impossibility of living in a house which literally monumentalises the fearful past. It is only when she achieves this moment of realisation that *Mad Puppetstown* begins to move towards its final resolution.

Although the novel ends before the renovation is complete, its last pages suggest a happy ending to a decorative horror story. Basil assuages Aunt Dicksie's fears that she is a superfluous presence in the house and that her legacy will be erased by the home improvements. Basil insists to Aunt Dicksie 'we need you awfully, Easter and I do. We couldn't bear Puppetstown without you' (278). Aunt Dicksie acquiesces, giving consent for the renovation project to continue and, implicitly, for shared control of Puppetstown's domain to be instituted. Privately, Basil understands this consent as a form of exorcism that once and for all expels the many ghostly fears that so impeded the earlier efforts to restructure Puppetstown. The renovation can now continue harmoniously governed by a triumvirate with each member utilising his or her styles, identities, and histories. As in the case of *Two Days in Aragon*, renovation in *Mad Puppetstown* entails rebuilding and improving, while at the same time memorialising the complicated history of an Anglo-Irish family and its home. Keane's novel thus suggests the reality of Ireland's troubled political legacy and its violent progress into nationhood. The literary genre of the post-Treaty Big House novel frequently deploys the burned house, the decaying house, or the house in (near) ruins to allegorise the status of the Anglo-Irish in Ireland after creation of the Free State. Despite the relentlessness of this trend, *Mad Puppetstown* and *Two Days in Aragon* suggest the difficulties at stake in developing a nuanced taxonomy of architectural metaphors in Big House texts and the problems associated with foreclosing the Big House as a signifier of decline, making her novels somewhat unique among her contemporaries. In imagining the possibility of a rebuilt life and a renovated home after the Anglo-Irish war, Keane as a writer/architect has laid the foundation for new explorations into the metaphorical potential of the Big House and the Big House novel.

'Dark, established currents':
Molly Keane's Gothic

SINÉAD MOONEY

This essay aims to suggest that the novels of Molly Keane can fruitfully be considered in the light of the Gothic mode. Her generic 'belonging' is interestingly problematic. What little criticism has been devoted to Keane's writing to date has tended to rely heavily on a biographical or light sociological reading, sponsored by the biographically-inflected introductions to the Virago reprints of the early work during the 1980s and 90s, after the success of *Good Behaviour*. The result has been the adumbration of a Keane who often appears to have been rescued from relegation to the sub-category of period 'woman's novelist' only by the ambivalent gravitas conferred by her insider status as perhaps the very last of the Big House novelists to chronicle from within the demesne the demise of her caste. Yet the political thrust of Keane's writing, her acidly comic social history and the implications of her best work's powerful attraction toward the melodramatic, the violent, the irrational, even the macabre, has been neutralised by the textual apparatus of the Virago texts. Dirk Bogarde's 1990 foreword to her 1949 novel *Treasure Hunt*, is typical in its insistent recruitment of the novel to the middlebrow, gossipy and domestic: 'Oh! indeed. There is malice here, but you'll hardly know it, it's like garlic in a properly cooked dish' (i).[1] The successful Keane 'recipe' is unambiguous, as is Bogarde's account of the play upon which the novel was based (which Keane co-wrote with John Perry), with its 'cast of dotty, beguiling grotesques', delighting a British audience 'exhausted, despondent, rationed, taxed and still recovering from a savage war' (iv). This casts Keane as very much the beguiling representative of an Ireland envisaged as eccentric escape or alternative reality. That *Treasure Hunt* the novel (as distinct from the admittedly tinselly play) adroitly interrogates the mutual confrontation of English and Irish national stereotype is nowhere indicated. Neither does Bogarde's account register Keane's Elizabeth Bowen-like analysis of national identity as performance rather than birthright, or her novel's knowing intertextual nods to *Castle Rackrent* and Chekov, still less the fact that *Treasure Hunt* appears at times to pre-empt Beckett's Gothic-absurdist play *Endgame* in its portrayal of what Terry Eagleton dubs 'that Hobbesian social order, the family' (1995, 188).

---

1 The Molly Keane/M.J. Farrell novels referred to in this essay are: *Full House* (1935; London: Virago, 1985); *Treasure Hunt* (1935; London: Virago, 1990); *Two Days in Aragon* (1941; London: Virago, 1989); *The Rising Tide* (1937; London: Virago, 1984); *Mad Puppetstown* (1931, London: Virago, 1985); and *Devoted Ladies* (1934; London: Virago,1984).

Bogarde is far from being alone in his tidying of Keane's work into a more benign form. Polly Devlin, in her much more considered 1983 introduction to the Virago reprint of *The Rising Tide*, is representative in appearing to feel some form of anticipatory apology is due for the novel's 'narrow horizons [and] elitist occupations'. She regards it as typical of Keane's novels in making 'no mention of political turmoil, though at the time in which it is set the issue of home rule was tearing the country apart' (vi). In this regard, for Devlin as for other commentators, Keane is 'akin to Jane Austen; in concentrating on the two inches of ivory of [...] her feeling for the minutiae of human behaviour', with 'houses, hunting and horses, her central themes' (vii). 'Sometimes I think I should have broadened my canvas', Caroline Blackwood reports Keane as saying, in her 1986 afterword to *Full House* (1935), but goes on to approve Keane's decision to write only what she 'really knows', so that, in her novels, '[t]here are no tricks, there are no deceptions' (316). This cult of the author as mere domestic documentarian of her caste, and the frequently reiterated myth of the young Keane's original turn to Mills and Boon authorship as an expedient to augment an inadequate dress allowance, robs Keane's fiction of much of the resources of art. She is thereby reduced to a domestic miniaturist, face turned firmly, if consciously, aside from unpalatable historical verities, classified as undemanding Irish entertainment earmarked for the British market. Alternatively, she is near the conclusion of the Big House novel, catergorised in recent years by critics such as Seamus Deane as an anachronistic, nostalgic post-Yeatsian subgenre. Add to this the novels' considerable social-realist investment in the luxurious or decaying social surfaces of Keane's Ascendancy world, along with the novelettish register which is their most common lingua franca, and Keane would appear an unlikely recruit to the Gothic, even at its most broadly defined.

I want to argue, however, that certain varieties of the Gothic provide both a hospitable environment for a consideration of Keane's novels, and a means of fruitfully accounting for the ways in which their deceptively well-behaved textual surfaces clash with a recurrent investment in entrapment and escape, in exorcism and nostalgia, sadism, in physical and psycho-sexual boundaries. Gothic, with its characteristic faculty for amalgamating and perverting other forms, permits a consideration of Keane's uneasy compound of psychological realism, irony, comedy, melodrama and popular romance. Keane's very career, after all, tends to be constructed as haunted by the brand of repeated anachronism central to the negotiation with the past which many critics take to be the crux of Gothic, beyond any specific concerns with the supernatural through whose vocabulary this negotiation is frequently mediated.[2] Her run

---

2 See the introduction to Robert Mighall, *A geography of Victorian Gothic fiction: mapping history's nightmares* (1999), xix.

of West End theatrical successes, and her career as M.J. Farrell, ended when her brand of drawing room comedy was rendered suddenly anachronistic by the advent of *Look Back in Anger* and *Waiting for Godot*. Devlin's introduction to *The Rising Tide* charts, in terms reminiscent of Gothic's fascination with doubling and metamorphosis, the story of 'the emergence of Molly Keane [...] from the ghost of the anonymous, sexless, MJ Farrell' (v).[3] Moreover, besides the Gothic elements inherent in her double persona, her insistently retrospective fiction – with its anxious solicitude for the houses, rooms and objects which mark places where the past can irrupt into the present – exemplifies Chris Baldick's requirement that, for a work to be Gothic, it 'should combine a fearful sense of inheritance in time with a claustrophobic sense of enclosure in space' (xix). Certainly, Keane's recurrent themes of various forms of inheritance, houses and the women who are locked into or out of them, amid the long eclipse of Ascendancy power, fulfil both elements.

Considering Keane's fiction as a whole, however, it is in the repeated patterns of involuntary recurrence through which her novels return to certain fixations, obsessions and blockages that Keane's investment in Gothic is most evident. Most notably, these 'returns' are to certain troubled periods in Irish history, chiefly the onset of the Great War and 1922. Plots, motifs and favoured symbols repeat themselves in a characteristically uncanny manner from novel to novel. This 'vocabulary' of Gothic tropes or stock features, which has provided the principal embodiments and evocations of personal and cultural anxieties from the eighteenth-century beginnings of the mode, is not difficult to trace in Keane's Anglo-Irish family sagas. Underlying and disrupting their social-realist façade is a pointed reversion to houses, heredity, power, the weight of the past, and taboo subjects such as matricide, incest, homosexuality, torture, the supernatural or uncanny. Essentially, Keane's houses are the locus through which she dramatises the determining mould of the past on the individual subject, particularly the female subject. The houses themselves, aptly described by Polly Devlin as 'emotional archaeological sites' (*Devoted Ladies* xi) are typically Gothic. An alluring façade of hearth and home, evoked with hallucinatory detail, gradually shifts into an imprisoning structure containing unheimlich domestic secrets. Furthermore, the texts continually encode the social and psychic processes whereby her characters, particularly her female characters, are disciplined to accept their places within the Anglo-Irish order.[4] Keane's watchful, sentient houses thus offer repeated and iconic instances of the interpenetration of Gothic and domestic horror. Finally, in their intra-

---

3 Molly Keane 'used the pseudonym M.J. Farrell 'to hide my literary side from my sporting friends', according to the flyleaf biographical information of the 2000 Virago reprint of *Devoted Ladies* (1934). 4 Margot Gayle Backus, *The Gothic family romance: heterosexuality, child sacrifice, and the Anglo-Irish colonial order* (1999), 177.

mural repetition of gendered external power structures, they become, as Randi Gunzenhauser argues in *Horror at Home*, the space of the Bewährungsroman – 'the space of probation or trial' – for the female subject (8).

Keane's work, I want to argue, does not simply evade a troubled and troubling history in a blinkered form of domestic novel, but can be read as continually revisiting troubling and essentially irresolvable themes. Of course, the Gothic writer does not, by definition, seize on history as a coherent field that is subject to authorial control. Her apparently conservative domestic narratives which appear to observe the narrative codes of 'Good Behaviour' in their byplay with horses and dogs, fox-hunting and racing, tend to be ambushed by eruptions from a different mode of writing, as though the macabre is continually inserting itself into Keane's daylight world. The uncanny friction between modes can give the reader 'as quick a shock as the sight of a skeleton sitting on a sofa might give, or the geniality of a friend suddenly turned to bitterness and accusation', as *Two Days in Aragon* phrases it (58–9).

In fact, Keane's work, when not tidied into a more benign and horsy form by her critics, enters into an uneasy engagement with the dead hand of history, the origins of Anglo-Irishness, and the handing-on of its codes and institutions via what Margot Gayle Backus in her study of Anglo-Irish Gothic calls a 'mediating Gothic vocabulary' (175). Against, or behind, what David Punter dubs the 'daylight images of the realist tradition', Keane's Gothic throws up a parodic, shocking asymmetry in which 'history passes through a series of distortions, perversions surface and are given concrete form' (1999, 37). By its nature, Gothic narrative circles pathologically round themes and events that are rarely susceptible to direct exposition. As Marie Mulvey Roberts suggests, the Gothic plot acts as 'a mirror diverting us from the Gorgon's gaze, that is, at least once removed from the source of trauma and taboo'; it offers the reader, thus, 'an uneasy and eerie dialectic between anxiety and desire' (xvii). The indirect nature of Keane's engagement with her actual historical moment has frequently led to her novels' political thrust being overlooked, as readers take at face value their intermittent nostalgia for an Ascendancy past seen as graceful.

However, Keane appears to have viewed the situation of the Anglo-Irish as itself inherently Gothic in its decline, rather as Elizabeth Bowen did in her fictional and non-fictional accounts of the *bois dormant* atmosphere of the Big House.[5] Behind the ceremonious rituals of Ascendancy living, there is something rather frail and impermanent about all her characteristically unheimlich houses, even when they do not share the fate of her Aragon and finally burn at the hands of the IRA. There is a sense that, like the eponymous house in

5 See for instance Bowen's 'The Big House', in Hermione Lee (ed.), *The Mulberry Tree*, (1986), 25–30.

Mad Puppetstown (1931), they are always liable to revert to savagery and ruin, a fate which the novels regard with mingled or ambivalent nostalgia and regret even as they repeatedly rehearse the doom of the Big House. Both Silverue and Ownestown in *Full House*, which have 'survived successive sad times of fire and terror' (103) are counterbalanced by the abandoned Big House in which a hunt ball is given, plangently 'empty as a box' and overgrown with 'sour nettles and elder saplings' (230). The Gothic permits an audience, whether envisaged as the British market towards which Keane makes frequent knowing, if satirical, concessions or as her own Anglo-Irish caste, either to face or avoid multiple implications encoded within its narrative. Thus, while Keane does at times write in more or less undisguised ways about the socio-political realities of the lives of the female inhabitants of the Big Houses, and the domestic power structures underpinning Ascendancy life as it moved towards its eclipse, her primary mode is essentially Gothic. Keane's version of this, in its multiple and insistent variations on themes of female alienation within the home, which also abuts upon the public sphere because of its cultural resonance as Big House, is thus doubly uncanny.

I have mentioned that certain modalities of Gothic are more useful to a consideration of Keane's work than others. I am isolating two strands within a famously multivalent term which, whether defined as a plot, a trope, a topos, a discourse, a mode of representation, conventions of characterisation, or a composite of all these elements, threatens to become meaningless because of its sheer magnitude and longevity. For much of its history, the Gothic has consistently been misconstrued as light entertainment, or else dismissed as a variety of transparent moral allegory whose denouement lays the ghost to rest and stakes the vampire: many commentators have been deluded by the apparently 'normative' endings of so many Gothic novels into perceiving them as unsophisticated fables of good and evil.[6] What emerges from the numerous more recent appraisals of the Gothic, however, is a tacit agreement that it is, as David Punter reminds us in his study, *The Literature of Terror*, 'neither escapist literature nor light reading' (96). Keane's deployment of components of Irish Gothic and Female Gothic plays knowingly with both escapism and the popular fiction mode.

Of course, Gothic narratives never escaped the concerns of their own times. It is useful to think of this mode in terms of what Annette Kuhn calls its 'cultural instrumentality' (1). The Gothic is of course rightly, if partially, understood as a cyclical mode that re-emerges in times of cultural stress in order to negotiate anxieties for its readership by working through them in displaced, sometimes supernaturalised, form. This is in turn relevant to the

6 MaryBeth Inverso, *The Gothic impulse in contemporary drama* (1990), 1.

specific regional variety of the Gothic variously known as Irish Gothic or Anglo-Irish, even Protestant Gothic, which, according to influential readings pioneered by Seamus Deane and Terry Eagleton, offers a displaced and oblique account of the eclipse of the once-ascendant Irish Protestant minority. Eagleton in particular adapts Frederic Jameson's concept of the 'political unconscious' to argue that Anglo-Irish Gothic may be read as the political unconscious of Anglo-Irish society, the place in which its fears and fantasies most definitively emerge, a 'fantastic sub-text' allowing repressed self-perceptions of the Ascendancy to be refigured in distorted but suggestive fictional form (1995, 188). At its simplest, this is to argue that the effulgence of Anglo-Irish supernatural stories written after the Act of Union, peaking in the nineteenth century with the works of Joseph Maturin and Sheridan Le Fanu, with their evocations of aboriginal guilt, demonic familiars and spectrally-besieged houses, condone a displaced expression of the anxieties of a beleaguered and paranoid minority. A depleted form of Irish Gothic does survive into the twentieth century, with its ever-increased contraction of the Protestant population, the burning of the Big Houses, and concomitant sense of ineffectuality and threat, in Yeats, Bowen, and Keane. Keane's fiction, as I have begun to argue, under the guise of the hunting romance or latter-day silver fork novel, in fact suggests grotesque truths about the Anglo-Irish past and its unwelcome legacies.

Concurrently, too, as feminist critics of the mode have seen for decades past, the Gothic has long confronted the cultural problem of gender distinctions. Even as early as *The Castle of Otranto*, women are the figures most confined, most fearsomely trapped between contradictory pressures and impulses.[7] As Kate Ferguson Ellis has argued in her study of eighteenth-century Gothic, Female Gothic novels beginning with Radcliffe, have been concerned with familial violence frequently directed against women and metonymically represented by the iconic presence of the haunted house in which women are confined (3). The Gothic text, then, offers a set of conventions to represent what was not supposed to exist, or which could not be spoken, notably female fears of domestic immurement for its resultant committal of a woman to an imprisoning biological destiny.[8]

I want to suggest that Keane is best considered within the variously overlapping or interlocking contexts of Irish and Female Gothic. Both are strongly figured in her novels, frequently in ways which underwrite each other, problematising the status of a relatively disempowered sex within an already beleaguered (if privileged) minority. Irish Gothic in its depleted Free State form

7 'Introduction', Jerrold E. Hogle (ed.), *Cambridge companion to Gothic fiction* (2002), 9.   8 See Juliann Fleenor, *The female Gothic*, ed. Julian Fleenor (1983), 15.

is most strongly evident in the notions of inheritance and the concomitant ruination of older powers, such as circulate obsessively through Keane's novels at a time when the question of who should inherit Ireland was paramount. Female Gothic, on the other hand, while drawing on the same matrix of Gothic tropes – supernatural threat, heredity, family secrets, houses, ancestral portraits – is evident in Keane's prioritisation of an exploration of relations between women and houses, horror and claustrophobia, the liminal, and mother-daughter relationships.

If David Punter is correct to identify the Gothic as offering us 'a language in which to address our ghosts', then Keane's redirection of the mode allows her to explore obliquely the origins of the Anglo-Irish self in racial guilt, iconic houses both menaced and menacing to their (female) inhabitants. Seemingly engendered by their habitats like autochthonous births, they are imprinted with the various codes of 'good behaviour' – a well-policed endogamy, the handing-on of a repressive ideology – amid a vision of history as an entropic recircling (Punter; 1999; ii). This oblique but distinct racial guilt looms large in many of the novels, often appearing in the text in the guise of the classic Gothic motif of the family curse:

> A cursed family inherits an unwelcome legacy. History moves on,
> progress is made, enlightenment replaces barbarism and superstition,
> but still the curse– initiated by sacrilege, usurpation or some unspec-
> ified dark deed – inexorably visits its punishment on successive gen-
> erations. (Punter; 1980; 80)

The usefulness of this trope as a method to explore Anglo-Irish colonial origins in territorial usurpation, and its relentless policy of endogamy in response to racial and sexual fears, is obvious. It is deployed, for instance, in *Full House*, a novel preoccupied with blood and breeding, from its passive patriarch's favourite hobbies, heraldry and cattle breeding, to the repeated mentions of 'Bad Blood and Insanity' which feature prominently in its involved Gothic plot of hereditary insanity blighting a pair of young lovers (218). An ancestral portrait gallery makes this conflation between architectural fabric and 'blood' visible; the dissipated ancestor, Mad Harry Bird, with his Hellfire Club 'eccentricities' – 'beating his wives, torturing cats, and keeping his daughters' heads shaved like billiard balls' (141) – which flower forth again in the insanity of his physically similar great-great-grandson, allow for the suggestion of moral patterns through the recurrence of physical traits. This endorses the association between Anglo-Irishness and disease, endogamy and racial degeneration, removing the scene of haunting from the supernatural to the somatic sphere. It also makes political points using physiology and pathology to stigmatise Anglo-Irish eugenics. Throughout much of *Full House*,

Sheena Bird looks liable to be sacrificed, until the revelation of her 'foreign' paternity saves her from the indifference of her legal father and his faithless wife, whose selfish beauty recalls that of her house, the 'unkind, inward-looking' Silverue (218).

In fact, endogamous heterosexuality is problematised throughout Keane. The prevalence of homosexual characters in many of her novels suggests the re-direction of tribal libido into less acceptable (and less fruitful) modes. It is not insignificant that the family names for the guest rooms in which the unfortunate English paying guests are to stay in *Treasure Hunt* – 'Bluebeard', 'North Spare', 'Old Nursery' and 'Iceland' – suggest the twin horrors presented to Anglo-Irish women: patriarchal marriage, or solitude, infantilism and coldness. On the one hand, Keane details mercilessly the fate of women who, like Enid French-McGrath in *The Rising Tide*, disastrously express a sexuality which confines them within biological roles; on the other are those equally unenviable figures, the celibate/governess/lesbian solitaries such as *Two Days in Aragon*'s pathetic Miss Pidgie, *Full House*'s Miss Parker, *The Rising Tide*'s Diana, confined to schoolrooms and nurseries which enact their permanently subjected status.

Concurrently, the spectres of both actual incest and miscegenation hang about Keane's novels, signalled by the frequent references to 'Leda and the Swan up to mischief as usual' in the family arms of the Big House Ballyroden in *Treasure Hunt* (111), a novel which features a sinister equation of father and bridegroom. The repeated motif of the African statues, 'two life-size black boys in Saxon porcelain' (*The Rising Tide* 277), appear in both *Two Days in Aragon* and *The Rising Tide* as a type of colonial awareness and miscegenation. Both petticoated 'meek slave' and 'pampered favourite', they remind us that the Anglo-Irish code regards intermarrying between Big House and farmhouse as being 'as wrong [...] as the love of black and white people' (*Two Days in Aragon* 15). Furthermore, by being deliberately sartorially aligned with the feminine, the statues also suggest the disempowerment of women who likewise oscillate between 'slave' and 'favourite' in this novel. Keane's unusually politically explicit *Two Days in Aragon* (1941), set during the War of Independence, and read by Margot Gayle Backus as a revision of Yeats's *Purgatory*, is characterised by both incest and miscegenation in its depiction of an incestuous relationship between a Big House daughter and a Catholic groom, who is himself the product of an act of Big House miscegenation (Backus; 194). When Grania Fox of Aragon believes she is pregnant by the IRA go-between groom Foley O'Neill, who is, unknown to both, her first cousin on the wrong side of the blanket, the illicit and unwittingly incestuous affair re-enacts a Gothically distorted version of a long-established pattern of sexual abuse of Aragon's servants by the family males. The secrecy of this intergenerational web of sexual exploitation is signalled in the architectural fabric of the haunted house at the centre of the text, with its hidden torture chamber containing 'ivory-headed cutting whips and other fine and very curious instruments' (193), and in the literally submerged 'little and green scattered skeletons on the river bottom' (122), the unwanted offspring of Aragon's raped servant girls. If Yeats's *Purgatory* 'scapegoats Anglo-Irish women for the increasing hybridity of post-treaty identity and the concomitant 'fall' of the Big House', as Backus argues, then Keane's most politically explicit novel, by retelling it, offers a percipient analysis of the ways in which male sexual abuse perpetuates a system of colonial domination under the aegis of the patriarchal family (177). However, *Two Days in Aragon* is atypical among Keane's novels for its very direct engagement with colonisation as Keane's conscious 'atonement for her contemporaneous attitude' (ix) and for its prioritisation of male abuses; the remainder of this essay will be devoted to a more typical, and less discussed, Keane 'Gothic', *The Rising Tide*.

The Rising Tide (1937), a family saga charting the inhabiting of yet another alarmingly sentient Keane house by three generations of the French-McGraths, offers an example of how, in Keane's work, aspects of Irish Gothic and Female Gothic both underwrite and undercut one another in a manner suggesting the mutually conflicting impulses of Gothic narrative. It is a novel crowded with locked doors, houses and rooms, charades, hide and seek, darkness, and the forbidden and unspoken. Maternal power is continually perceived and represented as uncanny, and cycles of generational submission and domination and taboo forms of sexuality all feature. Alongside this, Keane's habitual Anglo-Irish activities of hunting and ratting are omnipresent, to the extent of signalling, as Kristin Morrison has suggested, 'the hidden evils infesting the [Anglo-Irish] estate' (32–3). In its exploration of the Gothic dimensions of mirroring but conflicting stories of successive generations of Anglo-Irish women and an uncanny house, *The Rising Tide* constitutes a particularly strong instance of the Gothic plot. It offers a 'diversion from the Gorgon's gaze', in the sense of avoiding direct exposition of a source of trauma from which, nonetheless, it cannot quite look away. The novel's opening passage, an apparently arch and whimsical reminiscence of the years between 1900 and 1914, signals this tension between consciousness and unconsciousness, knowledge and avoidance, clearly:

> 'But we can't feel about those years really. Not in the way we feel about the War. There we are conscious. [...] the War is forced on us, horror is so actual. But those years, the years of our cousins' youth, avoid us and will not be known (5).

The war whose 'horror is so actual' here is of course the First World War, used by Keane chiefly as a means of killing off or maiming her often perfunctory male characters, the better to focus on feminine concerns. However, in a novel which climaxes in 1922, and which has as its chief themes regime change, the inheritance and usurpation of houses, and filial rebellion against older powers, the half-hidden reference to what *Mad Puppetstown* calls 'the other, little, bitter forgotten war' (123) in Ireland, is clear. References to 'a change at hand: a house waiting its new possessor – a house muffled in history and tradition about to be stripped and woken' (*The Rising Tide*, 149) cannot be innocent in this context. Nor can the nameless evil which haunts the Big House and which is transmitted through the French-McGrath bloodline and appears to be a form of racial guilt, specifically linked to the past, 'oppression' and 'power misused and grown weak and wicked' (94).

If Garonlea is not a haunted house in the usual sense of the term, it is, like the 'unhappy' Silverue in *Full House*, a house haunted by its lineage or bloodline, and past wrongs this lineage has committed, made manifest in Garonlea's malevolent unhappiness, lying 'like the breath of mould in old clothes on the people who live in such a place' (16). Thus, the story of the French-McGraths, their house, and the change of regimes to which it is subject over the course of the narrative, allegorically makes visible cultural changes and political upheaval. These, in turn, cause an anxiety that needs to be assuaged at some level, but whose 'horror' is too 'actual' to be directly dealt with within its code of narrative 'good behaviour'. Kristin Morrison is right to suggest that the secrets Keane codifies within the text 'themselves become metaphors for what is most hidden in the novel, and at the same time is most present: its actual historical moment'(33).

Certainly, the novel as a whole lends itself to interpretation in terms of a displaced Irish Gothic exploration of the demise of Anglo-Ireland via the fate of a deeply emblematic haunted house, which dominates the novel as a site of repeated contestation and usurpation. However, complicating and ironising this muted and partial political allegory, is an investment in the frequently uncanny feminine psychological terrain of female alienation, subjection and domination in the home. Essentially, it is maternity and specifically female abuses of power, which emerge as the locus of dark, occult forces in *The Rising Tide*, and provide the disquieting narrative impetus behind the text's multiple uncanny repetitions. For Keane's brand of Female Gothic is not that which seeks the enabling recovery of a lost or hidden maternal origin, but one that explores fears of maternal power, the spectre of cyclical maternal cruelty, and the demonic otherness of the feminine.

The Rising Tide's house, while not as obviously feminised as Keane's Aragon, was built with the dowry of a rich ancestress, and is a very clear avatar of its tyrannical pre-war chatelaine, Lady Charlotte, who, no Gothic victim, dominates both Garonlea and her weak husband, Sir Ambrose, with 'an almost supernatural power', and has 'as much authority over her children as any prison Governor' (42). Far from embodying the Yeatsian ideal of Anglo-Irish domestic architecture as an icon of aesthetic unity and civilised consciousness, Garonlea bears out Edna Longley's suggestion that the true ancestor of the twentieth-century Big House novel is less Castle Rackrent than *King Lear*: 'Real power having collapsed, the vacuum is filled by a distorted expression of that power [through which] the voices of Goneril and Regan sound' (125). Keane's passive patriarchs, of whom Sir Ambrose is typical, allow for her characteristic feminisation of history, her re-imagining of Anglo-Ireland as repressive matriarchy. Throughout her novels, she repeatedly depicts monstrous, phallic mothers as Gothic tyrants wielding the power of their usually feminised Big Houses, denying any form of agency to their offspring. In Keane's world, where libidos are more likely to be invested in houses than in other people, and where the formation of human beings, particularly women, by their homes is the more insisted upon because of the very tenuousness of the Anglo-Irish claim to 'belong', Garonlea and its chatelaine together constitute the novel's Gothic monster. Lady Charlotte, 'a shocking despot, really swollen with family conceit and a terrifying pride of race' (7) is an apt mate for her house. The Big House, in its monstrous perversion of the traditionally sacrosanct domestic hearth, is the savage, even vampiric, focus of all the social and psychic energies of the narrative in which 'all [is] finally subdued to the pattern of Garonlea' (66). Its unearthly combination of moated 'English manor' and a lurking animality suggested in its 'tigerishly striped' façade (149), finds an equivalent in Lady Charlotte's monstrous physicality. House and chatelaine are linked by strands of vampiric imagery of draining and depletion, and suggest a parodic Anglo-Irish Dracula, battening on Big House daughters and the Irish body politic alike.

As the Gothic tyrant here, unsettlingly, is the mother, smotheringly present rather than suggestively absent, the traditional Gothic haunted house in Keane's hands directly indicts 'maternal omnipotence' (61), rather than patriarchal tyranny. *The Rising Tide* depicts variously submissive or rebellious daughter-figures exploring their relation to this patriarchal maternal body which is grotesquely all too present. Maternal bodies in *The Rising Tide* – whether the faintly 'abhuman' body of Lady Charlotte, or the uncanny, indomitably preserved beauty of the novel's other mother-figure, her daughter-in-law and eventual alter ego, Cynthia – are presented as sites of abjection, places where numerous cultural and familial fears are thrown off and dissolve together.[9] While we are accustomed to the familiar template of rev-

9 See Kelly Hurley, 'British Gothic fiction, 1885–1930' in Jerrold E. Hogle (ed.), *Cambridge Companion to Gothic Fiction*, 190–3, on 'human bodies that have lost their claim to a discrete and integral identity [...] that occupy the threshold between two terms of an opposition, like human/beast, male/female, civilised primitive ...'

olution as parricide, wherein the newly independent nation throws off its colonising father, Keane is more interested in manners than in military conquest, and in politics as passed on by colonising mothers. As Declan Kiberd points out, and as Keane's novels, with their tyrannical, femininised Big Houses, are acutely aware, 'a house is never a mere setting, but a coded set of instructions as to how its occupants should behave' (376). This 'coded set of instructions' bears most heavily on women and children, for, Keane seems to suggest, it is mothers who compel their young to adopt the Anglo-Irish code, to be, as Declan Kiberd notes, '"sealed" and "finished", so that the social forms may survive the death of their contents' (370). The imagery of formation is significant: Garonlea's specifically Anglo-Irish unhappiness, likened to 'the breath of mould in old clothes' (16) is aptly echoed in the 'glass mould' of the Ascendancy code which upholds Cynthia, a later Garonlea mother, and justifies her 'masochistic pleasure in her treatment of [her] children' (136).

This, I want to suggest, is the other taboo subject; Keane's suggestion that this half-occluded political allegory is also an indictment of female, specifically maternal, power. While *Two Days in Aragon* or *Full House* largely project onto the distant past the ancestral abuses of women that haunt Aragon and Silverue, *The Rising Tide* links the hints of racial guilt or primal crime to ongoing domestic abuses. *The Rising Tide* also makes it plain that, unlike the sexual exploitation of servants in *Two Days in Aragon*, these are cyclical maternal abuses visited upon women by women. Women can be the agents of a repressive regime; the intermittent political allegory which recurs throughout the text's three generations is an affair entirely played out between women, with daughters attempting to negotiate with the dead hand of history imagined as maternal. With its double tale of mothering, the novel questions both the notion that women cannot collude with or be active agents of an oppressive regime, whether familial or colonial, and that maternal love is a natural part of the female psychic economy. Both the novel's Anglo-Irish mothers are sadists, with the narrative stating quite baldly of Cynthia and her children that she 'tortured the miserable little lives out of them [...] because she did not love them and needed to hurt them' (136).

It isn't, however, just that patriarchy is reimagined as matriarchy in *The Rising Tide*; in a characteristically Gothic manner, apparently stable binaries break down throughout, and characters undergo uncanny metamorphoses. This blurring of what initially appear to be opposing binaries, of course, is classically Gothic in dealing with fears of primordial dissolution that could obscure the boundaries between all western oppositions, generating the kind of uncanny effects which lead David Punter to nominate 'disequilibrium' as the trademark of the Gothic (1980; 43) The Gothic clearly exists in part to raise the possibility that all 'abnormalities' which we deny are deeply and pervasively part of ourselves. *The Rising Tide* features this merging of apparent opposites in the disquieting mirroring effects of its circuitous plot.

Counterweighting Lady Charlotte, Gothic tyrant and Anglo-Irish maternal vampire, is a 'rival queen' in the shape of her utterly modern daughter-in-law Cynthia and her house Rathglass, site of her rival 'court'. A libertarian site of female freedom and physical comforts, 'an altogether lighter and happier place' and 'a terrifying contrast to life at Garonlea' (122), Rathglass initially appears to incarnate forward-looking bourgeois sexuality and romantic love, challenging Garonlea's aristocratic emphasis on alliance and the past. *The Rising Tide* seems set to be predicated upon these two opposed houses, with their rival queens, facing each other across the valley, in a manner reminiscent of Emily Brontë's Wuthering Heights and Thrushcross Grange. The temptation to read the bourgeois, forward-looking Rathglass, with its anglicised Irish name as suggesting in some sense a republican future in direct opposition to the demonised Gothic mansion of Anglo-Ireland, is obvious. Some commentators have accepted the rebellious daughter-figure Cynthia as a republican figure, and have seen analogies between 'the Irish Free State and Cynthia's youth and beauty' (Morrison; 33). However, the uncanny doubleness or slipperiness of Cynthia as a figure is signalled by the fact that Rudiger Imhoff, for instance, reads Cynthia as occupying the other pole of the analogy, 'as an image of the decaying Ascendancy becoming the victim of its own self-indulgence' (195). In fact, as I will argue, she suggests aspects of both.

In any case, it would be uncharacteristically facile for a Keane novel to present Diana – the lesbian Garonlea 'daughter at home' – with a choice of self-expression at Rathglass and oppression at Garonlea. No sooner has this forward-looking new regime been posited, with its suggestion of alignment between the rebellious Cynthia and republican forces in terms of their shared revolt against the Big House, then it almost immediately collapses into its opposite term. Rathglass and Garonlea cease to be opposing houses and become disquieting doubles of one another.

Rathglass, which, though presented on the surface as an escape route from the glowering Gothic pile, Garonlea, is in fact the dower house for the mansion, and thereby as implicated in its ancestral wrongs. Furthermore it is acquired by Cynthia by the unscrupulous ejection of an elderly aunt, who possesses an Irish 'brogue', in a muted re-enactment of Garonlea's originary expropriation of Irish land. Diana, the novel's moral touchstone, is still economically exploited and sexually stunted here, as Cynthia's 'slave and shadow' (75). Most importantly, the initially attractive figure of Cynthia, romantically vital, cannily manipulating her 'myth-like glow of popularity' (74) and adept at playing the system for her own ends, is gradually deformed into an uncannily familiar variety of maternal viciousness after her young husband's death in the trenches. The 'sharp wolfish twist' laid bare by her bereavement sees her embark on a career of sexual power games, the 'religion and drug' of hunting (107), and, mirroring Lady Charlotte, taking a sadistic pleasure in the torment of her children. She is thereby revealed to be as saturated in the Big House code as the maternal enemy with whom she exists in a state of open warfare: 'You had to feel ashamed and embarrassed if your children did not take keenly to blood-sports, so they must be forced into them. It was right' (135). Rathglass, then, rather than offering an alternative or opposite way of life to the Big House regime, comes to mirror it in an unheimlich manner. Mirroring her house, Cynthia, over the course of the novel, transforms uncannily into Lady Charlotte's equally monstrous double. At first (as dutiful daughter-in-law) a narcissistic extension of Lady Charlotte, then a filial rival, she becomes finally a discomfiting and alienating counter-self, with the added complication of a complicated and demonised sexuality which slides from agonised widowed chastity to an increasingly desperate promiscuity in middle age, as her power fades and the Gothic cycle of victimhood and tyranny turns full circle in favour of her now-powerful children.

Cynthia's doubleness, her position as dangerous hybrid, is the wellspring from which the breakdown of binaries stems, and is frequently signalled in the text in classically Gothic manner. On the one hand, she is a rebellious daughter who attempts to stake the vampire of Lady Charlotte and Garonlea: when she inherits it in trust for her son. On the other hand, she herself becomes the 'chatelaine of Garonlea', her identity eliding into sentient architectural fabric, rather like her fictional sister, Daphne du Maurier's eponymous anti-heroine of *Rebecca*, whom she resembles in her ability to control spaces, horses or people and in her mastery of the masquerade of femininity. Cynthia's hybridity has its obvious political side. Her name, her manipulation of her glamorous chastity, and her association with queenliness and hunting all suggest Elizabeth I. She is associated throughout with the conquest and usurpation of space, particularly the destruction and recreation of Garonlea, and the clearing of trees – all these factors align her with her coloniser ancestors. Yet her takeover of the Big House is a purge of its previous inhabitants and a rejection of its past: she 'scour[s] the very shadow' of its former regime from the place, 'hurl[s] the unwanted ancestors into attics with their faces to the wall' (178), changes 'a whole world of tradition' (262), has 'won the house over from all its dismal hauntings' (189). In this, she is an uncanny figure, unsettling both the Anglo-Irish regime and its replacement, blurring them together as the novel's two houses blend and merge their (apparently) oppositional qualities. She offers an instance of the typical Gothic engagement with tropes of metamorphosis, a feminised Jekyll-and-Hyde composite, that counters Lady Charlotte's female Dracula. Cynthia's dangerous hybrid of Anglo-Irish hunter queen and maternal sadist is conveyed in intertextual nods; like Dorian Gray, her appearance 'amazingly young' (151), she confronts the portrait of a French-McGrath ancestress, a 'reserved [...] sanitary, asexual' double of herself (235). During her son's coming-of-age party, her son and her ex-lover are shocked by the contrast between her smoothly groomed back view and 'grotesque [...] distorted' reflection in a mirror: 'But was that haunted, hungry face the real Cynthia?' (169).

That Cynthia's eventual dethronement from her 'spiritual pedestal' (206) is accomplished via a costume ball at Garonlea is no accident; throughout, she is mistress of the costumes and disguises, veils and masks which are ubiquitous features of Gothic, according to Catherine Spooner (1). Judith Halberstam argues that while metaphors of masking and disguise generally indicate an 'authentic self' hidden underneath, in Gothic texts they 'consistently work to problematise that authenticity, making subjectivity a mere surface effect, multiple, performative and dispersed across a continuum of appearances'. This seems an apt description of Cynthia's 'perfectly-constructed façade' masking uncanny otherness (5–6). One of the issues Keane's writing addresses in *The Rising Tide* is how the masquerade of femininity and its formation is bound up with the inculcation of Anglo-Irish identity, imaged as both the physically and psychically monstrous Lady Charlotte and the ageing beauty Cynthia. Cynthia's life 'slipping on its decline', her falling short of her own 'unattainable ideal' (206–7), is congruent with the final slip into decline of Anglo-Ireland, signalled by the narrative's only mention of the Irish Civil War, which is being conducted 'much to the inconvenience of social life', although Garonlea, in line with its uncanny ability (like Cynthia) to represent coloniser and colonised, 'miraculously escaped burning by either party' (208–9). The water imagery which gives the novel its title links both a woman's desperate attempt to retain beauty and sexuality into middle age, and the end of an ageing regime, as tides rise, crest and turn, and the 'dark established currents' of Garonlea, previously vanquished by Cynthia's regime, align themselves with her children's nascent regime and reassert themselves against her weakening power (209). That her brief 'conquest' of the Big House is imaged as a specifically feminised form of aggression-as-makeover – 'we're going to change it so enormously [...] cut its hair, paint its face, give it some royal parties' (145) – suggests a sense of the merely cosmetic and temporary nature of apparent historical change. By the end of *The Rising Tide*, Keane's re-casting of Anglo-Irish history as feminine suggests a vision, half-rueful, half-satisfied, of the frailty of Anglo-Ireland's tenure in twentieth-century Ireland, viewed with the hindsight of 1937. The unattributed appearance in Diana's thoughts of a line from *Antony and Cleopatra* – 'Lady, the bright day is done and we are for the dark' (267) – implicitly dignifies Cynthia's eclipse even while the novel appears to endorse it.

The vanquishing of Cynthia by her now-powerful children, passionate about hunting and heartless exemplars of the Anglo-Irish code in which she drilled them, is achieved by an act of sartorial Gothic. Simon celebrates his majority with a period fancy-dress ball ('95 to '07). In a manner both eerie and carnivalesque, younger guests dress as their ancestors, and older guests dress as their own younger selves, in a Garonlea restored to its chill, claustrophobic 'haunted' self. The usual liberatory-transgressive element of sartorial tourism, in which alternative, empowering identities can be assumed, is curiously reversed: adults dress up as babies and as their own mothers; Lady Charlotte's three dutiful elder daughters corset themselves back into the constraints of a youth they have never escaped; Diana wears in public the night clothes of her youth, signalling in her case the suppression of the female sexual desire which is such an unsettling force in the narrative as a whole. While on the one hand, the costume ball resembles Mrs Dalloway's party as a half-comic, half-savage farewell to a dying, anachronistic upper-class caste, the party does not look ahead with any hope to the newly-established regime of Simon and Susan French-McGrath. As Cynthia is haunted by the clothes of her youth, 'that locked wardrobe of ghosts and memories' (289), and loses her lover to a younger woman at the masquerade, she emerges as merely an accumulation of outdated fashions – the anachronistic forms of an anachronistic regime. However, again like Daphne du Maurier's Rebecca, she remains, even when dethroned, the most vital figure of the novel, and her glamour, assertive sexuality, and energy are more attractive than her cold, clever children.

As Sue twice dresses up as an ancestress, Simon, via an uncanny blurring of gender boundaries, develops an eerie resemblance to his paternal grandmother, and willingly reawakens the family curse. Together with Garonlea, now 'his mate and equal in power', he enjoys the reawakening of past unhappiness as a 'blood-offering' to avenge the 'insults of freedom and coarse taking of pleasure' of Cynthia's regime (309). Again, the inheritance of an iconic house in 1922, amid a landscape rife with intimations of the death of an order hints at the emergence of Irish political independence. However, this implication is in turn contradicted by the enacting of an involuntary return in the novel's narrative logic, whereby Simon ends the novel poised to become another repressive figure, fulfilling his family destiny; nothing new, apparently, can happen in the Gothic plot.

Thus, while Cynthia manages in some sense a 'fitting exit' on her own terms, the novel does not subscribe to what it calls a 'super-conventional happy ending' (219). The staked vampire comes back to uncannily undead life, Garonlea in new hands reverts to its most oppressive self; the novel's end is profoundly ambivalent. While it has become something of a truism to align the Gothic with the transgressive, the end of *The Rising Tide* bears out a more nuanced approach, suggesting rather that the Gothic mediates the relationship between the force of transgression and the force that returns us to the status quo. The novel demonstrates that neither the personal nor the cultural past is dead, and that both can uncannily return. Both previous Garonlea regimes may have been monstrous, but the once-oppressed, now-powerful young who inherit Garonlea are not hailed with any particular approval by the novel. In their smug, incestuous asexuality, they most resemble Keane's other sibling or faux-sibling Big House inheritors, for instance the curiously sterile Easter and Basil in *Mad Puppetstown*, or the colourless Phillip and Veronica in *Treasure Hunt*. If Keane's conflicted brand of Anglo-Irish Gothic allows a kind of skewed or disguised confrontation with deep-seated historical, social or gendered dilemmas buried in individuals or groups, it offers no resolution. While her fictions explore the long-drawn-out death of an order with a mixture of fear and satisfaction, and confront the weight of the past with fear and hatred as well as nostalgia, they also manifest a disgust for a future imagined as no less sterile.

Contributors

MARY BREEN teaches in the English Department, University College Cork. She has published on Molly Keane and Kate O'Brien. Her main research interests are in Irish women's writing and contemporary fiction. Her current research is on the relationship between late eighteenth- and early nineteenth-century women's fiction and life writing

VIRGINIA BROWNLOW (NÉE KEANE) was born in Dublin in 1945 and brought up in Ardmore, Co. Waterford. She moved to London in 1969, where she met and married film historian, Kevin Brownlow. She collaborated on a number of research projects with her husband and also trained and worked as a special needs teacher for disturbed children. Her interests include writing, gardening, and travelling. The couple has one child, Julia and they divide their time between London and Ardmore.

MOIRA E. CASEY is an assistant professor at Miami University of Ohio, Middletown, where she teaches composition, British and Irish literature, and women's studies. She has published articles in *Colby Quarterly, Foilsiu,* and *Teaching English at the Two-Year College* and she is currently working on a book about Irish lesbian fiction.

SILVIA DÍEZ FABRE lectures in English literature at the University of Burgos, Spain. She works on the Big House novel. In this field of research she has published several articles. Her PhD is on Somerville and Ross's *The Real Charlotte*. She is the secretary of the Spanish Association for Irish Studies.

DEREK HAND teaches in the English Department in St Patrick's College, Drumcondra. He is interested in Irish writing in general and has published articles on W.B. Yeats, Elizabeth Bowen and on contemporary Irish fiction. The Liffey Press published his book *John Banville: exploring fictions* in 2002. He is a frequent reviewer of Irish fiction for the *Irish Times*. He is currently writing *A history of the Irish novel* for the Cambridge University Press.

VERA KREILKAMP is professor of English at Pine Manor College and visiting professor with the Irish Studies Program at Boston College. She is also co-editor (for literature and the arts) of *Éire-Ireland*. Her research fields are Irish landscape and visual art and Ascendancy fiction. She is author of *The Anglo–Irish Novel and the Big House* (1998) and editor of the catalogue for the exhibition Éire/Land (2002). More recently, she has contributed the chapter 'Fiction and empire: the Irish novel,' to Kevin Kenny (ed.), *Ireland and the British Empire* (2004) and 'The Novel of the Big House', to John Wilson Foster (ed.), *Cambridge Companion to the Irish Novel*, (forthcoming).

CAROLYN LESNICK is a PhD candidate at the University of Pennsylvania. She is currently working on a dissertation entitled 'Vamping as generic propriety: the Anglo-Irish Big House novel', which focuses on the novels of Molly Keane, Elizabeth Bowen, and Edith Somerville and Martin Ross.

RACHAEL SEALY LYNCH is an associate professor of English at the University of Connecticut. She has published articles and essays on recent and contemporary Irish writers, including Molly Keane, Edna O'Brien, Mary Lavin, and Liam O'Flaherty, in such journals as *Irish University Review*, *Twentieth-Century Literature*, and the *Canadian Journal of Irish Studies*. She is currently working on a book focusing primarily on Irish Protestant women from Isabella Shawe Thackeray to Molly Keane and Jennifer Johnston.

SINÉAD MOONEY is a graduate of UCC (BA 1993, MA 1996) and of the University of Oxford (DPhil 2002). Her research interests include the work of Samuel Beckett, modernism and Irish twentieth-century women's writing. She has published several book and journal articles on Beckett, and her monograph on Beckett in Northcote House's Writers and their Work series is in press. She is currently working on a monograph based on her DPhil research on Beckett and self-translation for OUP. She has been a lecturer in the Department of English, NUI Galway since 2002 and divides her time between London and Galway.

SARAH McLEMORE is a doctoral candidate in English at the University of California, Santa Barbara. Her PhD dissertation is entitled 'Modern terror: space and violence in British and Irish fictions, 1883–1922'. Her research interests include literary representations of architecture, British and Irish modernist novels, and issues of gender and sexuality in twentieth-century Irish literature.

KELLY J.S. McGOVERN is a doctoral student in the English Department at the University of Maryland, College Park. She earned her MA from Boston College, where she concentrated on Irish language and literature. Her research interests include twentieth-century Irish literature as well as gender and postcolonial theory

ELLEN L. O'BRIEN is an assistant professor of English and Women's and Gender Studies at Roosevelt University in Chicago. Her teaching interests include nineteenth and twentieth-century English and Irish literature, gender studies and feminist theory, and postcolonial literature and theory. She is currently completing a book on representations of crime in Victorian poetry and researching a book on street poetics and cultural politics in nineteenth-century Irish broadside ballads. Her articles have appeared in *LIT: Literature, Interpretation, Theory, Victorian Literature and Culture, Victorian Poetry*, and the *Canadian Journal of Irish Studies*.

SALLY PHIPPS (NEÉ KEANE) was born in Dublin in 1940. She was brought up in Cappoquin, Co. Waterford, educated at home and in France and England. She qualified as a teacher and married George Phipps in 1972. Encouraged by her friend Sean Dunne, the literary editor of the *Cork Examiner*, she became a freelance journalist. She collaborated with Molly Keane on an anthology, *Molly Keane's Ireland*, which was published in 1993. Her interests include travelling, cooking, walking and writing. She is currently writing a biography of Molly Keane.

ELLEN M. WOLFF has taught Irish literary and cultural studies at Boston College and the College of the Holy Cross (Worcester, Massachusetts) and now teaches at Phillips Exeter Academy, in Exeter, New Hampshire, USA, where she is Eleanor Gwin Ellis Instructor of English. She has written and presented on the work of Samuel Beckett, Elizabeth Bowen, John McGahern, Anne Devlin, and Fiona Barr, among others. Her new book, *'An anarchy in the mind and in the heart': narrating Anglo-Ireland*, is forthcoming from Bucknell University Press.

EIBHEAR WALSHE lectures in the Department of Modern English at University College Cork and his research interests include modern Irish fiction, Munster writing, Irish drama and Irish Lesbian and Gay writing. His biography of Kate O'Brien was published by Irish Academic Press in 2006. He was a section editor for *The Field Day anthology of Irish writing*, volume 4 (Cork University Press, 2002) and guest edited *The Irish Review* in 2000. His other publications include the edited collections, *Ordinary people dancing: essays on Kate O'Brien* (Cork University Press, 1993); *Sex, nation and dissent* (Cork University Press, 1997); *Elizabeth Bowen remembered* (Four Courts Press, 1999) and *The plays of Teresa Deevy* (Mellen Press, 2003). He co-edited, with Brian Cliff, *Representing the Troubles* (Four Courts Press, 2004).

ANDRIES WESSELS is professor of English at the University of Pretoria in South Africa. He was educated at the Universities of the Orange Free State, Oxford and South Africa. He has published articles on South African, Irish, comparative and modernist literature as well short stories and poetry translations.

GWENDA YOUNG is a lecturer in film studies in the Department of English, University College Cork. She has published articles on film in a variety of international journals and magazines. She also has an interest in Anglo-Irish literature, especially the work of Molly Keane.

Works cited

Anderson, Benedict. *Imagined communities: reflections on the origin and spread of national-ism*. New York: Verso, 1991.

Backus, Margot Gayle. *The Gothic family romance: heterosexuality, child sacrifice, and the Anglo-Irish colonial order*. Durham and London: Duke UP, 1999.

Bakhtin, M.M. *The dialogic imagination: four essays*. Ed. Michael Holquist. Trans. Caryl Emerson and Michael Holquist. Austin: University of Texas, 1981.

Bakhtin, Mikhail. *Rabelais and his world*. Trans. Hélène Iswolsky. Bloomington: Indiana UP, 1984.

Baldick, Chris (ed.). *The Oxford book of Gothic tales*. Oxford: OUP, 1993.

Barthes, Roland. *S/Z*. Trans. Richard Miller. New York: Hill and Wang, 1974.

Beckett, J.C., *The Anglo-Irish tradition*. Ithaca: Cornell UP, 1976.

Bence-Jones, Mark, *Twilight of the Ascendancy*. London: Constable, 1987.

Berger, John, *Ways of seeing*. London: Penguin, 1977.

Bhabha, Homi. 'Introduction: narrating the nation'. In *Nation and narration*. Ed. Homi Bhabha. New York: Routledge, 1990. 1–15.

Bowen, Elizabeth. *The Last September*. 1929; London: Penguin, 1952 and 1987; New York: Avon, 1979.

Bowen, Elizabeth. 'The Big House.' In *The Mulberry Tree: the writings of Elizabeth Bowen*. Ed. Hermione Lee. London: Virago, 1986. 25–30; *Collected Impressions*. New York: Alfred A. Knopf, 1950. 195–200.

Bowen, Elizabeth. *Bowen's Court*. London: Longmans, Green, 1942; Cork: Collins, 1998.

Boylan, Clare. 'Sex, snobbery and the strategies of Molly Keane.' In *Contemporary British women writers*. Ed. Robert Hosmer. New York: St Martin's, 1993. 151–60.

Breen, Mary. 'Piggies and spoilers of girls: the representation of sexuality in the novels of Molly Keane.' In *Sex, nation, and dissent in Irish writing*. Ed. Éibhear Walshe. Cork: Cork UP, 1997. 202–220.

Bristow, Joseph. *Empire boys: adventures in a man's world*. London: HarperCollins, 1991.

Bristow, Joseph. *Effeminate England*. New York: Columbia UP, 1995.

Brown, Terence. *Ireland: a social and cultural history, 1922 to the present*. Ithaca, New York: Cornell UP, 1985.

Burke, Edmund. *A philosophical inquiry into the origin of our ideas of the sublime and beautiful*. Ed. with an Introduction by J.T. Boulton. London: Routledge & Kegan Paul; New York: Columbia UP, 1958.

Cahalan, James. M. *The Irish novel* Dublin: Gill & Macmillan, 1988.

Cahalan, James. *A chronology of modern Irish literature and culture*. New York: G.K. Hall, 1993.

Cairns, David, and Shaun Richards. *Writing Ireland: colonialism, nationalism and culture*, Manchester: Manchester UP, 1990.

Casey, Moira. *The lesbian in the house*. Book in progress based on doctoral dissertation. University of Connecticut, 2003.

Castle, Terry. *The apparitional lesbian: female homosexuality and modern culture*. New York: Columbia UP, 1993.

Charnes, Linda. *Notorious identity: materializing the subject in Shakespeare*. Cambridge: Harvard UP, 1993.

Chen, Bi-Ling. 'From Britishness to Irishness: fox hunting as a metaphor for Anglo-Irish cultural identity in the writing of Somerville and Ross.' *Canadian Journal of Irish Studies* 23 (1977) 39–53.

Cleary, Joe. 'Postcolonial Ireland.' *Ireland and the British empire*. Ed. K. Kenny. Oxford: OUP, 2004.

Cleary, Joe. 'Toward a materialist-formalist history of twentieth-century Irish literature.' *Boundary 2* 31:1 (Spring 2004) 207–41.

Corcoran, Neil. *After Yeats and Joyce: reading modern Irish literature*. Oxford: Oxford UP, 1997.

Costigan, Giovanni. *A history of modern Ireland with a sketch of earlier times*. New York: Pegasus, 1969.

Coughlan, Patricia. 'The ear of the other: dissident voices in Kate O'Brien's *As Music and Splendour* and Mary Dorcey's *A Noise from the Woodshed*.' In *Sex, nation and dissent in Irish writing*. Ed. Eibhear Walshe. Cork: Cork UP, 1997. 103–34.

Cronin, Gearoid. 'The Big House and the Irish landscape in the work of Elizabeth Bowen.' In *The Big House in Ireland: reality and representation*. Ed. Jacqueline Genet. Savage, MD: Barnes and Noble, 1991. 143–61.

Deane, Paul. 'The Big House revisited: Molly Keane's *Time after Time*.' *Notes on Modern Irish Literature* 3 (1991) 37–44.

Deane, Seamus. 'The literary myths of the Revival: a case for their abandonment'. In *Myth and reality in Irish literature*. Ed. J. Ronsley. Waterloo, Ont.: Wilfrid Laurier UP, 1977. 317–29.

Deane, Seamus. *Celtic Revivals*. Boston: Faber, 1985. 28–37.

Deane, Seamus. 'Heroic styles: the tradition of an idea.' In *Ireland's Field Day*. Notre Dame, Indiana: U of Notre Dame Press, 1986. 6–8.

Devlin, Polly. 'Introduction.' *Conversation Piece*. 1932. London: Virago, 1991.

Devlin, Polly. 'Introduction.' *Devoted Ladies*. London: Virago, 1984.

Devlin, Polly. 'Introduction.' *The Last September*. Molly Keane. London: Virago, 1985.

Diez Fabre, Silvia. 'The literary representation of Anglo-Ireland in the work of Somerville & Ross and Elizabeth Bowen: towards a theology of space.' In *The representation of Ireland/s: images from outside and from within*. Ed. Rosa Gonzalez Casademont. Barcelona: PPU, 2003. 101–8.

Doan, Laura. *Fashioning Sapphism*. New York: Columbia UP, 2001.

Dollimore, Jonathan. *Sexual dissidence: Augustine to Wilde, Freud to Foucault*. New York: Oxford UP, 1991.

Donoghue, Emma. 'Noises from woodsheds: tales of Irish lesbians, 1886–1989.' In *Lesbian and gay visions of Ireland: towards the twenty-first century*. Ed. Ide O'Carroll and Eoin Collins. London: Cassell, 1995. 158–170.

Donoghue, Emma. *Passions between women: British lesbian culture, 1668–1801*. New York: HarperCollins, 1993.

Dooley, Terence. *The decline of the Big House in Ireland: a study of Irish landed families 1860–1960*. Dublin: Wolfhound Press, 2001.

Eagleton, Terry. *Criticism and ideology: a study in Marxist literary theory*. New York: Verso, 1976.

Eagleton, Terry. *Ideology: an introduction*. New York: Verso, 1991.

Eagleton, Terrry. *Heathcliff and the Great Hunger: studies in Irish culture*. London & New York: Verso, 1995.

Fekete, John. *The critical twilight*. London: Routledge, 1977.

Ferguson Ellis, Kate, *The contested castle: Gothic novels and the subversion of domestic ideology*. Urbana and Chicago: U of Illinois P, 1989.

Fingall, Countess of, Elizabeth Plunkett. *Seventy years young*. 1937; Dublin: Lilliput, 1991.

Fink, Bruce. *The Lacanian subject: between language and jouissance.* Princeton: Princeton UP, 1995.

Fitzgerald, Barbara, *We are Besieged.* London: Peter Davies, 1946.

Fleenor, Juliann, ed. *The female Gothic.* Montreal: Eden Press, 1983.

Foster, R.F. *Modern Ireland, 1600–1972.* London: Penguin, 1988; New York: Penguin, 1989.

Geertz, Clifford. *The interpretation of cultures.* New York: Basic Books, 1973.

Glendinning, Victoria. *Elizabeth Bowen.* New York: Avon Books, 1979.

Grosz, Elizabeth. 'Sexed bodies.' *Volatile bodies: toward a corporeal feminism.* Bloomington: Indiana UP, 1994. 187–210.

Gunzenhauser, Randi. *Horror at home* (1993), quoted in Susanne Becker, *Gothic forms of feminine fictions.* Manchester and New York: Manchester UP, 1999.

Hadfield, Andrew and John McVeagh. *Strangers to that land: British perceptions of Ireland from the Reformation to the Famine.* Gerrards Cross: Colin Smyth, 1994.

Halligan, Marjorie. 'Going beyond the Pale: from M.J. Farrell to Molly Keane: the development of a style,' MA thesis. Queen's University Belfast, 1999.

Hargreaves, Tamsin. 'Women's Consciousness and Identity in Four Irish Women Novelists'. In *Cultural contexts and literary idioms in contemporary Irish literature.* Ed. Michael Kenneally. Totowa, NJ: Barnes & Noble, 1988; Gerrards Cross: Colin Smythe, 1988. 290–305.

Harrington, John P. *The English traveller in Ireland: accounts of Ireland and the Irish through five centuries.* Dublin: Wolfhound Press, 1991.

Hildebidle, John. 'Kilneagh and Challacombe: William Trevor's two nations.' *Éire-Ireland* 28:3 (Fall 1993) 114–29.

Hogle, Jerrold E., ed. *Cambridge companion to Gothic fiction.* Cambridge: Cambridge UP, 2002.

Hurlbert, Ann. 'Visitations.' Review of *Time after Time*, by Molly Keane, and *Stones for Ibarra*, by Harriet Doerr. *New Republic*, 30 January 1984; 40–1.

Imhof, Rudiger. 'Molly Keane, *Good Behaviour, Time after Time*, and *Loving and Giving.*' Ed. Otto Rauchbacher. *Ancestral voices: the Big House in Anglo-Irish literature.* Hildesheim: Olms, 1992. 195–203.

Inverso, MaryBeth. *The Gothic impulse in contemporary drama.* Ann Arbor and London: UMI Research Press, 1990.

Keane, Molly [M.J. Farrell, pseud.]. *The Book of Nursery Cooking.* Dublin: Poolbeg, 1985.

Keane, Molly. *Conversation Piece.* 1932: Virago, 1991.

Keane, Molly. *Devoted Ladies.* London: Collins, 1934; Virago, 1984.

Keane, Molly. *Full House.* 1935; London: Virago, 1985 & 1987.

Keane, Molly. *Good Behaviour.* New York: Alfred Knopf; Dutton Obelisk, 1981; London: Abacus, 1982 & 1995.

Keane, Molly. *The Knight of Cheerful Countenance.* London: Mills and Boon, 1926; with a new introduction by Molly Keane in London: Virago, 1993. (*KCC*)

Keane, Molly. *Loving and Giving.* 1988; London: Abacus, 1989.

Keane, Molly. *Loving without Tears.* 1951; introduction by Russell Harty in London: Virago, 1991. (*LWT*)

Keane, Molly. *Mad Puppetstown.* London: Collins, 1931; Virago, 1985.

Keane, Molly. Introduction. *Molly Keane's Ireland: an anthology.* Ed. Molly Keane and Sally Phipps. London: HarperCollins, 1993. ix–xvii.

Keane, Molly. *Queen Lear.* New York: E.P. Dutton, 1988.

Keane, Molly. *The Rising Tide*. London: Collins, 1937; Virago, 1984.

Keane, Molly. *Taking Chances*. 1929, London: Virago, 1987

Keane, Molly. *Time after Time*. London: Abacus, 1983 & 1984. New York: Alfred Knopf, 1984; New York: Dutton, 1985. (*TAT*)

Keane, Molly. *Treasure Hunt*. 1952; London: Virago Modern Classics, 1990.

Keane, Molly. *Two Days in Aragon*. 1941; London: Virago, 1985, 1989 & 1992.

Keane, Molly. *Young Entry*. 1928; London: Virago, 1989.

Kearney, Richard. 'Faith and fatherland.' *Crane Bag* 8:1 (1984) 55–66.

Kelly, Patricia. 'The Big House in contemporary Anglo-Irish literature.' In *Literary interrelations: Ireland, England and the world, vol. 3: national images and stereotypes*. Ed. Michael Kenneally and Wolfgang Zach. Tübingen: Gunter Narr, 1987. 229–34.

Kelly, Hurley, 'British Gothic fiction 1885–1930'. In *Cambridge companion to Gothic fiction*. Ed. Jerrold E. Hogle. Cambridge: Cambridge UP, 2002.

Kinealy, Christine. *A death-dealing famine: the Great Hunger in Ireland*. Chicago: Pluto Press, 1997.

Kiberd, Declan. *Inventing Ireland: the literature of the modern nation*. London: Vintage, 1996.

Kreilkamp, Vera. *The Anglo-Irish novel and the Big House*. Syracuse, NY: Syracuse UP, 1998.

Kreilkamp, Vera. 'Review of *Mad Puppetstown* and *Two Days in Aragon* by M.J. Farrell.' *ILS* Fall 1986, 16.

Kreilkamp, Vera. 'Molly Keane's recent Big House fiction.' *Massachusetts Review* 28.3 (1987) 453–460.

Kristeva, Julia. *The powers of horror: an essay on abjection*. Trans. Leon Roudiez. New York: Columbia UP, 1982.

Kuhn, Annette. *Alien zone: cultural theory and contemporary science fiction cinema*. London: Verso, 1990.

Lasdun, James. 'Life's victims: recent fiction.' Review of *The life and times of Michael K.*, by J.M. Coetzee, *Marcovaldo*, by Italo Calvino, *The Philosopher's Pupil*, by Iris Murdoch, *Shame*, by Salman Rushdie, and *Time after Time*, by Molly Keane. *Encounter* 62 (1984) 69–73.

Lee, Hermione. Preface. *The Mulberry Tree*. By Elizabeth Bowen. London: Virago, 1986.

Lewis, Gifford. *The selected letters of Somerville and Ross*. London: Faber and Faber, 1989.

Lloyd, David. *Ireland after history*. Notre Dame: University of Notre Dame Press, 1999.

Longley, Edna. 'Three writers of the Big House: Elizabeth Bowen, Molly Keane and Jennifer Johnston'. In Longley and Gerald Dawe, eds. *Across a roaring hill: the protestant imagination in modern Ireland*. Ed. M. Longley and G. Dawe. Belfast: Blackstaff, 1985.

Loos, Adolf. 'Ornament and crime.' In *Crime and ornament: the arts and popular culture in the shadow of Adolf Loos*. Ed. Melony Ward and Bernie Miller. Toronto: YYZ Books, 2002. 29–36.

Lynch, Rachel Jane. 'The crumbling fortress: Molly Keane's comedies of Anglo-Irish manners.' In *The comic tradition of Irish Women Writers*. Ed. Theresa O'Connor. Gainesville: UP of Florida, 1996. 73–98.

Lyons, F.S.L. *Culture and anarchy in Ireland, 1890–1939*. Oxford: Clarendon, 1979.

Madden-Simpson, Janet. 'Haunted houses: the image of the Anglo-Irish in Anglo-Irish literature.' In *Literary interrelations: Ireland, England and the world, vol. 3: national images and stereotypes*. Ed. Michael Kenneally and Wolfgang Zach. Tübingen: Gunter Narr, 1987. 41–46.

Magnusson, Magnus. *Landlord or tenant?: a view of Irish history*. London: The Bodley Head, 1978.

MacCormack, William J. *Ascendancy and tradition in Anglo-Irish literary history from 1789 to 1939.* Oxford: Clarendon, 1985.

McAlindon, Tom. 'Tragedy, history and myth: William Trevor's *Fools of Fortune.' Irish University Review* 33:2 (Autumn/Winter 2003) 291–306.

Memmi, Albert. *The colonizer and the colonized.* London: Souvenir, 1974.

Mercier, Vivian. *The Irish comic tradition.* Oxford: OUP, 1962.

Mighall, Robert. *A geography of Victorian Gothic fiction: mapping history's nightmares.* Oxford: OUP, 199).

Mitford, Nancy, 'The English aristocracy.' Ed. Nancy Mitford. *Noblesse oblige: an enquiry into the identifiable characteristics of the Engli*sh *aristocracy.* Ed. Nancy Mitford. New York: Harper, 1956. 21–52.

Moore, George. *A drama in muslin.* Gerrards Cross: Colin Smythe, 1993.

Morrison, Kristen, 'Ancient rubbish and interior spaces: M.A. Butler and M.J. Farrell dis-Covered'. In *Visualising Ireland: national identity and the pictorial tradition.* Ed. Adele M. Dalsimer. Boston: Faber and Faber, 1993.

Mulvey Roberts, Marie, ed. *The handbook to Gothic.* Houndmills: Macmillan, 1998.

Myers, Kevin. 'We thought we would go on forever.' *Irish Times*, News Focus, 1 October 1980.

Nietzsche, Friedrich. 'On the uses and disadvantages of history for life.' In *Untimely Meditations.* Ed. Daniel Breazeale. Trans. R. J. Hollingdale. Cambridge: Cambridge UP, 1997. 57–123.

O'Brien, Ellen L. 'Anglo-Irish abjection in the "very nasty" Big House novels of Molly Keane.' *LIT* 10 (1999) 35–62.

Petre, Diana. Introduction. *Young Entry.* London: Virago, 1989.

Phipps, Sally. Interview with Rachael Lynch, June 2005.

Pritchett, V.S. 'The Irish character.' *At home and abroad.* San Francisco: North Point Press, 1989. 178–200.

Pritchett, V.S. *Lasting impressions.* London: Chatto and Windus, 1990.

Punter, David. *The literature of terror: a history of the Gothic from 1765 to the present* (London: Longman, 1980).

Punter, David. 'Ceremonial Gothic'. In *Spectral readings: towards a Gothic geography.* Ed. Glennis Byron and David Punter. Houndmills: Macmillan, 1999.

Quinn, John, ed. *A portrait of the artist as a young girl.* RTE: 1985; London: Methuen, 1986. *(POA).*

Rollins, Hyder E., ed. *The letters of John Keats, 1814–1821, vol. 1.* Cambridge, MA: Harvard UP, 1958.

Rich, Adrienne. 'Compulsory heterosexuality and lesbian existence'. In *Women, sex and sexuality.* Ed. Catherine Stimpson and Ethel Spector Person. U of Chicago P, 1980.

Schirmer, Gregory A. *William Trevor: a study of his fiction.* London: Routledge, 1990.

Sedgwick, Eve Kosofsky. *Between men: English literature and male homosocial desire.* New York: Columbia UP, 1985.

Showalter, Elaine. *Sexual anarchy, gender and culture at the fin de siècle.* London: Bloomsbury, 1991

Skeats, Sarah. 'Eating the evidence: women, power and food'. In *Image and power.* Ed. Sarah Skeats and Gail Cunningham. New York: Longman, 1996.

Somerville, E. and Martin Ross. *The Real Charlotte.* London: The Hogarth Press, 1988; Dublin: A&A Farmar, 1999.

Somerville, E.Œ., and Martin Ross. *The Big House of Inver.* 1925; London: Mandarin, 1991.

Somerville, E.Œ., and Martin Ross. *Irish Memories*, London: Longmans, Green, 1917.

Spooner, Catherine. *Fashioning Gothic bodies*. Manchester: Manchester UP, 2004.

Tocqueville, Alexis de. *Journeys to England and Ireland*. Trans. George Lawrence and K.P. Mayer. New Haven: Yale UP, 1958.

Tracy, Robert. *The unappeasable host: studies in Irish identities*. Dublin: University College Dublin P, 1998.

Trench, William Steuart. 'From *Realities of Irish life*.' In *The Field Day anthology of Irish writing*, vol. 2. Ed. Seamus Deane. Derry: Field Day, 1991.

Trevor, William. *Fools of Fortune*. 1983. London: Penguin, 1984.

Trevor, William. *The Silence in the Garden*. London: The Bodley Head, 1988.

Trevor, William. 'Beyond the pale.' *Selected Stories: Ireland*. London: Penguin, 1995. 64–86.

Trevor, William. *The Story of Lucy Gault*. London: Viking, 2002.

Weekes, Ann Owens. *Irish women writers: an uncharted tradition*. Lexington, Kentucky: UP of Kentucky, 1990.

Weekes, Ann Owens. 'A trackless road: Irish nationalisms and lesbian writing.' In *Border crossings: Irish women writers and national identities*. Ed. Kathryn Kirkpatrick. Tuscaloosa: U of Alabama P, 2000. 123–56.

Yeats, W.B., *Collected Plays*. Dublin: Gill and Macmillan, 1989.

Zerubavel, Eviatar. *Time maps: collective memory and the social shape of the past*. Chicago: U of Chicago Press, 2003.

Zizek, Slavoj. *The sublime object of ideology*. London: Verso, 1989.

Zizek, Slavoj. *Enjoy your symptom!: Jacques Lacan in Hollywood and out*. New York: Routledge, 1992.

Index